SYRACUSE LANDMARKS

SYRACUSE
An AIA Guide to Downtown and Historic Neighborhoods
Landmarks

Evamaria Hardin

Photographs by Jon Crispin

TO Joseph WITH
GOOD WISHES

Evamaria Hardin

Onondaga Historical Association / Syracuse University Press

First Edition 1993
93 94 95 96 97 98 99   6 5 4 3 2 1

Publication of this book is sponsored by the Central
New York Chapter of the American Institute of Architects.
This book is funded in part by the New York State Council
on the Arts and is published in cooperation with the Onondaga
Historical Association.

The paper used in this publication meets the minimum
requirements of American National Standard for Information
Sciences—Permanence of Paper for Printed Library Materials,
ANSI Z39.48–1984.   TM

Library of Congress Cataloging-in-Publication Data

Hardin, Evamaria.
Syracuse landmarks : an AIA guide to downtown and historic
neighborhoods / Evamaria Hardin : photographs by Jon Crispin.
        p.   cm.
    Includes index.
    ISBN 0-8156-2599-5
    1. Architecture—New York (State)—Syracuse—Guidebooks.
2. Historic buildings—New York (State)—Syracuse—Guidebooks.
3. Syracuse (N.Y.)—Buildings, structures, etc.—Guidebooks.
I. Crispin, Jon. II. Title.
NA735.S97H37 1993
720'.9747'66—dc20   92-35000

Manufactured in the United States of America

CONTENTS

Evamaria Hardin, the author of *Archimedes Russell: Upstate Architect,* works as an architectural historian in upstate New York.

Jon Crispin is a professional photographer based in central Massachusetts.

Journalist **Dick Case** is a longtime resident of Syracuse whose popular column appears in the Syracuse *Herald American.*

FOREWORD
Dick Case

Syracuse is a small apple among cities.

Our founders may have wished grander things for us. We were, by chance or design, put right in the middle of New York. Nowadays, the major east-west (Interstate 90) and north-south (Interstate 81) highways intersect here. We are still working on making something of this asset. I'll have to get back to you.

We are both small town and big city. A county seat. The marketplace of the region. Upstate headquarters. The courtroom of the Northern District of New York. Council fire of the Iroquois Confederacy. Home to the Dome. The town where the trains used to run down one of the main drags. Where Broadway shows and new laundry soap were tested. An old canal port modernized a bit, here and there. Big enough to be complicated and sophisticated. Yes, it's hard to find a place to park at a meter in the central business district 9 am to 5 pm.

Small enough to be comfortable. You run into a couple of your neighbors on Salina Street when you take a lunch-hour walk. And we are not embarrassed for our Irish mayor when he paints a green stripe down the street for the St. Patrick's Day parade.

It will take a couple of weeks to get an appointment with a dentist. The lines at Motor Vehicles aren't bad: you'll be out in an hour. The waiting at Heid's in Liverpool on a warm summer noontime might be a bit longer.

"Yeah. Gimme a double coney and a chocolate milk!"

Allow a couple of days for a letter to make it from one end of the city to the other. That's about six miles, north to south.

Truth is, we like our town because we are here. Each of us has a list of favorite things to do. That includes not doing anything.

I like to stand in front of buildings and wonder what's inside. Literally and spiritually. Some people like the zoo in Burnet Park. I've gone there for lunch. Grab a burger, sit on the patio, watch the elephants. Other citizens think it's fun to be downtown during the day in summer. Buy a dog and lemonade and sit in on the free shows in the squares. Or go to the Regional Market on Saturday morning.

Ride the trolley to Armory Square. Buy a cranberry muffin, then walk around the corner and price the terra cotta fireplaces and the puppets from Indonesia. Round the block and order a vegetarian lunch.

Or walk up North Salina Street, saluting the Sniper Monument as you pass. No, that's not the general's grave; he lies in Woodlawn Cemetery. Browse in the Eastern Orthodox bookstore. Buy a suit or an Oriental rug at the old Learbury plant.

You may wander the old German and Italian neighborhoods on the far North Side, east of Assumption Church and St. John the Baptist. You pass a monastery and the city's smallest house (812 Danforth Street) while walking on top of the old brewery tunnels. Look to the north: that red dot on the horizon is the elevator housing that looks like an old mansion on top of Penfield Manufacturing Company. To the west, a mansion of another sort rises, Carousel Center.

It's fun tracking University Hill. Check out Newhouse Center I, like the Everson Museum downtown, the interesting architecture of I. M. Pei. Across the street is the Hall of Languages, Syracuse University's first building, which has a totally different kind of charm. You'll want to stop at the rose garden in Thornden Park and prowl Oakwood-Morningside Cemetery, where you'll find one of the largest green spaces in the city. The dominant green thing in our town, by the way, is the mowed lawn.

Our first mayor, Harvey Baldwin, was buried in a mausoleum at the brow of Highland Street hill, in Rosehill, one of our cemeteries that isn't really a cemetery anymore. You'll think it's a park. We have plenty of those too, including Merry Widow, which is the size of a large phone booth. The only virgin woodland is in upper Onondaga Park, near Hiawatha Lake.

We have a band of rock running easterly out of downtown that may contain diamonds. Great blue herons nest at Webster's Pond, in the valley. Our last farm, in the Erie Boulevard East muckland, gets smaller by each growing season as commerce encroaches. The highest point in the city is the roof of Brighton Towers, the senior citizen apartments built on the old dumps at Brighton Avenue and Rock Cut Road.

There also are Eastwood, Tipperary Hill, Skunk City, Drumlins, Mount Olympus, Oil City, and Machiova, a tiny enclave of Polish culture on the West Side.

The Cardiff Giant was born here, as were the creator of David Harum (Edward Noyes Westcott), the Shubert brothers, and Charles Brannock, inventor of the Brannock Device to measure your foot for a shoe. By the by, Nettleton Shoes of Syracuse invented the loafer. And both the author of The Wonderful Wizard of Oz, Frank Baum, and the composer of "Somewhere over the Rainbow," Harold Arlen, were Syracusans.

The most interesting thing about the place where we live, though, is the way all of its thousands of parts fit together. I'm talking past, present, and future.

The man who buried his dog in his front yard on Lodi Street connects to the baker who brings hot bread out of the oven on wooden paddles at Columbus Bakery; they are neighbors. The painter of the house next to mine is the cousin of the secretary at City Hall who went out with the cousin of the sixth chair violinist in the Syracuse Symphony Orchestra.

My uncle used to cut meat for rich families on James Street. His mother took care of their kids. The cop in the district has a brother who is a firefighter. Their father's cousins were undertakers. The guy next to me on the bus at night is a doctor's son. His uncle's a priest who preached at my aunt's funeral.

Well, you get the idea.

We marry in the same churches, use the same dry cleaners and front-end mechanics, and vote in the same schools. Our dogs meet in the parks. We pass jogging. We slice the pepperoni and green peppers that circulate through the streets after dark in warm boxes of cardboard. We see each other's pictures in the papers and on TV. We invade the lives of strangers as wrong numbers on the phone. Sit side by side in the emergency rooms.

We connect.

Every minute of every day we do that. Somehow the pieces fit. Somehow it works.

PREFACE

This book is meant for visitors and residents, for architects and preservationists, for anyone who would like to know more about the architecture of Syracuse, New York, and its history. We believe that a city's buildings are to be understood not as mere freestanding objects but as expressions of its history, economy, and social needs. Our aim is to acquaint the reader with the city's rich diversity of architecture and the history with which it is intertwined. We hope that everyone who takes these tours by foot, by car, in a wheelchair, or at home in an armchair will find that there is something interesting to see and to read about in Syracuse.

Our second purpose in bringing you this book arises from the preoccupation with industry and trade that has given Syracuse its distinctive characteristics. That preoccupation has not always been sensitive to the community's architectural legacy. The city has lost several notable buildings by distinguished architects such as James Renwick, Minard Lafever, and Alexander Jackson Davis. Fortunately, in the last fifteen years there has been an increased awareness of the importance of preserving and adapting older buildings: a preservation ordinance is now in effect, there are community groups supporting preservation efforts, and there have been some successes in saving and restoring structures that would have surely seen the wrecker's ball in the climate of a generation ago. But in matters such as these, success is ephemeral. Unless there is a widespread public awareness of the need to cherish our architectural past, changing economic conditions could lead easily to a new era of neglect and destruction. The Central New York Chapter of the American Institute of Architects, the Onondaga Historical Association, and Syracuse University Press all see the publication and distribution of this walking tour guide as contributing to that public awareness.

We have chosen sites for their architectural and historical significance. National Register districts and sites are emphasized, as are the works of eminent architects or buildings that have won design awards. We also consider some more recent buildings—products of urban renewal efforts—that have had a more questionable impact on the urban landscape. In the discussions of architecture, we have chosen to give primary attention to building types rather than architectural styles. When specialized architectural terms could not be avoided, their definitions may be found in the glossary near the end of this guide. Although the guide focuses on downtown Syracuse, by touring other neighborhoods as well as selected parts of the Syracuse University campus, one can not only enjoy the community's diversity but also learn something about its development. This is by no means a complete guide of the city. Because of the constraints of space, many areas worthy of attention had to be left out. We hope that they will some day be the subject of a companion volume.

The introduction, "The Rise of a Commercial City," provides an overview of the history of Syracuse. A general map of the city indicates the location of individual walking (or driving) tours, which are arranged by geographic proximity. Each tour is preceded by a brief historical introduction, as well as approximate walking or driving times or both. Particular places or buildings are indicated on maps by numbers that are keyed to the text and to the photographs. Those historical and contemporary photographs that are not keyed to specific numbered entries are unnumbered. Names of architects and renovation/restoration dates follow the names, construction dates, and addresses of the buildings or places when that information is available. Various historic preservation designations are given:

HABS Historic American Building Survey
NRHD National Register Historic District (or part of the district)
NRHP National Register of Historic Places (individually listed property)
CSPD City of Syracuse Preservation District (or part of the district)
CSPS City of Syracuse Protected Site (individually listed property)

Names and addresses of buildings not on a tour but nearby and worthy of attention appear at the end of the tour without a number and are not included on the tour map.

Syracuse, New York   Evamaria Hardin
September 1992

ACKNOWLEDGMENTS

Many people have contributed to the completion of this book, and my heartfelt thanks go to all of them: Paul Malo, Tony Proe, and Michael Sellin read parts of an early draft and made useful comments. Francis E. Hares, Dennis J. Connors, and Edward Lyon spent long hours reading and commenting on the completed manuscript, as did Carrie Gannett. Syracuse University architecture students Karen Mehan, Garrett Ulm, Mark Cutone, Tushar Advani, Michael Allen, David Barata, Rebecca Doyle, Marin Flynn, Ronald Maggio, Sarah Mayberry, Michael Moss, John J. Veak, Robert Wildermuth, Christopher Berg, Peter Kliner, Harry Pettoni, Paul Berry, and Peter Mantis walked early stages of some of the tours and made helpful suggestions. Barbara Giambastiani Bartlett and Christine B. Lozner spent many hot summer days walking, driving, and mapping all the tours.

Judy Haven worked tirelessly for many months making the Onondaga Historical Association research files available to me. Without the OHA, Judy, and her staff, the book could not have been written, and I am deeply indebted to them. Special appreciation and thanks also go to Joanne Arany who was most helpful in providing Building-Structure Inventory Form material. Serving as a base of information for many of the downtown and neighborhood tours, the Building-Structure Inventory Forms were done under the auspices of the Landmarks Association of Central New York and the Preservation Association of Central New York. Part of the information for the Syracuse University tour was taken from Building-Structure Inventory Forms prepared by Dr. Harvey H. Kaiser and from *Syracuse University Alumni News*, 1984. The Walnut Park tour is based in part on Building-Structure Inventory Forms written by Professor Mary Ann Smith and her students. The tour of Sedgwick Tract is derived from research by Barbara Giambastiani Bartlett for the Preservation Association of Central New York. Information for the South Salina Street Historic District came in part from Building-Structure Inventory Forms prepared by Mary Ann Smith, Suzanne Kuehn, Lionel Julio, James Kutchins, and Brian Krafjack. The Oakwood Cemetery tour was written by Christine B. Lozner. Dennis J. Connors and the Onondaga Park Association provided information for the Salina and Onondaga Park tours respectively. A list of Onondaga Valley homes compiled by Carl Steere Myrus helped to identify houses discussed in that tour. I also thank R. Gregory Sloan, who provided access to papers and photographs in the collection of Oakwood Cemetery of Syracuse, Inc.

Many thanks go to the staff of the Syracuse University Archives and to Barbara Opar and her staff of the Syracuse University Architecture Library. The Koolakian family was particularly helpful in providing valuable information and historical photographs, and I am grateful to them. Other historical photographs and maps came from the Onondaga Historical Association, the Erie Canal Museum, the New York States Archives in Albany, and from the collection of Randall T. Crawford. I greatly appreciate their cooperation. I am grateful to Jean Henderson and Celia Harper for help with their respective church archives. Suzanne Good and Jane Tracy shared information on buildings in Onondaga Valley and Onondaga Hill with me, and I thank them for it. Special appreciation goes to all the building owners, architects, developers, and their assistants; and to preservationists who generously answered my many questions about various structures discussed in this book and who showed me through their buildings and their houses.

I am indebted to the staff of Syracuse University Press, and especially to the Director, Charles Backus, for their commitment and patience, and to the editor, Kay Steinmetz, whose scrutiny and careful attention improved the book considerably, for which I am most grateful. And although I would like to blame others for any mistakes and omissions, I am afraid they are all mine. Much of the success of a book like this belongs to the photographer, and my heartfelt thanks go to Jon Crispin for his fine work. It has been a pleasure to work with him. Maps are based on originals designed and produced by William Padgett Design, Erieville, New York, commissioned by the Central New York Chapter of AIA. I greatly appreciate the contribution of the designer of the book, Ed King.

The book could not have been published without money, and I thank the New York State Council on the Arts for its generous financial support. I am indebted to Dean Biancavilla and his committee and to Barbara Giambastiani Bartlett for their efforts to raise money in order to make this book a reality. I am grateful to the following individuals and organizations that have contributed funds: Sargent-Webster-Crenshaw & Folley; King & King Architects; James Jordan Associates Architects; Crawford & Stearns; Omega Design; Quinlivan Pierick & Krause; Bell & Spina Architects; R.J. Engan & Associates; Holmes/King & Associates Architects; Dean A. Biancavilla, AIA; John P. Goodman, AIA; Heritage Coalition, Inc.; Bristol-Myers Squibb Company.

A special note of thanks to two people: Mary Ann Smith, who introduced me to upstate architecture, and Larry Hardin, who has had much to do with my being upstate in the first place.

SYRACUSE LANDMARKS

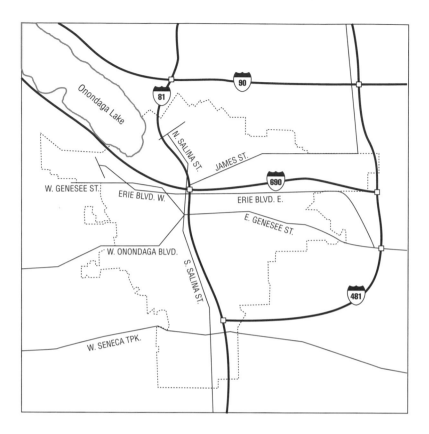

SYRACUSE: THE RISE OF A COMMERCIAL CITY

A glance at a road map immediately reveals two facts about Syracuse: it is at the geographical center of New York, and it lies at the intersection of the state's principal north-south and east-west thoroughfares. There has always been a crossroads here: first Iroquois trails, then wagon roads, followed in turn by canals, railroads, and finally interstate highways. Being at a crossroads makes a city possible, but having a product of its own to sell makes it grow and develop. It was an act of nature that gave the city its first trading commodity: an ancient sea had left deposits from which salt could be easily extracted. In an era before refrigeration, salt was a valuable commodity indeed. Ready salt and the Erie Canal transformed Syracuse from a crossroads into a city, and manufacturing and the railroad sustained it when the salt industry and canal faltered.

This is a city whose face has been shaped by commerce. Although something remains of an earlier period, especially in Hanover Square and Onondaga Hill and Onondaga Valley, in the middle of the nineteenth century Syracuse was a city in a hurry. Much of its architecture reflects that era of individualism, widely varied building styles, and explosive, unplanned growth. Those who look downtown for sustained elegance will be disappointed, but those who look for the visible manifestations of what propelled the United States during the past centuries will be amply rewarded.

As the city matured, growth shifted from the central city to its neighborhoods and suburbs, from commercial to residential construction. Just as downtown has good examples of every American commercial building type of the last two centuries, the outlying parts of the city are a veritable catalogue of the domestic architecture that was built in the United States during the last 200 years. Syracuse is not, like Colonial Williamsburg, a museum that evokes what is for most of us a fantasy image of our past but an ongoing, ethnically diverse city in which we can discover the more typical lives of our ancestors.

Native Americans and Early European Settlement

The story of Syracuse begins with an area covered with swamps and bogs, and with a vast forest surrounding a beautiful, pristine lake. That lake was named after the Onondaga Nation, which was in the geographical center of the territory occupied by the Iroquois League. (Iroquois was the name given to the Indians by the French; they called themselves Haudenosaunee—the People of the Longhouse.) Legend has it that the League of the Iroquois was founded by five separate peoples on the northern shore of Onondaga Lake. Two primary axes of movement through the territories of the "Five

Nations," one east-west, the other north-south, crossed the territory of the Onondaga. The symbolic longhouse of the Iroquois Confederacy was oriented along the east-west axis. The Mohawk guarded the eastern door, and the Seneca the western, while the Onondaga tended the council fire in the center. Along this axis the business of the league was conducted. The Cayuga aligned themselves with the Seneca to the west, and the Oneida joined with the Mohawk to the east. Later the Tuscarora joined the league, which thus occupied an area between the Genesee and Hudson rivers, although its influence extended well beyond the boundaries of the area that is now New York State.

The Onondaga rebuilt their villages throughout central New York approximately every fifteen years. Their houses were framed with saplings, bent to form a domed structure, and covered with elm bark shingles. Until the eighteenth century, fortifications consisting of rows of upright saplings surrounded the houses. Visiting Jesuits told of long houses arranged in rows, accessible by doors at either end. A central corridor held the cooking fires, with sleeping platforms for nuclear families placed to each side. A group of Onondaga settlements along Onondaga Creek named Onondaga Castle, was destroyed in 1779 by American Revolutionary soldiers in their retaliatory campaign against the Iroquois and their Loyalist allies on the New York frontier.

During the seventeenth century, the Europeans came, first as missionaries and explorers, later as traders and conquerors. In 1656, six Jesuits, ten soldiers and and forty warriors established a French outpost on the shore of Onondaga Lake, Ste. Marie de Gannentaha, which lasted for only two years. The first "re-creation" of this French settlement was completed in 1933 as part of a work relief program. It was replaced in 1991 by Ste. Marie Among the Iroquois, a historically more accurate reconstruction with an interpretive center (designed by Hueber Hares Glavin) that introduces us to the events and people of Ste. Marie and helps us understand the profound changes that the meeting of two distinct worlds created in this region as well as the determining role of the Iroquois in that balance of power for nearly 200 years. During the War of Independence, Iroquois allegiance was divided between British and American forces, whose power struggle eventually ended the league's supremacy. In 1790, a series of treaties was negotiated between New York State and the Iroquois Confederacy by which most of the native lands east of the Genesee River were taken away. Some Iroquois retreated to Canada, others to a reservation. The Onondaga were left with a tract of about 6,000 acres of their original territoriy south of the present city of Syracuse.

In 1782, the New York State legislature set aside a 1,500,000-acre area, known as the Military Tract, that encompassed the present Onondaga, Cortland, Cayuga, and Seneca counties, as well as portions of four others. The land was parceled out as bounty to American Revolutionary soldiers, but they represented only a minority of the settlers because many sold their land claims to speculators. In 1786, Ephraim Webster and Benjamin

Ste. Marie Among the Iroquois

Neukirk were the first to set up a trading post, Webster's Landing, where Onondaga Creek at that time emptied into Onondaga Lake. Because the course of the creek has been straightened several times since then, the exact site of the post is not known. Neukirk died shortly after their arrival, but Webster stayed on. Trader, trapper, soldier, spy, subject of many a tall tale, Webster spoke the languages of the Iroquois and lived with a Native American with whom he had children. Although he later married a European settler, he maintained good relations with his Onondaga neighbors, who had given him a square mile (Webster's Mile Square) of their lands in Onondaga Hollow.

It was through Webster's influence that Comfort Tyler settled here, along with Asa Danforth and his family. Webster had met Tyler and Danforth during a hunting trip in Montgomery County, where both men farmed. They were to play an important role in the development of that area. Before long, land-hungry, tax-weary Protestant New Englanders pushed their way westward along the Seneca Turnpike (now Route 173), the region's first east-west road. Those who stayed found a healthy upland location with good farmland, salt springs six miles to the north on Onondaga Lake, and a saw- and gristmill to provide for their immediate needs. Among these people were the founders of Syracuse.

Onondaga Hollow and Onondaga Hill, two early settlements along the Seneca Turnpike, were the core of what became the seat of government of Onondaga County, established in 1794. By 1810, the first Onondaga County Courthouse, a simple timber-frame building, was erected on the Hill, officially making it the county seat. The designation of county seat meant prestige, an influx of new settlers, and an increase in business; county court was held twice a year in frontier towns. It was not surprising that the Hill and the Hollow prospered. The surviving houses of the New Englanders tell us about their prosperity and the latest trends in architectural designs that had been inspired by classical architecture.

Salt

The dominance of Onondaga Hollow and Hill was soon to be challenged by a new development. Salt deposits, residues from an ancient salt ocean, became the source of salt springs that lined the shore of freshwater Onondaga Lake. In mid-seventeenth century, Father Simon LeMoyne, a French Jesuit priest doing missionary work among the Onondaga, had been invited by his hosts to drink from the bitter-tasting water. Quick to realize that he tasted salt, he boiled the brine and derived salt crystals. His report about the rich natural resources around Onondaga Lake, however, was met with skepticism once he returned to Canada. A century later, Sir William Johnson (superintendent of Indian affairs for the northern colonies), mindful of the British crown's as well as his own interest, acquired vast tracts of land in upstate New York, among them Onondaga Lake, and a strip of land containing the salt springs. The War of Independence intervened before his heirs could exploit the land for its riches, and after the Revolution the property reverted to New York State. A treaty provided for common rights for both the Onondaga and the European settlers. Everyone was in need of salt; appropriately named "white gold," it was used as barter before money became the regular currency.

As early as 1790, squatters set up their kettles on the southeast end of Onondaga Lake nearest the spring hole that was thought to be most productive of brine. Thus evolved Salt Point, later to become Salina and eventually Syracuse's First Ward, or the North Side. In 1794, James Geddes established his saltworks on the southwest corner of the lake and was the first to manufacture salt on a large scale. After the state took possession of the Salt Springs Reservation in 1797, Geddes surveyed the tract and laid out salt lots to be made available through public auction. Everyone engaged in salt manufacturing had to acquire the right to erect saltworks and to cut wood for fuel. An administrator was installed to oversee production and to levy taxes on salt, which for decades was an important revenue for New York State. At first salt was gained by boiling the brine. A later method was solar evaporation. Soon the landscape was covered with wooden well houses sheltering brine wells. Set into hills were stone pump houses from which brine would be pumped into reservoirs. There were salt blocks, so called because of the blocks that contained large vats for boiling the brine, and salt covers, shallow vats where brine was stored for evaporation. Although most houses where saltworkers and their families lived have been demolished, some of the Salina homes that belonged to salt manufacturers and administrators still exist. Making the necessary kettles and barrels became an equally important industry. Almost every farmhouse on the roads leading to Salina became a cooperage, and North Salina Street was originally known as Cooper Street.

Solar salt 'flats' near Spencer Street in Syracuse, c. 1895. Courtesy Onondaga County Parks Museum Office, Salt Museum collection.

As the demand for salt increased, great fortunes were made. Syracuse salt manufacturers formed one of the nation's first combines, the Salt Company of Syracuse, which was so successful that it was accused of being a monopoly, but was later exonerated. During the industry's peak years, salt flats stretched from Liverpool along the southern half of Onondaga Lake all the way to downtown Syracuse. The early Civil War years were especially profitable for the salt industry. After production reached a peak of 9 million bushels in 1862, the industry slowly declined as salt deposits were found elsewhere. The last salt block stopped boiling in 1890, and the last solar saltwork ceased operation in 1926. On the lakeshore near the site where

Salt Museum

Father LeMoyne first tasted the water from the salt spring stands the Salt Museum (1933; Leon Howe), designed and built as part of a work relief program. The building's exhibit gallery interprets the history of the local salt industry. A section of the building contains a re-created salt-boiling block built around a chimney that was part of a salt block erected in 1856.

One important survivor of the salt industry was the Solvay Process Company in the nearby village of Solvay, the first plant in the United States to produce soda ash. The Solvay process for manufacturing soda ash from brine and limestone was patented by Ernest and Alfred Solvay of Belgium in 1861. It remained a secret for almost twenty years until Rowland Hazard, a successful Rhode Island industrialist, and his engineer, William B. Cogswell, a native Syracusan, secured the U.S. manufacturing rights to the process. Well aware of the area's resources in the limestone and salt needed to make soda ash, Cogswell convinced his employer to erect the plant on abandoned salt land on the shore of Onondaga Lake, and the company was incorporated in 1881. Around the plant grew the village of Solvay. Most of the laborers who worked at Solvay Process immigrated from the Tyrol, and many of their descendants still live in Solvay. Solvay Process was known for its benevolent paternalistic labor practices. One of the company's projects was a kindergarten, the first in the area. When Frederick Hazard (son of Rowland) died in 1917, the mayor of Syracuse flew the flag at half-mast in honor of his "great contributions in dollars and in humanitarian leadership." The company merged with Allied Chemical and Dye Corporation in 1920, and sixty-five years later closed its doors in Solvay.

The Canals and Their Legacy

The Erie Canal established Syracuse's dominance over its rival settements to the immediate north and south. As a result of the boom of the early canal years, the villages of Salina and Syracuse merged to become the city of Syracuse in 1848. One year later, a local paper announced that 250 houses were under construction and that 500 more would be built in that year, thus giving a first glimmer of credibility to Harvey Baldwin's famous "Hanging Garden" speech of 1847. Baldwin, Syracuse's first mayor, predicted "a population of 100,000 souls and immense structures of compact buildings"; and he added, "our beautiful lake on all its shores will present a view of one continuous villa, ornamented with its shady groves and hanging gardens connected by a wide and splendid avenue." For this vision, Baldwin received only ridicule because Syracuse's beginnings had been less than promising. A map of 1810, drawn up by James Geddes, shows a well-established settlement of Salina to the north laid out in a gridiron plan. To the south was the future Syracuse: a crossroads in the swamp.

In 1804, James Geddes sponsored a bill to sell 250 acres of land in the Salt Springs Reservation to finance the construction of a road from Manlius to the west line of the salt reservation that would allow salt manufacturers to take their product to market. Thus Genesee Street and Syracuse came into being. The surrounding swampland tract was bought by Abraham Walton of Utica for $6,550. The "Walton Tract," the present site of much of downtown, did not have much to offer besides water to power mills, a basic necessity for settlers. Walton, who never moved here, built a gristmill in

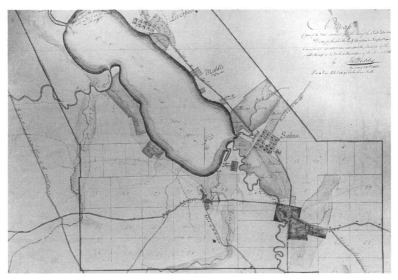

Syracuse and Salina, map 1810. New York State Archives.

1805 on the east bank of Onondaga Creek (where West Genesee Street now crosses). Soon two more mills, a school, and a church joined the Old Red Mill, creating a center of activity. A millpond to the south covered the area now occupied in part by Armory Square.

With the condition that a tavern be built, Walton sold one-half acre for $300 to an American Revolutionary soldier named Henry Bogardus, an ancestor of James Bogardus, inventor of the cast-iron building. Bogardus' Tavern (1806), a small one and one-half-story frame structure, faced the newly constructed road at its intersection with the wagon trail to Salina, on what is now the northwest corner of Genesee and Salina streets (the present site of the Syracuse Newspapers Building). This early crossroads, propitiously located in the central part of New York State, was to develop into an important transportation center.

The tract changed hands several times between 1814 and 1824, until a group of enterprising businessmen from Albany who saw beyond this "most unhealthy locality in the state" agreed to purchase the tract at $30,000 and gave the owner, Henry Eckford, a draft on the newly formed Syracuse Company in Albany, "the largest draft on Albany from the West up to that time." William James had established this new company with his New York City representative, James McBride, and his friends Isaiah and John Townsend. Moses DeWitt Burnet, James's brother-in-law, acted as the company's agent in Syracuse. These men gave their names to Syracuse streets, and their company was the first to improve and promote the tract systematically. William James was the grandfather of the famous James brothers, William, the philosopher, and Henry, the novelist, who were supported throughout their lives with money made from Syracuse property and salt.

The 1820s were important years for the fledgling settlement, then called Corinth. Joshua Forman, credited with being the father of Syracuse, moved from Onondaga Hollow to the south side of Clinton Square, where he lived in a frame house surrounded by a flower garden and a pine grove. The lowering of Onondaga Lake, along with a drainage system devised by Forman, reclaimed marsh lots that became usable land. A post office was to be established, and because there was another Corinth in the state, a new name had to be found. Having read a poem about the ancient Siracusa of Sicily, Forman's protégé, John Wilkinson, first postmaster and resident lawyer, saw similarities between the two: each had salt springs and a freshwater lake nearby. Thus Syracuse was named. Forman and Wilkinson laid out the village within the Walton Tract, and the rest of the land went into five- and ten-acre farm lots. One can only venture guesses about its appearance. Colonel William L. Stone, a visiting journalist from downstate, remarked to Forman that "Syracuse would make an owl weep to fly over it." Stone saw "a slab settlement with three frame buildings, a start for a brick tavern and two hundred people....It was the canal diggers who built the slab houses...pine slabs at a penny a piece were used...with plenty of nails the house could be made airtight and the roofs were of the same material."

The canal diggers were local people, mostly of New England origin. They had been hired by farmers, merchants, and professional people who lived along the water route that was to connect Lake Erie with the Hudson River. The enormous task began in 1817. Harsh working conditions and lack of sanitation killed many who built the 363-mile waterway through wilderness and malaria-ridden swamps. In the absence of engineering schools, workers and engineers had to learn their skills on the job. A fortunate coincidence was the discovery of natural cement near Chittenango in 1818 by Canvas White, an important canal engineer. It provided a mortar, "hydraulic cement," that hardened under water and was used for the construction of the Erie Canal.

As surveyed by James Geddes, the route ran past Bogardus' Corners. The completion of the entire waterway in 1825, the same year that Syracuse became a village, was celebrated with a relay of cannon fire along the route, with bands playing and people cheering. Because of its success in transporting goods and people, the Erie Canal had to be enlarged and deepened in midcentury. By then the Irish immigrants provided a ready labor force, giving credence to the often-repeated story that the Irish built the canal.

Revenues from the salt industry helped to pay for the Erie Canal, and in turn, salt merchants profited considerably from it, because much Onondaga salt was shipped along this waterway. Its branch, the Oswego Canal, opened in 1828 and led through Salina, which four years earlier had been incorporated as a village. Dividing the city into north and south, with the Oswego Canal making an east-west division, the Erie Canal physically shaped Syracuse and molded the appearance of buildings erected along its shores. Despite original pessimism and ridicule—Thomas Jefferson dismissed the idea of an east-west waterway as one just "short of madness"— the Erie Canal's success in providing easy access to markets, helping to open up the West, raising land values, and stimulating the growth of cities along its route, was soon acknowledged. Syracuse was a prime example: it had 600 inhabitants in 1820, and 2,565 in 1830. It grew to 11,014 in 1840, and ten years later the city had 22,127 people. When in 1829 Colonel Stone returned to Syracuse on a second visit, he spoke of "massive buildings" and "lofty spires of churches, well-built streets thronged with people" and described the change that had occurred within a decade as "one of enchantment."

More than a mere commercial force, the Erie Canal was a lifeline for many fugitive slaves and provided an escape route to freedom. It also brought entertainment. Revivalist preachers plied their trade up and down the Erie and saved souls along its banks. A publisher from Cooperstown floated his bookstores between Albany and Buffalo. Perhaps the most unusual attraction was an embalmed whale exhibited along the canal by an enterprising mariner who got his catch to Syracuse just in time for the 1890 New York State Fair. That was the first state fair to be held permanently in Syracuse, on farmland to the west of the city close to the Erie Canal and the New York Central railroad tracks. Twenty-two bridges spanning the "Grand Canal" provided vantage points from which daily life could be observed. During these early years, handsome homes were built along East and West Water Street, allowing their owners to keep a watchful eye on canal traffic and to enjoy a glimpse through a newly opened window into the outside world, perhaps finding it exciting and threatening at the same time.

Much of the excitement and doubtless some of the sense of threat was provided by the steady stream of European immigrants, who came initially to work in the salt industry and later to labor in manufacturing and commercial enterprises. Although "salt barons" were mostly of Protestant New England stock, salt boilers came from Catholic areas of Ireland and Germany, and later from Italy and eastern Europe. The initial waves of immigrants were followed successively by Armenians, Greeks, Canadians, northern and central Europeans, and Asians. Syracuse is still a city of ethnic neighborhoods. Part of the West Side, home for many of the Irish who were later joined there by Poles and Ukrainians, soon became known as Tipperary Hill. Its Irish roots are recognized by a traffic signal—the only one of its kind in New York State—in which the green light is placed above the red.

Building churches became increasingly important in a community that was facing problems of incorporating large immigrant groups. Church and temple not only seemed effective institutional forms of social control but also served as important social centers for many immigrants. Before churches were built, services were held in private homes or in schools, which, as a rule, preceded church buildings in Onondaga County. In the 1820s, three churches were built in Syracuse, and by 1851 there were nine churches in the city, including one synagogue. The Syracuse city directory listed forty churches (including three synagogues) in 1873, and one hundred churches (including eight synagogues) in 1918.

The Erie Canal was the conduit for ideas as well, and most of them were linked to religion. Syracuse, in the midst of a region where habitual revivalism occurred— the "burned-over district"—became a favorite stop for revivalist preachers, some of whom held the crowd's attention with their dramatic performances. William Miller, founder of the Adventists, had a large following in Onondaga County. After he announced the Second Coming of Christ in 1843, the faithful gathered in their ascension robes on the rooftops of downtown buildings. It was an anxious time for them, and children were frightened because they did not want to go to heaven just yet.

This religious fervor took many forms and imbued secular activities. Besides being used for religious purposes, churches also became focal points for the temperance movement, women's suffrage, and pro- and antislavery activities. Readily accessible by canal boat and train, Syracuse became a convention city that warranted the construction not only of hotels but of the Convention Hall on East Genesee Street (1858; Rufus Rose; now demolished). Many public and commercial buildings of that time were equipped with public halls to be used for social, cultural, and political activities. Two thousand suffragists gathered in the public hall of the old City Hall for the Women's Rights Convention in 1861. They were not popular, and Susan B. Anthony and Samuel J. May, pastor of the Unitarian church, were burned in effigy in Hanover Square.

But the Erie, the old "horse ocean" that inspired many romantic tales, had its dark downside. Packet boats, which brought visitors, new ideas, and immigrants, also brought two cholera epidemics. The canal was used for the disposal of waste generated by the very cities that owed their existence to it. The plagues of the Erie were said to be harlotry, blasphemy, drunkenness, rioting, and chills and fever. And there were other calamities, both major and minor. Local architect Russell A. King tells the story of his firm's predecessor, Archimedes Russell,who, after having driven his car into the canal waters, later relied on the driving services of Harry King, a teenager then and not yet an architect. Neither had a driver's license, which was not required in the early 1900s, and there was no rail along the canal to prevent these not-infrequent mishaps. Some survived the plunge, but some less fortunate drivers and pedestrians did not emerge from the canal waters alive. A more spectacular mishap occurred in 1901, when a bridge collapsed under the weight of a trolley. The worst disaster was a canal break in 1907, when a crack in the foundation caused by the collapse of the underground aqueduct of Onondaga Creek drained the canal for six miles. Small boats and a building were swept away in the torrent.

Although the opening of the new Greek Revival weighlock building in 1850 indicated that the canal business was going well, it gradually diminished under strong competitive pressure from the railroads. Even when canal tolls were abolished in 1882, the Erie Canal could no longer compete

Weighlock building, ca. 1900. Courtesy Erie Canal Museum, Syracuse

with this less expensive and faster means of transportation. Railroad owners effectively used their political power to oppose any improvements to the canal; consequently, this grand construction, once considered by some as "the Eighth Wonder of the World," died of neglect.

The electrically operated Barge Canal, completed in 1918, replaced the Erie. It followed a similar route overall but no longer flows through Syracuse. The original canal's Syracuse section became Erie Boulevard when it was filled during the 1920s, with hard landfill in Clinton Square and with soda ash deposited by Solvay Process in the western section. The banks of the remaining Erie Canal now offer recreation. The Oswego Canal metamorphosed partly into the Barge Canal system, partly into Oswego Boulevard and Interstate 81, which was built through the city in the 1960s, dividing Syracuse into east and west. Both Interstate 81 and Interstate 690, the latter creating a north-south division, facilitate out-of-town travel and remove long-distance traffic from city streets. But because they promote easy travel to the suburbs and neighboring shopping centers, they have also encouraged the flight of larger retailers from the downtown area.

Railroads

The railroad came to Syracuse in 1839, and by 1890 the city was connected with nine railroad lines. The first station was built at Vanderbilt Square. Strap-iron rails were laid along Washington Street, and trains sped through downtown Syracuse "at twenty miles an hour under favorable conditions." The railroads played an important part in the development of the city and changed its face. They themselves developed rapidly, from cars pulled by horses along wooden tracks to fancy locomotives with overnight sleeping and parlor cars gliding along iron rails. By the turn of the century, an array of shops, roundhouses, and yards related to railroading had been constructed throughout the Syracuse area. Trains crossed Salina Street, enticing hotel and retail business to move from Clinton Square to Vanderbilt Square and Salina Street. When the old train station was demolished in 1869, passenger stations were built to the west in the area of present-day Armory Square, resulting in lively building activities there of hotels, warehouses, and flophouses.

With an average of ninety train movements daily, twenty-nine crossing points, and locomotives billowing smoke into the air and covering building facades with soot, downtown Syracuse was busy, congested, and noisy, especially when streetcars joined trains in the 1860s. Horsepowered at first, they soon were replaced by the street railway, which was electrified in the 1880s. This new means of transportation allowed people who could not afford horse and carriage to travel inexpensively within the city and to the outskirts, away from the place of work. As a result, surrounding settlements such as Geddes, Danforth, Onondaga Valley, Elmwood, and Eastwood became part of Syracuse between 1886 and 1927. The villages of Lodi and

Syracuse had been united as early as 1834. Whereas during the second half of the nineteenth century James Street, Fayette Park, and West Genesee Street were enclaves of the well-to-do, the new "streetcar suburbs" became home for people with less money. Speculation and development became profitable as many realized the American Dream in these newly developing and now easily accessible parts of the city. There are stories of most-accommodating trolley drivers who would perform errands and deliver messages, and of a philanthropic family living on West Genesee Street who ran a private trolley line for their own and their neighbors' convenience. In 1939, buses replaced the electric trolleys, initiating the removal of miles of trolley tracks and a vast street-paving program.

Three years earlier, the New York Central had started to use an elevated route, and Syracusans celebrated their city's liberation from train traffic. The replacement of trains by automobiles was complete in the 1960s when the elevated railroad bed became Interstate 690. Most train stations disappeared from the face of the city, and Syracuse's last New York Central passenger station (1936; Frederick B. O'Connor; National Register of Historic Places) on Erie Boulevard became a bus station in the 1960s. As you are traveling west along Interstate 690, you may get a glimpse of lonely figures waiting on an abandoned platform for trains that never come. *Waiting for the Night Train* was sculpted by Duke Epolito and Larry Zankowski in 1982. Those who want to take a train now have to travel to Amtrak's passenger station in East Syracuse.

Waiting for the Night Train

Building the City

Change, often equated with progress, became a constant factor in building the city. Frequent fires played as important a role as the need to replace older buildings with larger, newer ones. As a consequence, there are but few pre–Civil War buildings left in Syracuse. Those that remain are simple in form and ornament, their design inspired by classical styles that were adopted for commercial, residential, and religious buildings. Writers of builders' guides, such as Asher Benjamin (1773–1845) and Minard Lafever (1798–1854), were highly successful in promoting classical revival designs at a time when there were neither architecture schools nor architectural journals in this country. Architects learned their trade by experience.

Although the majority of early local buildings were of wood, which burned easily, three-story brick buildings, a source of pride, were erected during the late 1820s and 1830s. (Salina led the way with a three-story brick building constructed in 1808.) Because of the soil's heavy clay content, brick making was a lucrative local business through most of the nineteenth century. A coat of whitewash, to which a dash of yellow ochre was sometimes added, helped preserve the soft brick of the early years. The various limestone beds of the region provided building stone as well as raw material for the production of lime. Limestone gypsum, another raw material discovered in this area, was used for the manufacture of fertilizer, Portland cement, plate glass, plaster of paris, and stucco.

The present appearance of Syracuse was shaped in the years after the Civil War, a time when salt manufacturing declined here. A diversified industry assured the city's economic prosperity. Candle makers, beer brewers, steel producers, and manufacturers of furniture and caskets, of bicycles, cars, clutches, and gears, of agricultural machinery, of typewriters and electrical devices, and of shoes, glass, and china (to name but a few products) availed themselves of Syracuse's good transportation system, its central location, and its ready labor force. Building activities that had declined during the Civil War boomed after the war years. Between 1860 and 1870, the wealth of the city more than quadrupled; 850 buildings were constructed within the city limits in 1868, at a cost of $2.5 million. Local architects were busy.

Most commercial buildings in Syracuse in the 1850s were constructed with load-bearing walls of brick or stone and a wooden framework for floors and roof. In 1851, the *Syracuse Daily Journal* announced "one of the greatest improvements of the day is the exchange of massive stone pillars in front of stores for smaller ones of cast iron, adding to light admitted to the interior and giving the front a lighter appearance." It was then erroneously believed that the use of cast iron as building material would make a structure fireproof. It seems that no buildings with full cast-iron fronts were constructed in Syracuse, but cast-iron lintels, ornamentation, and pillars—items that could be ordered from catalogues and shipped by canal boat or train—were readily employed.

By midcentury the heavy-timber frame used for dwellings had been replaced by the balloon frame, a light framing system that utilized machine-made nails and standardized lumber, by then readily available. The picturesque styles replaced Greek Revival temples and their vernacular variations. Bay windows, porches, and Carpenter Gothic ornamentation embellished houses. For design ideas, one might consult books by Andrew Jackson Downing (1815–1852), who worked with Alexander Jackson Davis (1803–1892), or by Calvert Vaux (1824–1895). Their designs resulted in a tradition of rural and suburban dwellings, villas for the well-to-do, and cottages for the middle class. Agricultural journals also informed their readers about house designs. Like other city dwellers, Syracusans soon began to move into houses where life was softened by surrounding lawns and trees, away from the urban harshness associated with the place of work. Most likely the house owner's money was made in a downtown commercial building, usually a rectangular block that fit into the urban grid and could be added onto when needed. Modestly ornamented, the designs of these Italianate and Renaissance Revival buildings were inspired by Italian Renaissance buildings that had served their merchant princes several centuries before.

The Industrial Revolution made it possible to have more for less. Post--Civil War architectural styles exhibit people's delight in highly ornamented objects that could be made by machines. Reproductions of houses designed in Second Empire and Queen Anne styles, in Stick style, and in eclectic combinations ornamented with Eastlake designs filled the pages of a multitude of pattern books, so called because they reproduced patterns of architectural details to scale. Drawings of plans and elevations could be purchased from the publisher for little money, and if the client wanted a custom-designed house, drawings would sell for 2 percent of the building's cost, in contrast to the 3.5 percent an architect would charge. Houses in many Syracuse neighborhoods might have been inspired by designs in pattern books, which provided a rich source of information for carpenters and builders. Whereas the floor plan of the earlier classically inspired house was often dictated by its symmetrical design, that of the house built during the second part of the nineteenth century was arranged according to function. Important improvements in heating, lighting, and plumbing made the house comfortable. Architectural journals first appeared in the second half of the nineteenth century and kept architects abreast of the latest developments in building technology and style.

By the 1890s, fireproof and steel-frame construction had arrived in Syracuse. This, together with the passenger elevator, made tall buildings possible, and rising real estate prices in downtown areas made them necessary. Although Syracuse was not as squeezed for space as were larger northeastern cities, tall office towers nevertheless took over part of the central business district. Symbolizing corporate power, their prestigious height soon overshadowed church steeples, which in an earlier age had been the focal points of the skyline.

As the commercial core of the city grew vertically, the horizontal spread of residential areas continued. The rapid growth of industrialism had generated not only products but a large urban middle class. Homeownership was an important ingredient in being defined as middle class. An 1890 survey indicated that 48 percent of families in the United States owned their own homes. In Syracuse in 1924, homeownership was 37 percent and remained below 50 percent through the 1950s. But there were some who thought it convenient to live in apartment houses in the city, a way of living never as accepted here as it was in Europe. The popularity of the apartment house for the affluent middle class grew to some extent in the United States during the latter part of the nineteenth century. There were 9 apartment buildings in Syracuse in 1898; twenty years later there were 128. Most of them have been demolished. Attempts have been made to reverse negative associations with living in an apartment in the city. Five apartment towers in the downtown area were constructed during the years of urban renewal in the 1960s and 1970s. Through the conversion of former commercial structures into apartment buildings, a trend in Syracuse since the late 1970s, developers and city planners have hoped to bring back city dwellers.

Commercial and public buildings of the late nineteenth and early twentieth centuries became larger. Their classical form and ornateness were in part fashioned after the buildings of the White City of the World's Columbian Exposition in Chicago (1893), where the architectural vocabulary of imperial Rome was used as a unifying style. It was hoped that a return to classical order in architecture together with urban planning (also brought to the public's attention by the World's Columbian Exposition) would bring beauty and harmony into cities that, excepting the gridiron plan, had grown haphazardly and lacked an overall design. The City Beautiful movement, sparked by Frederick Law Olmsted's (1822–1903) boulevards and park systems, and by the White City, provided the blueprint for city planning. What this came to in many cities, Syracuse among them, was attention to civic art rather than to an overall urban plan. The grand Beaux-Arts design (now diminished in size) of the Soldiers' and Sailors' Monument on Clinton Square is an example.

Before the late 1800s, planning in Syracuse had consisted mainly of subdividing land, arranging streets, and locating municipal buildings. General Elias W. Leavenworth, president of the village of Syracuse and second mayor of the city, had insisted on wide, tree-lined streets, many of which were laid out along Indian paths and wagon trails. A modern system of paved streets was created by straightening and leveling roads, filling in ravines and hollows, and bridging and sewering brooks. The public squares and some cemeteries of the early settlers evolved into the city's park system. A tree-planting program of elms and maples was started after the Civil War, and eventually elms arched over streets like cathedral ceilings. The Dutch elm disease of the 1960s killed most of them, as well as many maples, which deprived of shade could not survive.

During the first quarter of the twentieth century, less became more, and the smaller, simpler, and more economic house was now put forth as the American Dream. Locally influential in this trend was the Arts and Crafts movement, which flourished in New York State and in Syracuse during the end of the nineteenth and the beginning of the twentieth century and attempted to bring happiness by good design and fine craftsmanship. Influenced by English Arts and Crafts designs, Gustav Stickley (1858–1942) began manufacturing furniture in the Syracuse suburb of Eastwood in the 1890s. He also published *The Craftsman*, a journal that was to become one of the most influential Arts and Crafts magazines in the United States. Stickley redesigned the interior of his Syracuse home according to Arts and Crafts principles; the house, which still stands at 438 Columbus Avenue, is listed on the National Register of Historic Places. Other important Arts and Crafts proponents in Syracuse were ceramic artist Adelaide Alsop Robineau, whose home and studio still exist on Robineau Road, and architect Ward Wellington Ward (1875-1932), who built not only homes for the well-to-do but also several fine bungalows that exemplify the ideals of the small Arts and Crafts house.

Stickley's *Craftsman* was joined by such important tastemakers as *House Beautiful* and *Ladies Home Journal* as advocates of simple and economic housing. Much emphasis was placed on technological systems and on

Gustav Stickley House

landscaping. The number of rooms and partitions declined, floor plans opened up, and the kitchen became the central core. Houses were frequently ordered through mail-order firms, such as Sears, Roebuck and Company. The Architects' Small House Service Bureau, Inc. was organized in 1921 to provide home builders with designs for small, inexpensive houses, and in the early 1930s, Herbert Hoover's government launched a campaign to increase moderate-cost dwellings. Colonial Revival style houses, English Tudor cottages, and Mission style houses combined modern efficiency and comfortable associations with the past. Syracuse neighborhoods are visual reminders of all of these trends. Although the building of row houses, much used in larger northeastern cities, was little exploited in Syracuse, the multifamily house, especially the two-family residence, is a characteristic Syracuse institution. And here, as elsewhere, public housing made an appearance: between 1938 and 1940 Pioneer Homes was constructed on East Adams Street as the first U.S. Housing Authority project in the country.

Exodus, Urban Renewal, and Preservation

The Depression and the Second World War put a temporary halt to building activities and marked the end of Syracuse's great period of growth. The doldrums were somewhat alleviated by the construction of a handful of major Art Deco-inspired buildings. While the State Tower Building (1927) on Hanover Square was the tallest in the city, the Niagara Mohawk Building (1932) on Erie Boulevard West was the brightest. Four years later, the New York Central's fourth passenger station opened its doors to travelers on Erie Boulevard East, and a milestone in building technology was reached upon completion of the Onondaga County War Memorial on Montgomery Street in 1951.

Aided and abetted by improved highways, the steady exodus into suburbs and exurbs, which grew 70 percent during the 1950s, changed the character of many of the one-time urban residential areas and condemned the older inner-city districts to decay. Urban renewal, launched by the Housing Act of 1949, seemed to many city planners the panacea for urban ills. It was believed that once the old "eyesores" were replaced with modern buildings moneyed clients would come into the city, thus revitalizing downtown. Because progress was equated with newness, in Syracuse, as in other nineteenth-century industrial cities, many buildings marked with use and age gave way to parking lots and shiny new towers. The demolition of older housing stock forced a large migration of lower-income people to other areas of the city, particularly to the near South Side. The social and architectural fabric of the city changed considerably. Because the design of many of the new buildings of that era did not reflect the design of their remaining older neighbors, the architectural collage that ensued threatened to become an unsightly hodgepodge. Remarked Ada Louise Huxtable of the *New York Times*, "Syracuse's great consistency...had been its will to self destruction."

The loss of old buildings also meant the loss of the city's history. There were some who were alarmed by this, among them the late Syracuse University professor Harley J. McKee, who pointed to the importance and beauty of nineteenth-century buildings in Syracuse at a time when historic buildings for many people meant Williamsburg. Under his influence, SAVE—Society for the Advancement of the Visual Environment—was founded in 1967, one year after a national act was passed that provided for the establishment of historic preservation offices in every state. SAVE metamorphosed into the Landmarks Association of Central New York in 1976. It now exists as the Preservation Association of Central New York and was joined in 1989 by the Heritage Coalition, Inc. Local preservation groups work together with the Syracuse Landmark Preservation Board, an advisory group that reports to the Syracuse Planning Commission and the Syracuse Common Council on the local designation of historic resources. The Landmark Preservation Ordinance of 1975 also established a citywide system for the controlled protection of individually listed buildings and districts. Finally, the federal investment tax credit program of the early 1980s provided an important impetus for the revitalization of many of the older downtown buildings, some of which are adaptively reused and look better now than during their heyday.

Two publications reinforced awareness of our architectural heritage. In 1964, the Syracuse University School of Architecture published *Architecture Worth Saving in Onondaga County* (McKee et al.), and *Onondaga Landmarks* (Syracuse–Onondaga County Planning Agency), produced by the Cultural Resources Council of Syracuse and Onondaga County, Inc., came out in 1975. During that time the Design Section of the Syracuse-Onondaga County Planning Agency under the direction of Manuel Barbas identified downtown buildings for adaptive reuse in one of the first municipal planning studies.

On its brighter side, during the period of urban renewal some buildings designed by internationally known architects were constructed. The May Memorial Unitarian Society at 3800 East Genesee Street, the fifth church of the society, was completed in 1962. It was designed by Pietro Belluschi (Boston, Massachusetts) and constructed in association with the local firm of Pederson, Hueber and Hares, Architects; Glavin, Landscape Architect. The church was named May Memorial after the society's second minister, ardent reformer Samuel Joseph May (1797–1871), who is said to have been burned in effigy more than any other Syracusan. In 1964 President Lyndon B. Johnson gave the first phase of his famous Gulf of Tonkin speech at Syracuse University; the occasion was the dedication ceremony of the Newhouse Communication Center (Newhouse I), named after its donor, Samuel I. Newhouse. The building was designed by internationally known architect I. M. Pei. Ten years later Newhouse II was added by Skidmore, Owings & Merrill of New York. The notable Everson Museum of Art, I. M. Pei's other building in this city, opened its doors on the corner of State and Harrison streets in 1968.

May Memorial Unitarian Church, sanctuary

In the 1970s, New York State launched its Urban Cultural Parks program. Not a park in the traditional sense, the Urban Cultural Park invites the visitor to learn about the city's history and culture, to enjoy its architecture, monuments, and green spaces, and to support their preservation. There are fourteen parks in New York State, including the one in Syracuse. Each park emphasizes a particular theme; "Business, Capital, and Transportation" was the topic chosen for Syracuse. It will be the focus of a permanent exhibition to be housed in the Urban Cultural Parks Visitor Center at the Erie Canal Museum.

There are plans to clean Onondaga Lake, once beautiful and pristine but now polluted by those whose lives it sustained. Large-scale alterations in Syracuse's urban fabric have ceased, with the possible exceptions of the redevelopment of "Oil City" at the south end of Onondaga Lake and the city's plan to link Franklin Square, the Carousel Center, and the waterfront with the downtown area. Also, a conference center to the south of the War Memorial and the Everson Museum has been built. Although occasional new buildings will arise, most of the physical changes now consist of rehabilitating and adapting older structures. For the time being, at least, there has been a marriage between economics and a concern for maintaining the architectural links with a robust past. One can only hope that the union will be both lasting and fruitful.

WALKING TOURS

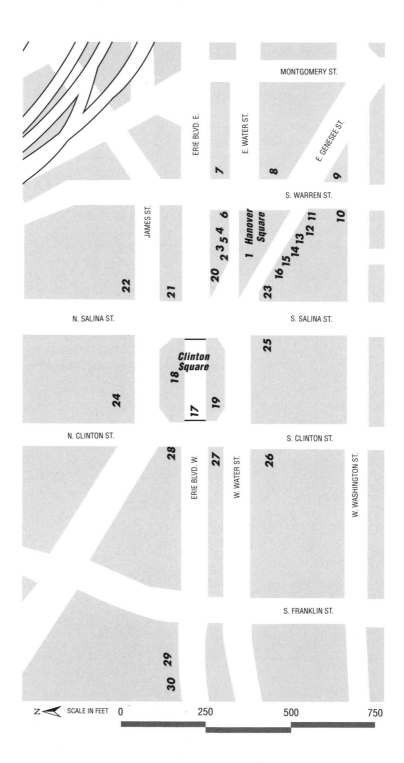

MONTGOMERY ST.

ERIE BLVD. E.

E. WATER ST.

E. GENESEE ST.

7

8

9

S. WARREN ST.

JAMES ST.

20 2 3 5 4 6

1 Hanover Square

12 11

10

16 15 14 13

23

22

21

N. SALINA ST.

S. SALINA ST.

25

Clinton Square

18

17 19

24

N. CLINTON ST.

S. CLINTON ST.

28

ERIE BLVD. W.

W. WATER ST.

27

26

W. WASHINGTON ST.

S. FRANKLIN ST.

29

30

N SCALE IN FEET 0   250   500   750

DOWNTOWN

Hanover Square and Clinton Square

Estimated walking time: 1 hour, 20 minutes (Nos. 1–30)

1. Hanover Square
Landscape architects: 1981, Balsley and Kuhl, New York
NRHD (except portions of the Phoenix and Franklin buildings) CSPD (except
the State Tower Building and portions of the Phoenix and Franklin buildings)

The name Hanover Square seems to have been used in the 1820s and
1830s, when the Hanover Arcade, a consortium of shops, was located on the
site of the State Tower Building. The first Syracuse city directory (1851) lists it
as Franklin Square; but Hanover Square it remained, although it was sometimes referred to as "Hangover Square" because of the many taverns surrounding it. The consumption of alcohol was alarming to many who lived
in a county that had 31 private schools, 88 churches, and 142 taverns. An
attempt by the citizens in 1846 to stop all sale of intoxicating drink proved
unsuccessful. In the early 1870s, journalist and printer Lewis Redfield had a
water fountain constructed in Hanover Square in the name of temperance
and in answer to the argument that one could not get a drink of water
downtown and so had to resort to stronger spirits. The fountain probably
died of neglect and was removed twenty years later. Syracuse was frontline

Hanover Square with Franklin Buildings, 1884, looking southeast.
Courtesy the Koolakian family

for the troops of the Salvation Army and the Rescue Mission who arrived in the city in full force in the 1880s and 1890s. Between trains, the old railroad depot (no longer existing) on Washington Street to the south of Hanover Square would be used frequently for temperance meetings.

Because of its location directly south of the Erie Canal and north of the railroad, Hanover Square functioned primarily as a transfer point and became the city's commercial district. The Erie Canal, which divided the city into north and south, also shaped the appearance of buildings along its banks, in this case on the north side of Hanover Square: their plain, functional facades fronted the canal (now Erie Boulevard), while architectural ornament was reserved for the side visible from the square.

Hanover Square was, and still is, a meeting place, imbued with stories real and imagined. Here "snake doctors" sold their patent medicines, speeches were delivered, public auctions were held, and crowds gathered to watch a one-legged man walk a tightrope. There were complaints in the 1860s that downtown streets were infested with cattle and hogs and that a sow had taken her litter to Hanover Square on a Sunday afternoon. Wooden platforms erected for recruiting purposes at the beginning of the Civil War were burned in a bonfire when the war ended. Hanover Square was the site of Abraham Lincoln's eulogy, when in 1865 his bier was brought through Syracuse on its way to the final resting place in Springfield, Illinois. The square later had its traffic problems, and carriage parking was banned in the 1890s. During that time, Hanover Square briefly became Veterans Park until Clinton Square was dedicated in 1906 as a site for the Soldiers' and Sailors' Monument. Like Clinton Square, Hanover Square was updated with a fountain and landscaping in 1981. The modern fountain seems too large for its space and does not relate to the buildings that surround it. This is regrettable, because these buildings have maintained their architectural integrity and are a textbook collection of popular styles of the nineteenth and early twentieth centuries, as well as visual symbols of the city's history. Hanover Square was the city's first Historic and Preservation District, a significant event in local preservation efforts.

2. Addition to the Gridley Building (No. 20), 1875

101 East Water Street
Architect: Horatio Nelson White, Syracuse
Interior renovation: 1899, Archimedes Russell, Syracuse
Renovation: 1974, Quinlivan Pierik Krause and Stopen, Syracuse

The addition to the Gridley Building was carefully designed to relate stylistically to the original Second Empire portion. Notice that the ornate facade faces Hanover Square. After the Syracuse Savings Bank was constructed with a passenger elevator, the Gridley Building, then known as the Onondaga County Savings Bank Building, also received a steam-powered elevator. During that time the elevator not only was a practical device but served as a status symbol as well.

3. Gere Building, 1894

121 East Water Street
Architect: Charles E. Colton,
Syracuse
Renovation: 1974–75, Curtin
Kane Gere and Ashley, Syracuse
NRHP NRHD CSPD

3. Gere Building

Built as a bank for James J. Belden and named after his father-in-law, Robert Gere, the Gere Building has been hailed as Colton's finest design. The old fireproof bank vaults still exist underneath the sidewalk. Since 1906, it has been occupied by various firms that enjoy an interior with marble flooring and wainscoting and the use of an open-screen elevator with a bronze well screen. Located on a narrow site between two adjoining office buildings, the Gere Building is distinguished by the design of the facade fronting Hanover Square. Here the architect uses the tripartite system of composition that corresponds to the classical column's base, shaft, and capital. In this case, the base is of gray granite and combines round-arched and rectangular openings in the style of Henry Hobson Richardson. In the shaft, windows are grouped vertically beneath arches, and the richly ornamented terra cotta cornice acts as the capital. Terra cotta designs on spandrels between floor levels and underneath the cornice were inspired by Louis Henry Sullivan's ornamentations, his answer to the European Art Nouveau, although they were more geometric than the European designs. Charles E. Colton was undoubtedly aware of buildings designed by Richardson and by Sullivan. They were frequently illustrated in architectural journals which were by then readily available.

Henry Hobson Richardson (1838–1886) was one of the most important and influential architects in the United States. He decisively influenced Louis Henry Sullivan (1856–1924), whose pursuit of a modern architectural style and love of ornament and functional form created a style named Sullivanesque. Of this the Gere Building is a good example. The building is listed in Marcus Whiffen's *American Architecture since 1780: A Guide to the Styles*

(1969). It was one of the earliest buildings on Hanover Square to be renovated.

When the building's architect, Charles Erastus Colton, died in 1914, he was hailed as having been "the most prominent architect in the city at the time." After he had worked in the office of Archimedes Russell, he established his own office in 1876. Colton was offered the position of state architect, which he declined because of pressing work.

4. Phoenix Buildings, ca. 1834
123–129 East Water Street
NRHD (portion of buildings) CSPD (portion of buildings)

The Phoenix Buildings are among the oldest surviving commercial buildings on Hanover Square and are so called because they replaced earlier wooden structures that were destroyed by fire. In the 1830s, the square often resembled a sea of mud, a condition that was changed in the 1860s when it was filled in, raising the street level by several feet. These commercial buildings were used as canal loft warehouses and served both the Hanover Square and the Erie Canal sides. Large doors in second stories through which cargo was hoisted with block and tackle are still visible on the Erie Boulevard side. Originally, these brick buildings were three stories high, and their facades were adorned with pilasters. They are now four-story buildings with plain facades and rectangular windows that have sandstone lintels ornamented with block designs and fine brickwork along the cornice line. Like the Franklin Buildings (**No. 13**) across the street, they are of the Greek Revival period (ca. 1820–1860), and although they are now without the columns and porticoes usually associated with the Greek Revival, they represent a type that was often built in this area.

4. Phoenix Buildings, c. 1860, looking northwest.
Courtesy Onondaga Historical Association.

5. The Consortium, ca. 1834 (one of the Phoenix Buildings)
123 East Water Street
Renovation: 1978–79, Hawley McAfee, Syracuse
NRHD (portion of building) CSPD (portion of building)

The Consortium was purchased in 1978 by the Consortium for Children's Services, Inc., a not-for-profit organization that runs a gift shop on the first level and has offices upstairs. It was one of the earlier buildings on Hanover Square to be renovated. It had been home to the Larned & Barker Drug Store and a leather goods manufacturer. The interior of the building can be seen during store hours.

6. Dana Building, ca. 1837
135–139 East Water Street
Addition: 1861
NRHD CSPD

Adjacent to the east side of the Phoenix Buildings, the Dana Building displays the same unornamented facade but does not continue the window arrangement of the adjoining structure. In 1861, a fourth story was added to conform to the height of its neighbors. Here, too, fine brickwork embellishes the cornice lines. In 1839, D. & M. Dana opened a dry-goods store on the northwest corner of Warren and Water streets, which became one of the principal establishments in the village. When barter was a necessity, many of the local farmers took their grain to the store and exchanged it for "store pay."

7. Grange Building, 1925
203 East Water Street
Architect: Edward Albert Howard, Syracuse
Renovation: 1982, JCM Architectural Associates, Syracuse
NRHD CSPD

The Grange Building was originally constructed as showrooms for Bresee Chevrolet and is now used for office and retail space. It encloses Hanover Square on the northeastern corner. Edward Albert Howard (1864–1935) had worked in the architectural office of James H. Kirby before he entered the office of Archimedes Russell, where he worked for twenty-five years.

8. State Tower Building, 1927
109 South Warren Street
Architects: Thompson and Churchill, New York
NRHD

"Syracuse was a thriving manufacturing and regional commercial center and did not have an 'ahead of the times' modern office building," said one of the original owners, Albert Mayer. The new building that would soon seem to be Syracuse's counterpart to New York's Empire State Building (1931) replaced the two Bastable Blocks (1863, 1893) that were destroyed by fire. The architects designed the State Tower Building with setbacks, obeying a zoning regulation that was in force in all major U.S. cities at that time. Tall buildings designed with setbacks allowed daylight to reach street level. The State Tower Building was not to occupy the whole site but was to be thin and graceful, allowing all places in the building to see daylight. L-shaped floors fulfilled the designers' concept. And according to the architects' vision, the building "should be ideal for big business and still have the finest small offices in Syracuse." The exterior was to give the illusion of sunlight even on gray days: the brickwork goes from darker to lighter shades as it nears the top, which also seems to increase the building's height. Ornamentation and materials used are representative of Art Deco; a shiny brass entrance leads into a small lobby with brass fixtures, an elegant mailbox, and colorful ornament, probably inspired by Native American designs.

8. State Tower Building

9. S. A. & K. Building, 1869 (now City Hall Commons)
200 East Genesee Street
Additions: 1894, 1985
Renovation: initial work, 1985, Robertson Strong Apgar, Syracuse; completion and present plan, JCM Architectural Associates, Syracuse
NRHD CSPD

This Renaissance Revival style building was originally known as the Granger Block, named after owner and builder General Amos P. Granger, a prominent local politician. It replaced two other buildings, both demolished by fire, and was renamed in 1898 by the then well-known local law firm Sedgwick, Andrews, and Kennedy, which bought the building and occupied part of it. Its plan is triangular to fit the site and from certain angles resembles the Flatiron Building in New York. The brick structure was originally four stories and received three more in 1894. The original height appears in the form of a belt course between the fourth and fifth levels. A greenhouse, added in 1985, is used as a public space. Now owned by the city, the building houses municipal offices. The original limestone pavers may be seen at the northwest corner of the pedestrian area between the greenhouse and the State Tower building.

10. Larned Building, 1869

114 South Warren Street
Architect: Horatio Nelson White, Syracuse
Alterations: 1890s, 1950s
Renovation: 1991–, JCM Architectural Associates, Syracuse
NRHD CSPD

When in 1869 the railroad station in Vanderbilt Square was torn down, the construction of the Larned Building (on the site of the Tremont House) and the Granger Block hailed the area's transformation from railroad-related activities to principally office and retail use. Both buildings were sought-after downtown business addresses. Granger's business partner, Samuel Larned, had made his fortune selling supplies to passing boats from his own canal boat. Designed by Horatio Nelson White as a "fine modern-style block," the building was built and named by Larned's heirs in his honor. The Second Empire style being the modern style at the time, the Larned Building received a mansard roof punctuated with mansarded towers at the principal corners as well as two shorter towers. In the 1890s, the mansard roof was reconstructed into a full story, and the roofline was leveled and received a cornice. The large Second Empire style windows on the second level near the street corner still exist. The ornate cast-iron window caps were mass-produced components that could be ordered through trade catalogues. Earlier storefronts, obscured by mid-twentieth century changes that were also made in the interior, are being restored to their 1890s condition, with retail space at street level; the upper stories serve as a parking garage and share access with the Vanderbilt parking garage on East Washington Street. Says Joseph C. Maryak of JCM Architectural Associates, "this is a *very* adaptive reuse."

Horatio Nelson White (1814–1892) learned his trade by practicing it and became a successful and prolific architect who designed numerous religious, commercial, residential, and educational buildings in Syracuse and central New York.

11. Post Building, ca. 1880 (former Post–Standard Building)

136 East Genesee Street
Renovation: 1991–, JCM Architectural Associates, Syracuse
NRHD CSPD

The first edition of the *Post–Standard* was published in this building in 1899. The structure was built on a narrow lot and has a facade designed in the Richardsonian Romanesque mode. The organization of windows grouped vertically under a large arch is representative of the style. Textural variety is achieved by using brick with sandstone trim. The renovated building will be adaptively reused.

12. Colboy Wholesale Jewelers, ca. 1870 (former Snow Drug Building)

134 East Genesee Street
Renovation: ca. 1980, JCM Architectural Associates, Syracuse
NRHD CSPD

This building on a narrow lot replaced Franklin Building No. 7 (**see No. 13**). The structure's mansard roof with small circular dormers are of the Second Empire style. A rhythmically organized three-bay facade is enlivened by a variety of arched openings and contrasting colors and by incised ornamentation on pilasters and keystones. Together with the adjacent building (**No. 11**) and the Gere and Gridley buildings on the north side of Hanover Square, it illustrates ornate post–Civil War architecture. Originally the building was used by the Snow Drug Company, established in Syracuse in 1854, which advertised remedies such as "mugworth and horse nettle root."

13. Franklin Buildings, ca. 1822–39

132–128 East Genesee Street
NRHD (portion of buildings) CSPD (portion of buildings)

This group of commercial structures originally had step-up entrances. In the 1860s, they became level with the street when Hanover Square was filled in. Lower levels were occupied by dry-goods stores, and upper stories functioned as warehouse, storage, and office space. They are the counterpart in age and stylistic features to the Phoenix Buildings (**No. 4**) on the north side of the square.

14. Koolakian's Men's Clothing Store, ca. 1822–23 (Franklin Buildings Nos. 5 and 6)

132–130 East Genesee Street
Addition: 1853
HABS NRHD (portion of building) CSPD (portion of building)

Constructed of granite, the building was originally freestanding and known as Granite Block or Granite Store. It later became Franklin Buildings Nos. 5 and 6. Its main floor received a rear addition of fifty feet in 1853, and its step-up entrance and entire first floor were lowered one foot to match the present street level. Apart from these and minor alterations to the store area made by the Koolakians, who have owned and occupied the building since 1956, this, the oldest downtown structure, is little changed, according to Robert G. Koolakian's extensive research. As compared with the two adjacent Franklin Buildings, it has its original roofline, and it is the only one built of granite. The interior woodwork was done with a straight saw, and nails and locks were handmade. The original windows have been restored.

Old documents make reference to the "Granite Store," whose history is closely connected to the development of the village of Corinth, officially renamed Syracuse in 1825. The first occupant, Kellogg & Sabin, ran a store there. John and Isaiah Townsend of the Syracuse Company owned the building in the 1820s and 1830s, and a salt scale and counterweight found by the Koolakians indicate that a salt inspector may have plied his trade here. In the 1860s, local architect Archimedes Russell occupied the third floor at about the time he was leaving Horatio Nelson White's employ. Most interesting is the building's connection with the Daguerreotype process of early photography. Photographer John M. Clark established his first sitting room and studio on the fourth floor, the "oldest in the city," and "one of the oldest in the country," according to Robert G. Koolakian, citing the Syracuse Standard of 1851. In an index of photographers who practiced in Syracuse from 1841 to 1900, Cleota Reed (1985) listed about thirty-five, and according to the Koolakians' research, "half of them practiced in the 'Granite Store' at one time or another." The famous Civil War photographer George N. Barnard, the photographer of Sherman's campaign, was associated with Clark's studio, which he bought in 1853. Barnard also rented space in the top two floors of the adjacent Owen Building (Franklin Building No. 4), which was connected with Clark's studio by a walk-through.

15. Sam Young Shoe Store Inc., ca. 1839
(former Owen Building [Franklin Building Nos. 3 and 4])
128–122 East Genesee Street
NRHD (portion of building) CSPD (portion of building)

At one time, the village well was located on this site. Part of the originally four-story Franklin Building No. 4 was built as a manufacturing plant for billiard balls and cues, which were made with a lathe powered by a windmill on the roof of Franklin Building No. 3. In 1871, the process was converted to steam power. The Owen Billiard Room was advertised as being "one of the leading resorts in town." In the early 1890s, the two upper floors, once rented by photographer George Barnard, were razed and the structure was altered.

16. Flagship Securities Building, 1896
(former Bank of Syracuse Building)
120 East Genesee Street
Architect: Albert L. Brockway, Syracuse
NRHD CSPD

The former Bank of Syracuse Building was the first steel-frame structure in Syracuse. Its modern frame is hidden behind a symmetrical Beaux-Arts marble facade. Stone replicas of ancient Sicilian coins in the pediments above both entrances remind the passerby that Syracuse was named after the ancient Siracusa in Sicily. The replica of the coins was also used on the bank's checks. Originally the building was planned to conform in height to the adjacent Onondaga County Savings Bank, but its growth remained stunted. Contemporary newspaper accounts preserved at the Onondaga

16. Flagship Securities Building (former Bank of Syracuse Building)

Historical Association wrote in glowing terms about the "little gem in marble." The interior was appointed with marble floors and wainscoting, and the tellers sat behind ornamental brass cages. The core, the two-story banking room, could be viewed from a gallery reached by winding stairs, and various offices were located several feet above the main room. The building has been recycled to house a restaurant in the basement and offices upstairs.

Albert L. Brockway (1864–1933) studied architecture at the École des Beaux-Arts in Paris and was in partnership with John P. Benson and later with Alfred Taylor. He served as the first chairman of the first Syracuse Planning Commission (1918) and received a personal award from Governor Theodore Roosevelt for the most constructive plan for the extension of the State Fairgrounds, for which he designed three buildings. As professor of architecture at Syracuse University, he revised the curriculum to follow more closely the methods of teaching at the École des Beaux-Arts.

17. Clinton Square
Landscape architects: 1981, Balsley and Kuhl, New York

Joshua Forman, who built his residence and set up his law office on the northwest end of Clinton Square, named the area after Governor De Witt Clinton, who was a strong proponent of the Erie Canal venture. The square has been the historic center of Syracuse since its modest beginnings. Its face has changed repeatedly and considerably since early north-south and east-west roads came together here and weary travelers rested at Bogardus' Tavern. The crossroads was colloquially called Bogardus' Corners. The owner of the tavern, Henry Bogardus, called the junction South Salina and his inn, the South Salina House. The simple frame structure, built in 1806, was held together with manufactured nails, the latest in building technology. Enlarged, it later became the Mansion House and was located on the north side of the square, now the northwest corner of Genesee and Salina streets. The settlement was also referred to as Milan, and when Sterling Cossit bought and operated the tavern in 1815, the four corners were then known informally as Cossit's Corners. Timothy Cheney, an early Syracuse builder, told of a journey he made with his father in the early 1800s from Onondaga Hollow to Salina to get a wagonload of salt. They stopped at "the Corners," and as they looked around, they saw no other building but the tavern; everything was in a "natural state."

By 1828, the Erie and Oswego canals had joined the crossroads as transport corridors. All four routes intersected within a three-block area in the rapidly growing village, leaving Clinton Square as a natural outdoor meeting

Syracuse House with Onondaga County Savings Bank (l) and Wieting Block (r), ca. 1869, looking south. Courtesy Onondaga Historical Association, Syracuse

Clinton Square with Erie Canal, 1890s, looking east. Courtesy Randall T. Crawford

place. On the south side of the square, the "yellow block," a brick building painted yellow, housed the "most fashionable stores of the village." The Syracuse House, an inn and a busy stagecoach stop, was an early brick structure built in the 1820s at the site of the present Onondaga County Savings Bank. When four stories were added to the building, it was hailed as being the largest building in the area of its day. From its porches, visitors could watch comings and goings on the Erie Canal. It was a lively place, and most travelers found it comfortable enough, except Charles Dickens, who when visiting in 1869 described it as the "worst inn I have ever seen...a hotel surprisingly bad...a triumph in that way...located in a most wonderful out-of-the-way place which looks as if it had begun to be built yesterday and were going to be knocked together with a nail or two tomorrow." Its competitor was the Empire House, which in 1845 replaced the Mansion House on the north side of the square. Designed by William B. Olmstead, it was described as "surpassing anything in beauty that had been seen in the city so far."

There were activities in Clinton Square—to be watched from the bridges crossing the Erie Canal—and there were festivities. The most spectacular one was the great New Year's Day feast in 1870, when brewer John Greenway invited the poor to a public barbecue. Twenty thousand people came to feast, but few were poor. The square was a place for ice skating and parades, for balloon ascensions and celebrations, for business and barter. Immigrants who came on packet boats and disembarked at Clinton Square were quite often hired on the spot by local businesses. Until 1899, a farmers' market was held here. Along the south side, three successive Wieting Blocks (1852, 1856, 1882; the last two by Horatio Nelson White), with their public halls that were often used for entertainment, as well as the Wieting Opera House (1882; Oscar Cobb, Chicago), underlined the square's importance as a place for cultural activities. Theaters developed around Clinton Square, and the city became a tryout center for Broadway.

For half a century, Clinton Square was also courthouse square. There had been two earlier county courthouses, the first located at Onondaga Hill and the second at a compromise location between the villages of Salina and Syracuse. With the placement of the third Onondaga Courthouse (1857; Horatio Nelson White) at the north side of Clinton Square, Syracuse's position as county seat was assured. In 1918, the Erie Canal was officially closed, and the section that ran through downtown was filled in and metamorphosed into Erie Boulevard in 1923. Streetcars and automobiles replaced packet boats and horse-drawn carts. Retail business had moved south to Salina Street several decades earlier, and Columbus Circle became courthouse square. The character of Clinton Square has changed. In 1981, part of the old canal bed wall was exposed, and a fountain with landscaping designed by Balsley and Kuhl of New York completed Clinton Square's new look.

18. Soldiers' and Sailors' Monument, 1911
Design: Clarence Howard Blackwell, Boston
Sculpture: Cyrus E. Dallin

Erected in 1911, after years of political bickering, the Soldiers' and Sailors' Monument is a prominent feature of Clinton Square and is dedicated to the men of Onondaga County who lost their lives in the Civil War. Of Beaux-Arts design, the monument was created by Clarence Howard Blackwell. The bronze groups and reliefs are by sculptor Cyrus E. Dallin, who, like Blackwell, had studied and worked in Paris. Changes to the monument's plaza, originally 152 feet by 52 feet, were made over the years. The focal point of the monument is a granite pylon, topped by a stone sphere that is held by stone eagles. The north and south facade of the pylon are covered with sculpted reliefs of trophies, while two bronze groups cast in Paris occupy the east and west facades. *Call to Arms,* on the east side, is portrayed by a heroic winged victory. The four figures beneath represent the four branches of the service. *Incident at Gettysburg,* on the west side, depicts an incident at the battle of Gettysburg when Color Sergeant Lilly knelt down under fire to mend the broken flagstaff with his belt. He was mortally wounded in another battle and is buried at Oakwood Cemetery. This particular sculptural group did not make it to Syracuse in time for the dedication on 21 June 1910. Dallin returned to the United States, leaving his assistant

Frederick MacMonnies in charge. The assistant got married, went on his honeymoon, and understandably forgot to cast the figures. But, bronze being more eternal than love, the figures eventually got here.

19. Jerry Rescue Monument, 1990
(see also No. 6, Downtown Abolition Sites tour)
Sculpture: Sharon BuMann, Central Square, N.Y.

On the west end of Clinton Square, facing the Amos Block, stands a monument that commemorates Syracuse's participation in the abolition movement. Dedicated in 1990, the Jerry Rescue Monument celebrates the deliverance of an escaped slave who had been incarcerated by federal agents. The monument is placed on an elevated star-shaped base; the star symbolizes hope, and the elevation underlines the importance of the incident. Three figures, larger than life, depict Jerry, shackles broken and his face and body expressing intense agony, Bishop Loguen, and Reverend Samuel J. May, who assist him in his quest for freedom. Reflecting action and vitality, this most recent addition to Clinton Square engages and involves the viewer. In the back of the brick walls are plaques describing the famous incident and the symbolism used in creating the monument.

The three grand bank buildings facing Clinton Square (**Nos. 20–22**) were built in the fashionable styles of the day and announced to all that Syracuse was prosperous and a sound investment. Stimulated by canals and railroads, Syracuse and its economy grew rapidly, and within less than fifty years Syracuse changed from barter to banking. The business of money exchange started in salt warehouses, where a depositor received a cer-

19. Jerry Rescue Monument with Soldiers' and Sailors' Monument (l.)

tificate on the amount of salt stored. This, in turn, could be used as money. For the sake of convenience, banking could be done from canal boats. Before 1830, when Syracuse's first financial institution, the Onondaga County Bank, was founded (liquidated in 1856), Syracusans who wanted to use a more conventional bank had to go to Auburn. By 1870, there were thirteen banks in the city.

20. Gridley Building, 1867
101 East Water Street
Architect: Horatio Nelson White, Syracuse
Addition (**No. 2**): 1875, Horatio Nelson White
Interior renovation: 1899, Archimedes Russell
Renovation: 1974, Quinlivan Pierik Krause and Stopen, Syracuse
HABS NRHP NRHD CSPD

The oldest of the three bank buildings that still flank the east side of Clinton Square, the Gridley Building was originally built as the Onondaga County Savings Bank, incorporated in 1855. It stood on a site formerly occupied by three successive "Coffin Blocks" (part of the original Phoenix Buildings), so called because the first of the three was built of wood and seemed to resemble a coffin. Onondaga limestone, brought from the Onondaga Nation's land to a stone yard at the Dey Brothers site, was used for the bank's construction, consisting of iron beams in combination with masonry partitions. This was considered to be quite progressive for the time and

View from Clinton Square looking east toward Hanover Square, 1854. The Coffin Block is to the right of the bridge. Photograph by George Barnard, Courtesy Onondaga Historical Association.

described as being fireproof. In 1875, a fifty-foot addition—an exact match to the existing building—was constructed to the east, fronting Hanover Square (**No. 2**). The architect chose the then-fashionable Second Empire style, popular in the 1860s and 1870s, for its design. The Gridley Building's mansard roof and dormers as well as the projecting and receding planes of the detailed facades are hallmarks of the style. Characteristic of many buildings erected along the canal, the facade fronting the waterway (now Erie Boulevard) is less ornate than the facades facing Clinton and Hanover squares. When the building was constructed, the city agreed to close a public right-of-way to the canal in exchange for a four-faced clock in the tower, which was to be maintained by the bank. The clock was put back into operation when the structure was renovated.

In 1897, the bank moved to its new building across the street (**No. 23**), and two years later, the older building was sold to businessman Francis Gridley, who hired Archimedes Russell to renovate the interior. It was then that the Salina Street entrance was closed. In 1974, this became the first downtown building to be renovated for adaptive reuse, an event that sparked preservation efforts. The exterior was cleaned and windows were replaced, a difficult task considering the multitude of sizes and shapes. Interior partitions were removed; interior brick walls, oak wainscoting, and cast-iron stairways were cleaned; the pressed-tin ceilings were restored. The old bank vaults on the basement level are vestiges of the building's former life. A small plaza with trees and benches enhances the front of the building facing Clinton Square.

21. Syracuse Savings Bank Building, 1875 (now Fleet Bank of Central New York)
1 Clinton Square
Architect: Joseph Lyman Silsbee, Syracuse
Renovation: 1928, Melvin L. King and Harry A. King, Syracuse
Interior murals: 1971, Hall Groat
HABS NRHP

The savings bank movement was promoted by Governor De Witt Clinton. New York State savings banks stimulated commerce by investing in Erie Canal and railroad bonds. The Syracuse Savings Bank was incorporated in 1849 and was the first bank in the one-year-old city of Syracuse. Harvey Baldwin, Syracuse's first mayor, was the bank's first treasurer. The construction of the present building was largely fireproof. The tower of 170 feet, containing bank vaults and elevator, made it the city's tallest building of the day and emphasized its importance. Banking facilities occupied the basement and first floor, and offices were in the upper stories. The passenger elevator, the first in a Syracuse building, would bring one to the top, from where there was a splendid view. There the architect Joseph Lyman Silsbee had his offices.

Popularized by English art critic John Ruskin, the High Victorian Gothic style, of which the Syracuse Savings Bank Building is a fine example, was

21. Clinton Square with former Syracuse Savings Bank Building (l) and Gridley Building (r), looking east

also called Venetian Gothic. Undeservedly and merely because of its location on two canals, Syracuse was sometimes referred to as "the Venice of the North." It stands to reason that the city should have several fine "Venetian" Gothic buildings; besides the Syracuse Savings Bank, there are the White Memorial Building and the building that now houses Colella Galleries at 123 East Willow Street. Notice the picturesque roofline on the Syracuse Savings Bank Building with its turrets and steeply pitched gables. Trefoil ornamentation, pointed arches banded in red and tan sandstone, finely sculpted details, and a variety of textures and colors, the latter inherent in the materials used, are characteristic of the style and attest to the skills of designer and stone masons.

The entrance was changed when the Erie Canal became Erie Boulevard, and apart from minor changes the exterior still is as originally designed by Silsbee. A major renovation in the late 1920s included a steel-frame rebuilding. Hall Groat's murals depict scenes from the city's history. The Syracuse Savings Bank became a canonical example of High Victorian Gothic architecture in the United States and was included and illustrated in various books on American architecture.

Silsbee (1848–1913) studied architecture at the Massachusetts Institute of Technology (MIT), worked in the offices of Ware and Van Brunt and later of Ralph Emerson of Boston, and came to Syracuse in 1873. The Syracuse Savings Bank Building was Silsbee's first important commission. Silsbee and Archimedes Russell were the first instructors in the Department of Architecture, established at Syracuse University in 1873. Between 1882 and 1885, Silsbee kept offices in Buffalo, Syracuse, and Chicago. He moved to Chicago in 1884 and eventually closed his other offices. Frank Lloyd Wright was briefly employed in Silsbee's Chicago office.

22. 100 Clinton Square
The most prominent of this complex of four buildings is the
former Third National Bank Building, 1886
Architect: Archimedes Russell, Syracuse
Interior alteration: 1912
Addition: 1926, Albert L. Brockway, Syracuse
Renovation of three adjoining buildings: 1985, Schleicher-Soper, Syracuse; renovation of the last building to the north: 1988, Jane Podkaminer, Syracuse
Mural: Corky Goss
NRHP (former Third National Bank Building)

The former Third National Bank Building is fun to look at. The exterior of the building shows an abundance of textures and forms characteristic of the Queen Anne style, in which the building was designed. There are steeply pitched dormers and entrance gables; a second-level bay with a conical roof punctuates the street corner; a swirling "pie" motif stretches across fourth-level windows; flowers ornament the two main gables as well as the trefoil above the side door facing James Street, which in its center holds a sunflower, the popular Queen Anne motif. Trenton pressed brick and Carlisle red sandstone provide textural variety. In 1912, the interior was altered, and the addition to the north (1926) is stylistically consistent with the existing structure.

The Third National Bank, organized in 1864, occupied the main floor and the basement level; other floors were for office rental until 1945, when the building was purchased by the Veterans' Administration for their headquarters. Legend has it that at one time a banker occupied a fancy penthouse on top of the building with a bathtub "big enough to float a canal boat" and a huge hand-carved fireplace flanked by carved wine closets. His windows overlooked "Robbers' Row" on lower James Street, a string of vaudeville houses and sleazy saloons shaded by a papier-maché "palm garden." The building, together with the adjoining structures that once served as warehouses with retail business on the street level, is being adaptively reused as office space. A mural on the north facade depicts salt crystals rising out of Onondaga Lake.

Archimedes Russell (1840–1915) apprenticed with a builder-architect in Boston before he came to Syracuse in 1862, when he worked for Horatio Nelson White. He set up his own office six years later and became very successful in and around Syracuse during a time of rapid growth.

23. OnBank, 1897 (former Onondaga County Savings Bank)
101 South Salina Street
Architect: Robert W. Gibson, Albany
Interior design: Angelo Magnanti
Interior murals and ceiling painting: 1931, William T. Schwarz
Restoration of interior: 1988, Allen Silberman of Crown Restoration,
New York
NRHP

The institution was originally known as Onondaga County Savings Bank. It moved from what is now the Gridley Building into its present building located on the erstwhile site of the Syracuse House, where the bank was located in its early years of existence. One of Syracuse's first steel-frame structures, the eleven-story Second Renaissance Revival building represents an early phase of skyscraper development. Here a two-story base supports two six-story shafts crowned with three-story capitals, which correspond to the tripartite system of the composition of a classical column. A copper cornice, hidden by a balustrade, divides the tenth and eleventh stories. Above the Salina Street entrance the cast-stone head of an Onondaga Indian pays tribute to the original inhabitants of this area. The superb Renaissance Revival interior was created by Angelo Magnanti, who also designed the interior of the Supreme Court Building in Washington, D.C. The plaster panels for the bank's interior, originally cast from molds and fabricated in Italy, were beautifully restored in 1988. In 1931, former Syracuse artist William T. Schwarz added a painted replica of a thirteenth-century astronomer's map complete with the signs of the zodiac, as well as ten murals depicting scenes from Onondaga County's history, as part of a public works project. A canopy on the exterior that had been added when the mezzanine was created in 1958 was removed in 1989, thus opening the windows to their original two-story height.

Demolition of Syracuse House, 1897. Photograph by I.U. Doust, courtesy the Koolakian family

23. OnBank, interior

Bank buildings were among this architect's specialties. Robert W. Gibson (1854–1927) studied architecture in Britain, emigrated to the United States in 1888, and established an office in Albany. He designed the Episcopal Cathedral of All Saints, among other buildings, in Albany and a number of Episcopal churches in upstate New York. Gibson moved to New York in 1888, where he continued a successful career.

24. Syracuse Newspapers Building, 1971
Clinton Square
Architects: Ginsberg Associates, New York

The 230,000-square-foot complex occupies the north side of the square and replaced the third Onondaga County Courthouse (1857; Horatio Nelson White) and other structures. The modern building is the home of the *Syracuse Herald American, Herald-Journal,* and *Post-Standard.* Eighteen presses, able to print 70,000 copies per hour at full speed, are visible through windows along the sidewalk on the North Salina Street side of the building.

The *Herald-Journal* had its beginning with the *Western State Journal,* founded in 1839 by Vivus W. Smith and his brother Silas. The *Journal* had its home in various downtown buildings and was burned out several times. Perhaps the most famous building occupied by the *Journal* in its early years was a brick structure on the west side of Clinton Square, later called the Journal Building and subsequently the Jerry Rescue Block. In the early 1850s, it housed the offices of the *Journal* and the police station. It was from this building that a former slave, William Henry ("Jerry"), was freed by antiabolitionists, and the event became known as the "Jerry Rescue" (see also the Downtown Abolition Sites tour). Although the *Journal* had various owners, publishers, and editors over the years, the Smith brothers and Vivus's son, Carroll Earll Smith, were the dominant forces in the paper's editorial policies throughout the nineteenth century. And, despite strong misgivings, Carroll Smith hired Grace Dwight Potter, the first woman reporter in the *Journal's* history, in 1897.

At the turn of the century, William Randolph Hearst bought newspapers nationwide as a vehicle to help him in his quest for the presidency. One of them was the *Syracuse Journal*. In 1939, the *Syracuse Herald-Journal* came into being when Samuel I. Newhouse merged the *Syracuse Journal* and the *Syracuse Herald*. Established in 1877, the *Syracuse Evening Herald* was the first paper in the city to publish cartoons. The *Post-Standard* goes back in part to Vivus Smith, co-founder of the *Onondaga Standard* in 1829. When Vivus changed party affiliations, the *Standard* was taken over by his brothers. The voice of the local Democratic party supporting abolition and women's suffrage, it became the *Daily Standard* and a competitor of the *Syracuse Post*, a Republican paper; the papers merged, and the *Post-Standard* came into existence. In 1944, the paper was purchased by Samuel I. Newhouse and was published from 1955 on by Stephen Rogers, now president of the Syracuse Newspapers.

25. Atrium at Clinton Square, 1972
(former Edwards Department Store)
2 Clinton Square
Architects: Welton Becket and Associates, New York

This modern four-level building is part of One Lincoln Center, a downtown revitalization project on South Salina Street. Considering the climate, the designers planned this structure as a series of setbacks and overhangs to offer pedestrians protection from rain and snow. It was originally built to house the new Edwards Department Store.

26. James Hanley Federal Building, 1977
100 South Clinton Street
Architects: Sargent Webster Crenshaw & Folley, Syracuse
Sculpture: Sol Lewitt

The modern James Hanley Federal Building consists of four rectangular blocks of varying heights. The play with rectangular forms is repeated in narrow window bands and in the ribbing of the concrete blocks. Of reinforced poured concrete and glass, the structure houses federal courts and offices. The arrangement of building blocks on a platform represents "the last phase of the development of tall buildings" and emphatically anchors the southwest corner of Clinton Square. Enter the entrance platform, look back toward West Water Street, and you will see the ornate facade of the Amos Block framed by the Courthouse portico of the James Hanley Federal Building; here old and new enhance each other. A minimalist sculpture entitled *One, Two, Three* stands on the platform, repeating the building's stark geometric forms rather than complementing them.

27. Amos Block
from plaza of
James Hanley
Federal Building

27. Amos Block, 1878
210–216 West Water Street
Architect: Joseph Lyman Silsbee, Syracuse
Renovation: initial work, 1987, Holmes/King & Associates Architects,
Syracuse; structural and exterior renovation:
1987– , James Kilcy, Binghamton, N.Y.

NRHP

Jacob Amos, a one-time mayor of Syracuse, built the Amos Block for his wholesale grocery business. It replaced the Empire State Mills Building, probably incorporating remnants of that earlier property. The structure was at one time part of a row of canalside buildings constructed for commercial purposes (shown by the functional facade facing Erie Boulevard). The space in the building was allocated for storage in upper levels and for wholesale grocery business at street level, with access from Water Street. By adding window bays and half a story to the center section and by altering the roofline, Silsbee organized the facade, giving it a new face that is Romanesque, polychrome, and texturally varied. The building seriously deteriorated, and major renovation work began in the summer of 1987. A contiguous four-story commercial structure of 1910 was beyond the point of reclamation and was torn down. There are plans to renovate the interior of the building for adaptive reuse.

28. Clinton Exchange, 1928 (former Federal Building)

4 Clinton Square
Architect: James A. Wetmore, Washington, D.C.
Renovation: 1985, DalPos Associates, Syracuse;
preservation consultants, Crawford & Stearns, Syracuse
Interior: dePolo/Dunbar, New York

By the time this building was constructed, the Erie Canal had outlived its usefulness and the "dirty foul-smelling ditch" was filled in and became a motor route. This had little effect on the design: a door added to the Erie Boulevard side was sufficient. The building was designed in the Neoclassical Revival style, which was often employed for public buildings during the beginning of the twentieth century.

The wedge-shaped structure is faced with limestone, and its slightly curved main facade is distinguished by a portico with tall Doric columns. The groin-vaulted foyer is resplendent with green-veined marble walls and columns, brass stair railings and fixtures, and terrazzo floors inset with marble medallions. Daylight enters through rows of tall round-arched windows that open to exterior and interior vistas. The two-story courtroom in the center of the second floor displays rich classical ornament and now serves the Pyramid Companies as a conference and telecommunications center. For fifty years, the building was home to the city's main post office, to a U.S. district court, and to other federal agencies. The Pyramid Companies, a real estate and investment firm specializing in the construction and operation of shopping malls, bought the building in 1984 to house its corporate headquarters.

28. Clinton Exchange

29. Niagara Mohawk Building

29. Niagara Mohawk Building, 1932
300 Erie Boulevard West
Architects: Bley & Lyman, Buffalo, and Melvin L. King, Syracuse
Sculpture: Clayton B. Frye

Described as a "cathedral of light," "a fruitcake," an "exuberant example of Art Deco Drama and Decor," the building is locally known more prosaically as the NiMo Building. The Niagara Mohawk Power Corporation, a statewide group of power companies that merged in 1950, occupies the building as its headquarters. Its Art Deco ornamentation is of the most opulent. The structural steel frame of the Niagara Mohawk Building is arranged in setbacks, is sheathed smoothly in aluminum, black glass, and stainless steel combined with gray brick and polished stone, and is ornamented with chevrons, parallel bands, and zigzags. The building advertised its product: light was an integral part of its ornamentation. Helium tubes and conventional incandescent lights illuminated the exterior at night, underlining the richness of ornamentation. The sunbursts above the two principal entrances on the south and east facades were of neon and helium, silhouetting the shape of New York State. During World War II, the light show was discontinued.

Above the main entrance, a helmeted warrior angel, twenty-eight feet high, spreads its hard-edged wings twenty feet. The statue, designed by Clayton B. Frye and fabricated by Mackwirth Brothers of Buffalo, was named the *Spirit of Power* in a citywide contest. The sun setting directly behind the figure, as well as its slightly lowered head, suggests that this

29. Niagara Mohawk Building, detail

Buck Rogers angel is bravely fighting the forces of darkness to bring light to the people below. The stainless steel alloy for the sculpture was developed by Crucible Steel in Solvay and is believed to have been used in architecture for the first time on the Niagara Mohawk Building. A few years later, Crucible Steel supplied the same material for the Chrysler Building in New York. The ornate lobby, considered to be the most important space in the building, rewards all who come to pay their bill: apart from Art Deco motifs of green Carrara marble, Vitrolite, metal, wood, and smooth stone, there are four Vitrolite glass murals depicting aspects of the power industry. Incandescent lights illuminate chromium-plated metals used on lighting fixtures, stair rails, and wall surfaces, and produce their own interior light show. Originally, part of the lobby contained a demonstration kitchen, which is now given over to offices. Part of the basement was occupied by a large demonstration auditorium. The overall message is clear: there is a cleaner, brighter future to be called into being by a flick of the switch. The building stands as a symbol of the modern world, of the potentialities of progress. Its ascending features point toward the future.

30. Niagara Mohawk Office Building, 1976
300 Erie Boulevard West
Architects: King & King Architects, Syracuse

The reflective curtain wall of the modern building mirrors the ornateness of the adjoining older structure. The building is best seen from the Interstate 690 ramp near West Street.

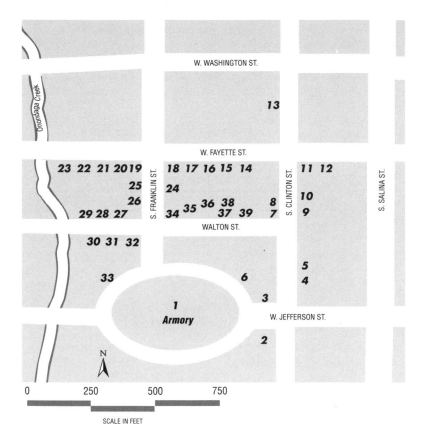

W. WASHINGTON ST.

Onondaga Creek

13

W. FAYETTE ST.

23 22 21 20 19 S. FRANKLIN ST. 18 17 16 15 14 S. CLINTON ST. 11 12 S. SALINA ST.

25 24 10

26 9

29 28 27 34 35 36 38 8 9

37 39 7

WALTON ST.

30 31 32

5

33 6 4

3

1
Armory

W. JEFFERSON ST.

2

N

0   250   500   750

SCALE IN FEET

Armory Square

NRHD

Estimated walking time: 1 hour, 30 minutes (Nos. 1–39)

From its modest beginnings, Armory Square played an important part in the city's industrial life—quietly so in the early 1800s, when a millpond and later solar salt-evaporation vats covered most of the area. Soon after the millpond and its surrounding swamp were filled in with dirt from Prospect Hill in 1849, noisier occupants arrived on the scene: within a decade, the first armory, home of the Fifty-first Regiment, was erected. Guardsmen trained in the oval-shaped Regimental Park, later known as Jefferson Park, and stables lined the streets. A crescendo was reached when the railroads came to town and two railroad companies built their terminals here. With them came hotels, boardinghouses, flophouses, shops, warehouses, factories, and people, as well as many fires that destroyed and damaged buildings. When in the 1930s the railroads were removed from the streets of downtown Syracuse, many of Armory Square's activities were removed as well. Buildings deteriorated and people left. But there were some who saw beyond the crumbling bricks. Undaunted by rot and decay, a group of entrepreneurs, architects, and artists looking for low rents and spacious studios bought and renovated derelict buildings in the 1970s. They formed the Armory Square Association, Inc., and Edward Butler, its first president, named the neighborhood Armory Square. Since then, many others have followed the example of these urban pioneers. There is a renewed vitality; the buildings are busy again, housing offices, studios, apartments, shops, and restaurants.

A wide range of buildings coexist within the district's boundaries: although they may not share a roofline, a modest one-time stable sits comfortably near an imposing commercial structure. Cast iron, the building material that revolutionized construction techniques of the nineteenth century, is used in many of the buildings. There are no multistoried iron fronts to be found here, but cast-iron columns are used in combination with heavy timber post-and-beam construction. Because many of the buildings were designed as warehouses and light manufacturing facilities, they were constructed to carry heavy floor loads, have experienced little settling, and are in good structural condition. Their exterior walls are faced with brick, and many have cast-iron storefronts. A number of buildings also have cornices, window caps, sills, and ornamental features of galvanized sheet metal, a material often used during the second half of the nineteenth century to imitate architectural elements of stone and wood. Durable, lightweight, and economical, they could be ordered from the manufacturer through trade catalogues. By then, pressed-metal products were also available in sheets or coils and could easily be nailed to the surface and painted, a fact readily acknowledged by nineteenth-century building owners. Many of the buildings' open loft spaces have pressed-metal ceilings, their design sometimes matched by wooden columns wrapped in embossed sheet metal. Aluminum siding of the late twentieth century, popular with many house owners and maligned by preservationists, is a direct descendent of these earlier pressed-metal products. Main facades of the larger buildings in Armory Square display Italianate and Renaissance design principles because they satisfied the owners' love of ornamentation without being too expensive. Although their function determined a utilitarian design, warehouses, more so than factories, were perceived as civic monuments and emblems of family enterprises—a credit to the city. Those that remain in Armory Square give credence to that.

1. Fifty-First Regiment State Armory, 1874, 1907

236 West Jefferson Street
Architects: 1874, Horatio Nelson White, Syracuse; 1907,
George L. Heins (state architect)
Alterations: 1930s
Renovation: 1991– , Schopfer Architects, Syracuse
NRHD

In 1857, the state legislature made a decision to build a series of armories in upstate New York.

Two years later, the first armory on this site and the second largest in the state, designed by Horatio Nelson White, opened its doors to the Fifty-first Regiment. While additions to the three-story brick building were being made by White in 1872, a fire swept through the building, destroying the old portion but leaving the additions intact. A new and larger armory rose from the ashes. Completed in 1874, it served the ten companies of the Fifty-first Regiment until George L. Heins planned the present building, completed in 1907.

The structure was designed to serve various functions: to store arms and equipment, to house offices, to drill soldiers, and occasionally to entertain them, together with their families and friends. The western end of the building housed the cavalry, and the stable of 1876 is still attached. The infantry was quartered in the eastern part. An arched-roof auditorium connects the two sections. The drill hall in the center is of steel-frame construction.

The castlelike style of the armory was meant to convey the building's particular social function. Some argue that the citizen militia, which later became the National Guard, felt equivocal about violent labor strikes that erupted frequently during the second half of the nineteenth century. It was hoped that a defensive bulwarklike structure would inculcate a martial spirit among the guardsmen while creating reassuring images of security for the citizens. But one wonders how reassuring this architectural show of force might have been for the citizens. Whereas builders of the medieval fortress made provisions to bring townspeople inside during times of emergency, the medieval "keep" is not duplicated in armory buildings. Their design instead seems to convey the impression of wanting to keep people out.

Plans are underway to remodel the armory for more hospitable purposes. It will be occupied by the Milton Rubenstein Museum of Science and Technology and by offices. The drill hall will be used by the National Guard until a new armory is built.

1. Fifty-First Regiment State Armory

2. Former D.L. & W. Railroad Station, 1941
500 South Clinton Street
Architect: Frederick B. O'Connor, Syracuse
Alterations: ca. 1961
NRHD

The Delaware, Lackawanna & Western Railroad came to town in 1848 and built its first small passenger station at West Onondaga and Clinton streets. A second, larger station was built next to the armory and was replaced by the present, "completely fireproof" structure, which has a polished granite base and is faced with buff-colored bricks and limestone trim. The interior was trimmed with aluminum and had travertine floors. Service was provided for passengers until the late 1950s. Since its sale in 1961 and subsequent remodeling, the former station has functioned as an office building, a bus terminal, and a restaurant. Before it received a front addition, the small flat-roofed building had a streamlined appearance not unlike that of sleek express trains that ran along city streets in the 1940s. Its Modernistic design symbolized speed and transportation despite the sobriquet "Delay, Linger and Wait" sometimes given to the D.L. & W. by weary travelers, who might journey by deluxe coach from Syracuse to Hoboken within seven hours.

3. 200–202 West Jefferson Street, 1927 (former Dome Hotel)
Architect: Gustavus Young, Syracuse
NRHD

This corner has been the site of several hotels. Designed by Gustavus Young (1871–1956), the present building, the tallest in the district, was used as a hotel from the time of its construction until 1986. The flat-roofed, eleven-story block is one of four in the district to be of steel-frame construction, a mode of building established in Syracuse by 1896. The brick-covered facades are articulated by the regular rhythm of window openings. The two-story base, of light-colored stone, shows modest Neoclassical ornamentation.

4. Loew's Landmark Office Building, 1928
423–437 South Clinton Street and 362 South Salina Street
Architect: Thomas W. Lamb, New York
Renovation, exterior: 1987, Dal Pos Associates, Syracuse; preservation consultants, Crawford & Stearns, Syracuse
Interior: 1986–, Wolniak & Associates, Syracuse
NRHD

This is the rear facade of the building that houses the Syracuse Area Landmark Theatre, originally Loew's State Theatre, with its entrance on Salina Street. The second floor windows mark the location of the dressing rooms. The exterior of the steel-frame structure, ornamented with Neoclassical detailing, expresses its interior function; a theater is on its lower levels, and office space occupies the upper stories. The interior of the Landmark Theatre is discussed in the tour of South Salina Street and Vanderbilt Square.

5. 415–417 South Clinton Street
6. 410–416 South Clinton Street / 214 West Jefferson Street, 1914
NRHD

Modest ornamentation embellishes the facades of these commercial buildings. Notice the wooden cutout designs above the fourth-story windows and the finely detailed cornice in **No. 5**, which received a top floor addition in 1910. **No. 6** is a steel-frame structure and has been owned and occupied by Onondaga Music since the building's completion. Copper is used on exterior panels and bars dividing windows. Easier to work than most other metals, copper was often used for ornamental work in architecture.

7. Neal and Hyde Building, 1883
318–322 South Clinton Street
Architect: Asa L. Merrick, Syracuse
NRHD

The imposing brick building with sandstone trim served as a dry-goods warehouse and store until the mid-1900s, when the roofline lost its gabled turrets. The keystone in the central arch bears Salem Hyde's initials.

Neal and Hyde Building (l) and Donohue Building (r), late 1800s.
Courtesy Onondaga Historical Association, Syracuse

Weighty and Richardsonian Romanesque, with rusticated stone trim and large arches, the structure conveys the prosperity of the dry-goods firm that built it. The company advertised itself as being "exclusive jobbers of hosiery, notions, fancy goods, tailors' trimmings and other articles incident to these lines." The firm that evolved into William Neal and Salem Hyde continued a business that was established in Syracuse in 1864 by Charles Chadwick.

Asa L. Merrick (1848–1922), a native Syracusan, served as a mason's apprentice before he opened his architectural office in 1879. He won commissions for several churches and many public school buildings in this city.

8. Donohue Building, ca. 1885
312–316 South Clinton Street
Renovation: 1991–, Billings Architects, Syracuse
NRHD

The physician Florince Q. Donohue may have had the health and happiness of his patients in mind when he asked his architect, who is unknown, to build this architectural gem as a clinic, office, and residence. The building functioned in these capacities until the early 1900s and later housed a bakery as well as apartments. In its most recent incarnation, it will be an office building with retail stores on the ground level.

Queen Anne style elements, such as a variety of textures of brick and terra cotta, as well as a rhythmic division and an ornate gable with two circular windows, make the main facade a visual delight. The forms and ornamental program of Queen Anne were mainly used for residential architecture, and only a few commercial structures of that style were built in Syracuse.

9. Butler Building, ca. 1866, 1893
321 South Clinton Street
Addition: 1893
Partial renovation of interior: 1981–83, Schopfer Architects, Syracuse
NRHD

The Butler Building is and is not a five-story structure, as Stephen Karon, the present director of the Discovery Center, likes to point out. It started out with two stories that are 120 feet deep. About thirty years later three stories, each 50 feet deep, were added. The main facade facing Clinton Street features arches into which windows are grouped vertically, thus underlining the illusion of a full five-story block. Pilasters with ornate capitals that separate window bays are Neoclassical Revival elements, and the storefront is of cast iron.

The building was home to various businesses related to furniture and household items as well as to tobacco importers and wholesalers. The ground floor has been occupied by the Discovery Center of Science and Technology since 1981. The Discovery Center is planning to move to the Armory building and hopes to open its new home there in the near future.

10. 307–313 South Clinton Street, 1870s
NRHD

The building at 307–309, originally built as a foundry, was occupied by the Galvanized Iron Works. In the early 1900s, a fifth story crowned by a galvanized metal cornice was added to the structure. The adjacent building at 311–313 once served as a factory, with lodgings, probably for its workers, in the upper stories. Its facade is ornamented with Renaissance Revival features such as cast-iron keystones in its arched windows and a metal pediment. The latter is most likely an early twentieth-century addition. Both buildings were later owned and used by Witherill, a local dry-goods company.

11. Kirk Block, ca. 1870
127–129 West Fayette Street
Addition: ca. 1910
NRHD

The patchwork of architectural elements on the exterior are like "remembrances of a building's past," recalling a number of changes that have been made over the years. The top floor was added during the first decade of the twentieth century, and part of the facade fronting South Clinton Street was ornamented with Neoclassical elements of pressed metal. Fine brickwork and ornate window surrounds are architectural remains of this once-Italianate building. As a residential hotel, it was one of many hotels and boardinghouses built in response to thriving railroad activities in the area. The building faces a parking lot across the street that at one time was the site of the Burns Hotel (1870s), which later became the St. Cloud and then the Temperance Hotel.

St. Cloud Hotel, 1940s. Courtesy Onondaga Historical Association, Syracuse

12. Chamberlin Building, 1870s
113–117 West Fayette Street
Renovation: 1985, R. J. Engan & Associates, Syracuse
NRHD

Originally known as the Keeler Block, the building was largely occupied by printers. W. H. H. Chamberlin, owner of a stationery business, bought the structure in the 1930s and renamed and remodeled it. The facade is ornamented by its rhythmic fenestration, a belt course enclosing the fifth floor, and a metal cornice with paired brackets, thus making it stylistically compatible with the neighboring buildings designed in the Italianate and Renaissance Revival traditions.

13. 250 South Clinton Street, 1990
Architects: Herbert Newman & Associates, New Haven, Conn.

This Post-Modern building is the latest arrival in Armory Square and is not part of the Historic District. It holds the street line and relates to its older neighbors in height, in the articulation of its facades, and in the surface materials that were used. The combination of brick, cast stone, granite, and glass is of the twentieth century, yet it coexists comfortably with earlier nineteenth-century brick construction. The round-arched entrance leads from an exterior courtyard into a marble and granite lobby with cherry-paneled walls. Large fluted pillars present themselves as focal points, but unlike their hardy ancestors, they shoulder no responsibilities. The lobby, sometimes called the "urban threshold," has become as important an image to corporate identity as have the building's form and facade.

The block of commercial buildings stretching from 215 to 245 West Fayette Street once contained some of the largest and most handsome stores in the city. Some have cast-iron storefronts and large plate-glass windows (by then readily available). Several of these buildings have modest facades on Walton Street. Although individual buildings vary in height and architectural ornament, they nevertheless form a coherent group because they are similar in scale and proportion.

14. 215–225 West Fayette Street, ca. 1871
Architect: Archimedes Russell, Syracuse
NRHD

This Italianate brick structure was built as a retail store and warehouse. Originally known as the Tallman Block, it was named after its original owner, a wholesale and retail grocer, and was advertised as "one of the best business blocks in the city." Ornate metal window caps give the facade a rich decorative effect. Once crowned with an Italianate metal cornice, the top floor with its cornice was removed in the 1930s.

15. Piper-Phillips Block, ca. 1872

227 West Fayette Street
Renovation: 1987, Riley & Associates Architects, Syracuse
NRHD

The Italianate theme is continued in the exterior design of this business block, exemplified by ornate metal window caps and a metal cornice with brackets along the roofline and above the cast-iron storefront. The building was constructed in three sections, which is indicated on the exterior by brick pilasters. The first floor consisted of three storefronts; its upper stories, ornamented with fine brickwork along the cornice line, were used as a residential hotel for railroad employees. The hotel was abandoned when the railroads left the area in the 1930s. The Bentley-Settle Company used the central and eastern storefront as their main office until 1973. Originally, a horse stable connected the structure with the Bentley-Settle Building facing Walton Street (**No. 39**).

15. Piper-Phillips
Block

16. Seubert-Warner
Building

16. Seubert-Warner Building, 1880s
239–241 West Fayette Street
Renovation: 1985–87, Crawford & Stearns, Syracuse, and Dan Leary
Architect, Syracuse
NRHD

Seubert & Warner, manufacturers and retailers of cigars, were the original owners. The building was also used as a paper and printers' warehouse. Windows with sandstone lintels are grouped in recessed arches ornamented with fine brickwork. Brackets support an Italianate cornice as well as one above the storefront. Apart from the Italianate cornices, the facades of this and the adjacent building (**No. 17**) are different from those of their neighbors to the east. They are less ornate, and the designers manipulated brick and stone to lend visual interest to the facades fronting West Fayette Street.

17. 243–245 West Fayette Street, 1888
Architect: attributed to Charles E. Colton
Renovation: 1985-87, Crawford & Stearns, Syracuse, and Dan Leary
Architect, Syracuse
NRHD

This four-story building was erected for retail and wholesale business and was formerly used by the Garret Paper Company. Here the textural variety of the building facade was achieved by combining rough-cut stone with the smoothness of brick. The simplicity of the design stands in contrast to that of the building's more ornate neighbors. Both **Nos. 16** and **17** were known as the Seneca Buildings after the paper company that owned and occupied them during the twentieth century. Between 1910 and 1911, the Bijou Theater, the first movie theater in town, was located here.

18. Hogan Block, 1895
247–259 West Fayette Street
Architect: Charles E. Colton, Syracuse
Renovation: 1985–87, Crawford & Stearns, Syracuse, and Bennetts Turner Sloan, Syracuse
NRHD

The structure was built by attorney Thomas Hogan to house retail business, restaurant, and warehouse. Together with the other large commercial blocks erected in the city in the 1890s, such as the Yates Hotel, the Dey Brothers Department Store, and the Kirk Fireproof Building, the Hogan Block was an expression of the city's business prosperity. It was indeed "evidence that life is lively and progressive," as had been suggested three years earlier by the *Syracuse Daily Standard* at the opening of the Yates Hotel (now demolished). The solidity of form, the organization of facades, and the embellishment with Neoclassical ornament, design features that might, so it was hoped, inspire confidence by association in the business establishments of their owners, point to the Renaissance palazzos of Italian merchant princes. Again a mixed-use building after its renovation, the Hogan Block combines apartments, offices, and shops under one roof.

19. Crown Bar & Grill (former Crown Hotel), 1876
301–307 West Fayette Street
Renovation: 1990, Crawford & Stearns, Syracuse
Interior: Linda Pizzica
NRHD

Together with adjacent buildings along West Fayette Street (**Nos. 20–22**), the Crown Hotel was one of a series of buildings erected here between 1869 and the 1880s in response to the railroad. At present, the Crown Hotel houses a restaurant on the ground level and offices upstairs. Notice the fine brickwork around the windows and doors, and the ornamental metal cornices with paired brackets. The Italianate building faces a parking lot that was once the site of the New York Central Railroad Station (1895; W. L. Gilbert, New York), an imposing Richardsonian Romanesque structure.

Concerns about the "crows nest of wooden balloon structures" that were built in this area in mid-nineteenth century and that were dangerous because of their inflammability were well founded. Many of them, in addition to some built of brick, were destroyed by fire. Of a solid block of buildings fronting this section of West Fayette Street, only three are left. Their Italianate facades are embellished by fine brickwork.

20. C. M. Gibbs Company, Inc., 1870s
309–311 West Fayette Street
Minor renovation: 1991–
NRHD

The commercial brick building is being used as retail, warehouse, and storage space.

21. 315–317 West Fayette Street, 1870s
Renovation: 1984, Lynne Mishelanie
NRHD

Here two adjacent buildings share almost identical architectural ornament. 315 West Fayette Street once housed a livery stable and later a bakery. After renovation it became home to a beauty parlor downstairs and an apartment on the upper level; next door is a restaurant.

22. Stag Hotel, 1870s
321–323 West Fayette Street
NRHD

The small brick structure built as the City Hotel was one of the first hotels in the district and is one of the few remaining ones in Armory Square.

23. Millpond Landing, ca. 1887
329 West Fayette Street
Architect: Horatio Nelson White, Syracuse
Addition: 1896
Renovation: 1989, Schopfer Architects, Syracuse; preservation consultants, Bero Associates, Rochester
NRHD

The last structure on the street within the Armory Square Historic District, it was originally built for wholesale grocer A. S. Coan & Company as a three-story building. In 1896, a fourth story was added. During much of the twentieth century, Lerman Carpet Corporation owned and used the building as a warehouse. After having served a variety of warehousing functions since its beginnings, the structure has recently been given new life as an office building.

24. Labor Temple, 1887
309–315 South Franklin Street
Renovation: 1983–85, Crawford & Stearns, Syracuse
NRHD

Built by businessmen Jacob and Charles Crouse, this was originally known as the Crouse Building. Penfield and Wilcox Bedding Manufacturers occupied it, as did the Penfield Manufacturing Company. When in 1927 it became the office location for various local labor unions, the building's name was changed to Labor Temple. Exterior ornament is abundant and

24. Labor Temple

well executed. It includes a multicolored main facade with richly detailed brick ornamentation, a combination of round-arched and rectangular windows, a vertical grouping of windows under a Richardsonian arch in the central section, and wooden cutout panels in third-level windows. Having been renovated, the building offers amenities of urban living: well-lit, high-ceilinged apartments and a restaurant on the ground level.

25. 306 South Franklin Street, 1870s
Renovation: 1990, Crawford & Stearns, Syracuse
NRHD

This three-story, two-bay brick building has the distinction of being the narrowest structure in the district. It has an unassuming facade, and only the cornice line with its ornamental brickwork calls attention to itself. It was at one time divided from the Crown Hotel (**No. 19**) by an alley, but both buildings are now connected on the second story.

26. 308–310 South Franklin Street, ca. 1900
Renovation: ca. 1981; 1991–, H. F. Buffington Construction Management, Syracuse
Interior: Donald Sweet, Buffalo
NRHD

The bow-fronted structure was originally built as a commercial laundry. Two floors are now recycled for use as a restaurant. The third level functions as residential space. At present, the building claims to be a daughter of San Francisco's Painted Ladies. With its detailing emphasized by contrasting bright colors, the building's facade demands attention.

27. Misener Building, 1873
204–210 Walton Street and South Franklin Street
Addition: 1930
Renovation: 1980s, 204–210 Walton Street; partial renovation of
South Franklin Street: 1991– , Holmes/King & Associates Architects,
Syracuse
NRHD

The four-story commercial block with ground floor display windows is U-shaped in plan and organized around an open court. It was built as Gray Brothers' Boot and Shoe Factory, and the local paper noted that "each floor was a large well-lighted apartment." The sign advertising Gray Shoes above the third story is still visible. Proud of their product, the owners of the firm exuberantly proclaimed that "the reputation of Gray Brothers for fine work is second to none in the country."

In the 1920s, Misener, manufacturers of hole saws, bought the building and later constructed a three-story addition. The brick facing of the steel-frame addition on Walton Street harmonizes with the material used in the older building. Steel-frame construction brought abundant light into the interior and, along with fireproofing, made the twentieth-century factory safer and more efficient than its nineteenth-century predecessor. Part of the building fronting South Franklin Street is adaptively reused.

210–214 Walton Street, 1918. Courtesy Onondaga Historical Association, Syracuse

28. Eureka Crafts, ca. 1850
210 Walton Street
Renovation: 1982, Eureka Crafts
NRHD

Originally built to house stables, this is one of the oldest structures in the Armory Square Historic District. In the 1950s, the company that owned the brick building advertised its product by covering the exterior with aluminum sheeting. The structure now houses a craft store and studios. The present occupants include artists and craftspeople who were among the first to move to Armory Square at the time of its rebirth.

29. 212–214 Walton Street, 1860s
Renovation: 1987, Thomas Fabbioli, Syracuse
NRHD

The two-story building was originally built as a stable. It is now occupied by offices upstairs, and a restaurant and a beauty shop downstairs. Good brick detailing on many of the buildings in the area, such as one sees here, indicates that there were bricklayers in the city who understood their craft.

30. McArthur, Wirth & Cooney Building, ca. 1899

221–223 Walton Street
Renovation: 1989–90, Riley & Associates Architects, Syracuse
NRHD

Fire-damaged, slated for demolition, and called an eyesore not too long ago, the building now brightens the westernmost border of the Armory Square Historic District near Onondaga Creek, which, in its heyday, regularly flooded basements of nearby buildings. Onondaga Dynamo Works built and first occupied the three-story warehouse structure. McArthur, Wirth & Cooney, a supplier of tools and machinery for butchers and packers, owned the building for most of the twentieth century. A recent occupant was Cooney Air Conditioning and Refrigeration. Like its immediate neighbors, the building is of heavy post-and-beam construction, but its curtain-wall type facade and a prominent skylight in the center bay give it distinction. The commercial lofts have been recycled into offices, and retail business is on the ground level.

31. 215 Walton Street, ca. 1872

Renovation: 1988–, William S. Elkins, Jr., Syracuse
NRHD

The facade is distinguished by Neoclassical features executed in brick. Windows have corbeled hood moldings and are grouped in recessed arches embellished with dentils. Apart from that, the "Chicken Building," as it is unofficially called, exhibits an almost self-deprecating sense of humor. Two chickens etched into the glass of the doorway in the entrance point toward the building's immediate past as a chicken packinghouse. The present owners were concerned that the particular smell connected with that enterprise might never leave the building, but, to their pleasant surprise, it did. In the back of the entrance lobby toward elevators and stairs, part of a rail system recalls the time when the building was used as a beef-packing warehouse. The track on which parts of slaughtered animals were moved to be weighed now presents itself as a handsome ceiling sculpture. At one time, the building may have been used as a warehouse for Crouse-Hinds Company, because an underground tunnel connects it to the structure at 310 West Jefferson Street (**No. 33**), the remains of the building that formerly housed Crouse-Hinds. The building at 215 Walton Street now houses offices and studio space.

31. 215 Walton Street, detail

32. Hall-McChesney Building, ca. 1897

402–412 South Franklin Street and Walton Street
Partial renovation: 1976, Edward Butler, Syracuse
NRHD

The publishing, printing, and bookbinding firm that originally gave the building its name was started by Charles E. Hall in 1878 and became Hall-McChesney in 1882. The large commercial block was built in two sections, each with a slightly different window arrangement. The south section has a cast-iron storefront, and brick pilasters divide its facade into five bays. The three-bay storefront of the north section is supported by banded masonry piers. The denticulation on the stepped roofline—a popular exterior design feature in the district—visually unifies the block.

The building has the distinction of having been the first in Armory Square to be renovated. Said Edward Butler, who bought it in the early 1970s: "The area was so down and out, I thought I would start something. I'm the guy who started it all, that's why they call me the Mayor of Walton Street." A first tenant was the *Syracuse New Times,* continuing the building's traditional association with printing and publishing. The paper was published here between 1979 and 1987, at which time more space for people and cars was needed, and the business moved reluctantly. The paper began as *Orange Penny Saver* in 1969 in the White Memorial Building on Vanderbilt Square and has continued as the *Syracuse New Times* since 1970.

32. Hall-
McChesney
Building

33. 310 West Jefferson Street

Renovation of remaining part of the building: 1990, VIP Structures, Syracuse

This is all that is left of the building that housed the Crouse-Hinds Company between 1900 and 1913 before the company moved to the north side of town. Crouse-Hinds was established in 1897 to manufacture electrical products. Fire destroyed most of the structure, and in 1990 VIP Structures of Syracuse rehabilitated the remains; Central Music Supply, Inc. now occupies the building, which is not part of the Historic District.

34. Frankton Building, ca. 1903, 1920s

138–144 Walton Street and 315–317 South Franklin Street
Alterations: 1920s
Renovation: 1981, R. J. Engan & Associates, Syracuse
NRHD

One of the earliest buildings to be renovated in Armory Square, the Frankton Building started out as a carriage repair shop. As automobiles replaced carriages, the structure was altered to accommodate cars in need of repair. At that time, a large part of the ground floor was open, and cars were driven up a ramp to the second story. Stairs have replaced the ramp, offices occupy the upstairs, and stores are below.

35. 136 Walton Street, mid-nineteenth–early twentieth centuries

Improvements to the second story: 1990, Edward M. Basta, Syracuse
NRHD

According to landscape architect Edward M. Basta, the back part of the building dates to the mid-nineteenth century, whereas the front might have been built in the early twentieth century. The two-story commercial building was constructed to carry heavy loads, and it has been recycled to house offices upstairs and a vending machine company on the first level.

36. 134 Walton Street, 1908

Renovation: 1986, Crawford & Stearns, Syracuse
NRHD

Originally built as an ice cream factory, the building has been occupied by various enterprises, such as wagon makers, grocery dealers, and manufacturers of billiard tables. Another example of adaptive reuse, the two-story commercial building is now home to the architectural firm that renovated the building and to a restaurant.

37. 128–130 Walton Street, 1860s

Renovation: second story, 1987, Hull Corporation, Syracuse; first story, 1990, Mark DiGiacomo, Skaneateles, N.Y.
NRHD

The small brick building, embellished with fine brick detailing along the cornice line, was built as a stable to serve a building on West Fayette Street. The first story has been adaptively reused as office space. The second level was originally the hayloft. It has a large door on the north facade through which heavy loads could be lifted.

38. Walton Court, 1986
Landscape architects: George W. Curry, and Land Scapes Inc., Syracuse

Seven buildings facing Walton, West Fayette, and South Franklin streets are grouped around a handsome courtyard to which they have access. The space originally functioned as a service area, and its history has been carefully re-interpreted: access ramps for people with impaired mobility mimic loading docks that were in back of the Hogan Block (**No. 18**) and one of the Seneca Buildings (**No. 16**). The original cobblestones found underneath the asphalt pavement could not be used in the reconstruction and were left in place under the new brick pavement, which relates to the surrounding brick structures.

39. Bentley-Settle Building, 1895
120–124 Walton Street
Renovation: 1987, Riley & Associates Architects, Syracuse
NRHD

The brick building visually dominates the north side of Armory Square. The grouping of windows under arches stresses its verticality, and fine brickwork ornaments the stepped roofline. The Bentley-Settle wholesale grocery firm built the structure as a warehouse, and its advertisement is still visible on the west facade of the building. The firm was organized in 1896 when R. E. Bentley purchased the interests of wholesale grocers G. N. Crouse & Company, and continued as a wholesale business until 1973. The recycling of the building into artists' studios a few years later was one of the earliest conversions in the district. Emphasis was on open, rough spaces with low rents suited to the needs of artists and craftspeople. A hydraulic elevator moved the new occupants and their goods. At present, the building is occupied by offices and retail business. During renovation a closed-in court with a skylight was created. It connects with the Piper-Phillips Block, which fronts West Fayette Street (**No. 15**). The appearance of the building's former function as a warehouse is maintained well here and is underlined by a large scale, original to the building, that is set into the floor.

Many of the artists have moved further west, where they occupy the Delavan Center at 501 West Fayette Street (not included in the walking tour), an industrial building formerly used by various manufacturers of agricultural machinery.

Plans call for a new building, **Center Armory, 1992–**, designed by Schopfer Architects of Syracuse, for residential and commercial use; it is to be constructed on the parking lot now north of the Armory.

Clinton Square ERIE BLVD. E.

W. WATER ST. **Hanover Square**

E. WASHINGTON ST.

11 *12* *14*
10 *13*

E. FAYETTE ST.

9

8
7

S. CLINTON ST.

S. SALINA ST.

6

S. WARREN ST.

MONTGOMERY ST.

5

E. JEFFERSON ST. **Columbus Circle**

E. ONONDAGA ST.

3 *4*

MADISON ST.

2

HARRISON ST.

1

N

E. ADAMS ST.

| 0 | 500 | 1000 | 1500 |

SCALE IN FEET

South Salina Street and Vanderbilt Square

Estimated walking time: 50 minutes (Nos. 1–14)

South Salina Street

South Salina Street, named after the saline or salt springs that supplied Syracuse with its "white gold," was originally a wagon trail, leading from the salt springs near Onondaga Lake to Onondaga Castle in Onondaga Valley. Then there were rolling hills south of the intersection of Salina and Jefferson streets. Coming down from the Lodi springs, Yellow Brook cut a ravine through South Warren and East Onondaga streets, crossed Salina Street south of Jefferson Street, and emptied into the millpond on Armory Square. Some liked to go fishing there; in the 1820s, one man built a boathouse next to his house on South Salina Street and kept his fishing boat on Yellow Brook. When in 1878 the Butler Block (later Betts Block) was built, workmen found remnants of an old bridge that once crossed Yellow Brook.

In 1823, brick was manufactured on the west side of the street between Jefferson and East Onondaga streets, but the mud made it difficult for the owner to deliver the merchandise. When the swamps near Fayette Park were drained, Yellow Brook became nearly dry. In the early 1830s, South Salina Street was leveled and the ravine filled in. The street was paved by mid-century and citizens rejoiced; the dreariness and gloom had passed. "What a change," someone wrote in a local paper, "while there was mud everywhere but ten years ago, the street is now crowded with promenading ladies and gentlemen and fine teams, and is the most beautiful and businesslike part of the city."

The trains crossing Salina Street from the station on Washington Street had stimulated business north of Jefferson Street. The area south of Jefferson Street, today the 400 block and beyond, remained predominantly residential until the end of the nineteenth century. A number of local physicians had their homes and offices there in fine Italianate houses, surrounded by gardens and shaded by tall elms. Amos Westcott, erstwhile mayor of the city and a dentist, who is reputed to have moved dentistry from the barber chair into respectability, lived there. So did his son Edward Noyes Westcott before he moved into a Silsbee-designed house on James Street (now demolished), where he wrote *David Harum* while dying of tuberculosis.

The commercialization of the 400 block came with the Dey brothers, who built their store on the southeast corner of South Salina and Jefferson streets in 1893, replacing Milton Price's Second Empire style house. Milton Price's dry-goods store in the Washington Block at the corner of South Salina and East Jefferson Street became the nucleus of the E. W. Edwards Department Store, and Price's eccentric behavior generated a treasure trove of anecdotes. The "Merchant Prince" was fond of fine horses and practical jokes. Folks did not seem to mind that he would gallop into downtown stores on horseback or that their fashionable top hats would be flattened by

Intersection of South Salina and East Jefferson Streets, Dey Brothers (r), 1906. Photograph by George G. Koolakian, courtesy Onondaga Historical Association, Syracuse

his riding crop, because they would always be handsomely reimbursed by him after the joke was over and the damage assessed. After all, the M. S. Price Store was well stocked with high-quality top hats. The carpet department was on the first floor of the store, and expensive carpets were spread out for display. To prove that his rugs were of the best quality, as advertised, Milton Price would drive his team of horses and carriage through the front door and over the rugs from time to time.

By the end of the nineteenth century, Salina Street and its immediate area had become the predominant retail district and remained so for about fifty years. Downtown was the place to shop, to eat, to go to the movies. J. Myer Schine operated three downtown theaters. The Schine Student Center at Syracuse University was a gift of the Schine family. Another distinguished theater family, the Shuberts, or "the boys from Syracuse" as they were called, started their successful careers in Syracuse. The Shubert-Endowed Chair for Drama at Syracuse University shows that their hometown was not forgotten.

The decline of this area began in the 1950s, when strip shopping centers and malls opened on the outskirts of the city. Businesses in the central part of the city closed their doors as quickly as shopping malls were built in the suburbs, making the latter the focus for retail business. Downtown changed from a predominantly retail center to a multipurpose area. The

Galleries of Syracuse, a multiuse building that opened in 1987, symbolizes this change. Pedestrian skyways were built by the city and private enterprise in the 1970s as an attempt to protect downtowners from inclement weather. A facade restoration for buildings on the east and west side of the 300 block is planned. The local firm of MacKnight Architects/Planners was commissioned to restore the facades of ca. fifteen historic properties.

1. 500 South Salina Street Building, 1929 (former Chimes Building)
500 South Salina Street
Architects: Shreve Lamb Harmon, New York,
and Frederick B. O'Connor, Syracuse
Renovation and addition: 1970

This fourteen-story office building replaced the Florence Apartments and is modestly Art Deco. Clad with cut stone and trimmed with bronze, the Chimes Building was one of the important new office buildings of its day. It was claimed to have the fastest elevators in the city, and there were chimes on the fourteenth floor that could be played manually or electrically. They struck every fifteen minutes and played a two- or three-minute musical melody every hour. But no matter what time of day it was, the chimes always struck when Syracuse University won a football game. They were located next door to the penthouse, which was occupied by the architect's office. "They made conversation difficult at times," said local architect Francis E. Hares, "but people got used to it." The chimes were discontinued after World War II. In 1970, the structure was rebuilt within its frame, remodeled, and received an addition. It again became the "cornerstone" of downtown, as it had been in 1929. In 1931, its architects designed the Empire State Building in New York.

2. Empire Building, ca. 1910
472 South Salina Street
Renovation: 1981–86, Ashley Associates, Syracuse

The reinforced concrete building is U-shaped in plan and originally housed offices as well as the Empire Theater, which was located in back and is now a parking lot. The ground level facing Salina Street was occupied by retail business. Here, as in all other commercial buildings on Salina Street, every square foot was valuable and densely occupied. The first- and second-level exterior facing Salina Street was altered when the building was renovated. The interior was converted into a modern office building and received a new, enlarged lobby, but a handsome brass mailbox, the building directory, and the name plaque (originally on the exterior) are original to the building. Here, as in the former Chimes Building, architects like to be on top of things: a former wooden storage shed on top of the eighth floor is now a penthouse and is occupied by the architects who renovated the building.

3. U.S. Post Office, Downtown Station, early 1900s
(former Rudolph Building)
444 South Salina Street
Renovation: 1982–83, Hueber Hares Glavin, Syracuse

The Rudolph Building, named after the jewelry chain that occupied it, housed five stores on the ground level and offices above. It was renovated to be reused as a downtown post office branch when the Federal Building (the former U.S. Post Office) on Clinton Square became headquarters for Pyramid Companies.

4. The Galleries of Syracuse, 1987
400 block South Salina Street
Architects: Joseph Bogdan Associates, Toronto,
and King & King Architects, Manlius, N.Y.

Six buildings were razed to build the Galleries of Syracuse, a multipurpose structure that houses shops, restaurants, office space, and the Onondaga County Public Library. The reflective glass exterior was designed to harmonize with the surrounding buildings and seems to dematerialize the structure. A striking feature is the floor-to-roof pedestrian gallery that cuts diagonally across the complex. The design of this diagonal plan emerged from a pedestrian traffic pattern study: people walk from the corner of South Warren and East Onondaga streets to the corner of South Salina and East Jefferson streets. This resulted in a building divided into two triangles, one for the library, and one for office space, with retail business on the first and second floors on both sides.

Two existing buildings that previously housed the Addis Company (1926) and Dey Brothers Department Store (1893) are connected to the

4. The Galleries of Syracuse

new structure. Notice the fine Art Deco tile facade of the former Addis Company store on the south end of the Galleries. Once a handsome Second Renaissance Revival block, designed by Archimedes Russell, Dey Brothers Department Store on the north end suffered severely over the years. Modernized bit by bit, its brick facade was finally covered with a skin of marble to keep up with the bland face of the former Sibley's building across the street, which had replaced the Keith Theater in 1967.

5. Syracuse Area Landmark Theatre and Loew Building, 1928
362 South Salina Street
Architect: Thomas W. Lamb, New York
Restoration of the lobby: 1982, Allen Silberman of Crown Restoration,
New York
NRHP CSPS

The Second Renaissance Revival Loew Building, constructed by the Loew Corporation of New York, houses offices and Syracuse's most extravagant theater. Thomas W. Lamb (1871–1942), designer of many movie theaters and of the second Madison Square Garden, followed Marcus Loew's advice: "Leave room for the projector and make it High Class." When the Hindu-Moorish fantasy land opened as Loew's State Theater, the glamorous audito-

5. Syracuse Area
Landmark Theatre,
interior

rium was the talk of the town. Said its creator: "The grand foyer is like a temple of gold set with colored jewels, the largest and most precious of which is a sumptuous mural. It represents a festive procession all in oriental splendor …It is pageantry in its most elaborate form and casts a spell of the mysterious and to the occidental mind, of the exceptional."

In the 1960s, threatened by competition from suburban theaters, Loew's started to deteriorate. The opulent furniture, the Tiffany chandelier, designed by Louis Comfort Tiffany and Lockwood de Forest for Cornelius Vanderbilt's New York mansion, and the Wurlitzer pipe organ were sold. A group of citizens, concerned about the theater's imminent demolition for parking space, formed the not-for-profit Syracuse Area Landmark, Inc., solicited funds, had the theater listed on the National Register of Historic Places, and purchased it in 1977. Five years later, Allen Silberman of Crown Restoration restored the lobby. The only remaining downtown theater, the Landmark Theatre again functions as a place for entertainment, conventions, meetings, and ceremonies. A restoration plan for the Landmark Theatre has been submitted by Bell & Spina, Architects Planners of Syracuse. Be sure to go inside and look at the lobby. Guided tours of the theater can be arranged.

6. 325 South Salina Street

In 1913, the building was home to the Syracuse Trust Company, and later to the Marine Midland Trust Company. Notice the finely detailed facade and the stone sculpture flanking the facade above the entrance. The two figures symbolize thrift and waste.

7. Wilson Building, 1897
306 South Salina Street
Architect: Charles E. Colton
Renovation: 1984–, R. J. Engan & Associates, Syracuse

In 1897, fire destroyed the Dillaye Block and some of its adjacent buildings. One year later, the Dillaye Memorial Building, named after the prominent local lawyer Henry A. Dillaye, was rebuilt. It became known as the Wilson Building when Wilson Jewelers bought it in 1943. There were stores on the main floor and offices upstairs. At present, the whole building is used as an office structure. A handsome Beaux-Arts-inspired main facade, obscured for a number of years by a modern front, faces Salina Street. A stone balcony supported by large volutes above the fourth-floor windows gives emphasis to the central section of the main facade. The pedimented and columned entrance with cartouches and volutes is noteworthy.

South Salina Street and First Presbyterian Church, ca. 1860, looking south.
Courtesy Onondaga Historical Association, Syracuse

8. Pike Block, 1855

300 South Salina Street
Architect: G. P. Randall, Syracuse
Renovation: initial work, 1986, R. J. Engan & Associates, Syracuse

Henry Pike of New York built this business block on Salina Street. The Syracuse High School occupied rooms there between 1854 and 1861. In 1878, a business college rented rooms upstairs, and there were stores on the ground level. Liston & Witherill Inc. Dry Goods Store (later renamed Whitlock and Witherill) became the owners in 1894. At one time, Witherill occupied five buildings in the downtown area, including the adjacent Chamberlin Building. The Pike Block faced for some time Minard Lafever's First Presbyterian Church (1849; demolished) at the southeast corner of South Salina and East Fayette streets. The facade of the commercial block has been restored to its 1870s appearance, with the exception of second-story windows and the storefront facing Salina Street, which are of more recent vintage. At present, there are offices in the upper levels with restaurants below.

G. P. Randall, the designer of the Pike Block, worked in this city from 1851 to 1856, at which time he moved to Chicago.

9. Lincoln Plaza, 1973

One Lincoln Center
Architects: Welton Becket and Associates, New York;
plaza, Hueber Hares Glavin, Syracuse
Sculpture: Angelo Savelli

This two-and-one-half-block project, which included the tower for the Chase Lincoln First Bank, the former E. W. Edwards Department Store (now the Atrium at Clinton Square), and a 1,200-car garage, was considered to be a major step in a $30-million urban renewal project. Characteristic of some modern architecture, the building relinquishes its relationship to the street: the tower is set back and placed on a plaza. This represents the last stage in skyscraper development, featuring one or several tall buildings grouped on a plaza of limited space. The plaza is embellished with a steel sculpture entitled *Empedocles,* unfortunately somewhat obscured by a Centro bus shelter.

In 1824, the Kirk Tavern stood on this site. William Kirk, a wagon maker, took it over in place of a wagon owed to him by the original owner. He later invested in New York railroad stock and became one of the wealthiest men in Syracuse. Kirk Park and Kirk Avenue on the South Side still bear his name. His son, the "Honorable William B. Kirk, mayor of the city, capitalist, Vice President of New Process Hide Company and Kirk Brick Company," as he was listed in *Boyd's Directory,* built the Kirk Fireproof Building. Designed in 1897 by Charles E. Colton for this site, it was the first in the city to deserve this name. It was later known as the City Bank Building and was torn down in 1970 to make room for the present structure.

10. Salina Place, ca. 1900
205 South Salina Street
Renovation: 1988, Anthony Fiorito, Syracuse

In 1895, Charles E. Chappell and Francis E. Bacon opened a modest dry-goods store in the 200 block. They were successful and over the years bought, remodeled, and enlarged adjacent buildings. They also occupied stores in the neighboring White Memorial Building. During the 1960s, the ornate facades of 205 South Salina Street were covered with a modern windowless skin. Restoration of the facades and renovation of the interior into a modern office building make this a fine companion to the renovated White Memorial Building next door. A lobby was created when the building was renovated, and the central portion of the building was opened up to become a four-story atrium to which the offices above have visual access. A skylight brings light to the main floor. New pressed-metal ceilings, oak pilasters along the walls, and new marble floors were installed.

The 200 block of South Salina Street became an active part of town in the 1880s. In 1876, the prestigious White Memorial Building (**No. 11**) was erected on the southeast corner of Salina and Fayette streets. Dennis McCarthy built a large business block (1895; Charles E. Colton) for his dry-goods store, D. McCarthy & Sons, on the present site of the Onondaga Plaza. A host of other stores nearby kept Syracusans supplied with hardware, china, shoes, "laces and fancy goods."

Vanderbilt Square

When in 1839 the railroad came to town, it was decided that trains should run along Washington Street, then called Railroad Street. A Greek Revival train station was built by Daniel Elliot (1788–1843) on Washington Street between Salina and Warren streets for the Auburn and Syracuse Railroad. A bell announced incoming and outgoing trains, but it seems to have been difficult to keep people off the tracks. Police officers would run ahead of locomotives shouting to people to keep off and sometimes beating them off with their billy clubs.

Trains crossed Salina Street and brought changes to downtown. In the 1840s, two hotels and a block of stores replaced wooden dwellings, nearly all painted white with green shutters and surrounded by lawns, shrubs, and picket fences. Retail business moved from the Clinton Square area toward the passenger terminal on Washington Street, making Salina Street and Hanover Square into main shopping areas. When in 1869 the old train station on Vanderbilt Square was pulled down, passenger stations moved to Armory Square. Syracuse became known as the city where trains ran right through downtown. They blackened building facades, impeded traffic, and held up fire engines. Citizens' protests were ignored by high-handed railroad company owners and managers, whose policies were in line with Commodore Cornelius Vanderbilt's dictum, "the public be damned." Liberation came in 1936 when trains moved to elevated tracks north of downtown.

Vanderbilt Square, 1915, looking west. Courtesy Onondaga Historical Association, Syracuse

11. White Memorial Building, 1876

201 South Salina Street
Architect: Joseph Lyman Silsbee, Syracuse
Renovation: 1984, Anthony Fiorito, Syracuse;
preservation consultants, Crawford & Stearns, Syracuse
NRHP

This was the second important building that Silsbee designed in downtown Syracuse. Like the Syracuse Savings Bank that had been completed one year earlier, the White Memorial Building was designed in the High Victorian Gothic style with a richly detailed polychrome facade. The slate roof is crowned with an iron cresting. The building was named after the brothers Horace, Hamilton, and Andrew D. White, who were involved in the banking business that was housed in the previous building located on the

11. White Memorial Building, detail

site. Their bank, Syracuse National Bank, and their offices occupied the second story of the new building. There were offices on the third and fourth floors, and the fifth floor underneath the "French" (mansard) roof was to be used as a masonic hall. It was also one of the earlier buildings to have a passenger elevator, which made the upper stories as rentable as the lower ones. Stores occupied the first level along Salina and Washington streets. "In a growing city like Syracuse, we can hardly have too many buildings of this kind," proudly exclaimed a reporter of a local paper. An important long-term tenant of the White Memorial Building was H. J. Howe Jeweler, which occupied the first story of the building from 1895 until the 1970s, when the business moved to a suburban mall. A restaurant now occupies the first floor and the basement. After having been renovated and cleaned, the building is again resplendent with colors and details that had been hidden for decades by historic railroad soot. On Washington Street a steeply pitched gabled entrance, rich with Gothic Revival ornament and guarded by gargoyles, leads into a small lobby, beautifully restored.

12. University Building, 1897
120 East Washington Street
Architects: Green and Wicks, Buffalo
Renovation of lobby: 1985–87, Crawford & Stearns, Syracuse

Built by Syracuse University on donated land and formerly the site of the Remington Block, the building originally housed the university's law school on the main floor, which it shared with the Syracuse Commercial Bank. The rest was office space, except for the eleventh floor, which was occupied by the Citizens Club. One half of the roof space was leased to the Citizens Club as an outdoor space; the other half was a public roof garden. In 1965, the building was remodeled, and although the university sold the building in 1971, the name remains. It is now used as an office building with retail business on the main floor.

The ten-story Beaux-Arts building is an example of the Renaissance palazzo gone vertical. Starting in the late 1880s, the composition of tall

12. University Building, detail

buildings corresponded to the parts of a classical column: base, shaft, and capital. In this case, two seven-story shafts with a one-story capital rest on a two-story base. The towers are connected by a receding central section and a three-story entrance block. The building's steel frame is faced with granite and brick, and has a richly ornamented facade, terminated by an ornate metal cornice, perhaps best appreciated by standing on the sidewalk and looking up. It was reputed to be "thoroughly fireproof." An elaborate entrance, embellished with fluted columns, garlands, and sculpture representing progress and education, leads the visitor into a lobby with a marble staircase, a wrought-iron balustrade, and Neoclassical ornamentation.

13. C. W. Snow Building, 1888
216 South Warren Street
Architect: Archimedes Russell, Syracuse
Addition: 1911, Russell and King, Syracuse
Renovation: 1925, Albert L. Brockway, Syracuse

The Snow Building abuts the University Building's south facade on Warren Street. It was built for C. W. Snow, a wholesale druggist. The wall-bearing brick structure with concrete slabs reinforced by steel beams was originally eight stories high and Syracuse's first tall building. It is difficult to imagine today how impressive this building was as it towered over its four-story neighbors. Archimedes Russell, who had served as fire commissioner and as president of the Board of Fire Commissioners, claimed that it was the best fireproof structure in the city. To provide a home for the Citizens Club and to conform to the height of the adjacent University Building, Archimedes Russell and Melvin L. King added two stories in 1911. When in 1925 Merchants National Bank & Trust Company of Syracuse purchased the structure, Albert L. Brockway was hired to rebuild it. High above the street, almost underneath the cornice, a stylized flower motif attests to Russell's fondness for that Queen Anne symbol.

14. Key Bank, 1915, 1924
201 South Warren Street
Architects: Mobray and Uffinger, New York
Addition: 1928, T. Walter Gaggin, Syracuse
Renovation of the interior: ca. 1960, Hawley McAfee, Syracuse

Originally built as the main office for the First Trust and Deposit Company, the Neoclassical Revival building now houses Key Bank's main offices. The institution became Key Bank in 1980. The bank's history goes back to 1832 because it regards the Bank of Salina as its ancestor. The building is of steel-frame construction and faced with granite, marble, and terra cotta. The pedimented entrance is flanked by modified Corinthian columns. Fluted pilasters articulate the facades and lions' heads embellish the attic level, which is faced with terra cotta tiles. The size of the building was doubled when additions were made to the south. In the early 1960s, interior renovations included the addition of a mezzanine, the covering of plaster columns, and a fourth-floor remodeling.

A number of buildings closely connected with the history of the city were located on this site. One of them was Cook's Coffee House, the location of the Coffee House Riot of New Year's Eve of 1844 when a drunken brawl between Salina "Salt Pointers" and Syracusans finally laid to rest the Salina-Syracuse rivalry and led to the founding of Syracuse as a city. The two villages merged to receive a city charter in 1848 and Salina became Syracuse's First Ward. Later, the Vanderbilt Hotel was located here, named after Commodore Cornelius Vanderbilt, who stayed for a night and left his portrait. And then there was the famed Yates Hotel (1892; Archimedes Russell), said to have had the longest bar in the county, a popular watering-hole for local politicians. The six-story building that covered a city block was demolished in 1971 and replaced by a parking lot.

Two buildings in the immediate area but not on the tour are:

Syracuse Building, 1927
224 Harrison Street
Architect: Paul Hueber, Syracuse
Addition: 1931, Starrett Brothers and Eakin, New York

The building, first (and now again) known as the Syracuse Building, began as a two-story building of concrete, a base for a planned later addition of four floors. Paul Hueber occupied offices on the second floor until 1970 when the firm, by then Hueber Hares Glavin, moved to West Onondaga Street. In 1931, the building's exterior was redesigned and six stories were added, using steel-frame construction. On the exterior, modest Art Deco ornamentation was used along the roofline and on the entrance, which has since been changed. Because the work was done by Starrett Brothers and Eakin, the building was renamed the Starrett-Syracuse Building, later to become the Syracuse-Kemper Building when Kemper Insurance became the owner. In the 1930s, the studios for WSYR Radio, also designed by Paul Hueber, occupied space in the building.

The Lawyers Building, 1941
433 South Warren Street
Architects: King & King, Syracuse
Renovation of the interior: 1981, Schopfer Architects, Syracuse

This handsome Modernistic building can easily be overlooked but should not be. It is the only one of its kind in downtown Syracuse. The flat roof and rounded corners of the abbreviated top story, the smooth terra cotta surface and horizontal band of windows create the streamlined effect characteristic of Modernistic buildings that were popular in the 1930s and 1940s. The small lobby in front of the elevator with its brass and aluminum door contains mirrored panels (recycled from a nightclub down the street), giving the illusion of a larger space.

According to Roger Scott, one of the present owners, the building originally consisted of two separate structures, one of concrete and steel, the other of heavy wood construction. When the WFBL radio station moved in, King & King joined the two buildings, giving it its present face. In 1981, the law firm of Scott, Sardano & Pomeranz bought the building. A bowling alley in the basement was then covered, and the third floor and the lobby were renovated. The building houses offices; the half story on top, which gives the building the appearance of an ocean liner, contains the elevator shaft and the air-conditioning system.

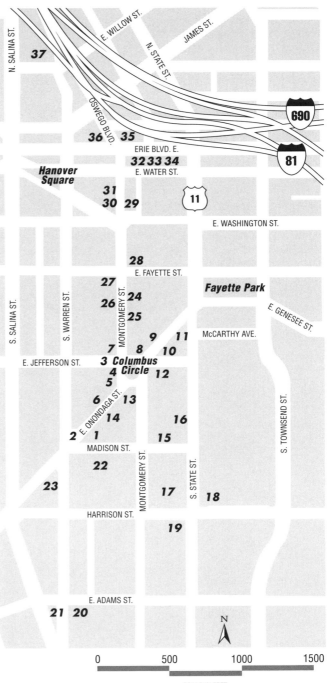

N. SALINA ST.

E. WILLOW ST.

JAMES ST.

N. STATE ST.

37

OSWEGO BLVD.

690

36 **35**

ERIE BLVD. E.

81

32 33 34

E. WATER ST.

**Hanover
Square**

31

30 **29**

11

E. WASHINGTON ST.

28

E. FAYETTE ST.

27

Fayette Park

S. SALINA ST.

S. WARREN ST.

MONTGOMERY ST.

26 **24**

25

E. GENESEE ST.

9 **11**

McCARTHY AVE.

7 **8** **10**

E. JEFFERSON ST.

3 Columbus

4 Circle **12**

5

S. TOWNSEND ST.

6 E. ONONDAGA ST. **13**

14

2 **1** **16**

15

MADISON ST.

22

MONTGOMERY ST.

S. STATE ST.

23

17 **18**

HARRISON ST.

19

E. ADAMS ST.

21 20

N

| 0 | 500 | 1000 | 1500 |

SCALE IN FEET

Columbus Circle and Montgomery Street

Columbus Circle Area

NRHD (buildings immediately surrounding Columbus Circle)
CSPD (buildings immediately surrounding Columbus Circle except
the former Wesleyan Methodist Church)

*Estimated walking time: 1 hour, 30 minutes (**Nos. 1–23**)*

It may not be its official name, but Syracusans know it as Columbus Circle. Those who work in nearby office buildings and stores know it as a place to spend the lunch hour on a pleasant day, to sit around the monument fortified with sustenance from the munchie wagons. Here fountain and flowers, people and pigeons coexist in harmony. At an earlier time, Library Circle, as it was called (and later St. Mary's Circle), was a quietly residential place with several churches within walking distance. Religious buildings were traditionally placed near their congregations or at sites easily accessible to them. As people moved away from the inner city, many downtown churches lost their original function. Some were demolished; others have been adapted for other purposes. There are six church buildings in this immediate area, and four of them are still "working" churches. The other two have been adaptively reused.

During the beginning of the twentieth century, the character of the circle

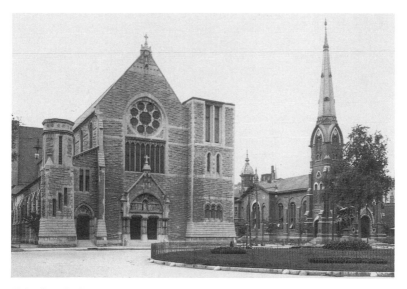

Columbus Circle with St. Mary's (l) and Central Baptist Church (r), 1890s, looking northwest. Courtesy Onondaga Historical Association, Syracuse

changed when the Syracuse Public Library and the fourth Onondaga County Courthouse were built here. With the courthouse came more people and the distinction of being the center of county government, a distinction that had formerly belonged to Clinton Square. During the course of the twentieth century, important civic and commercial buildings replaced older structures, and the rerouting of traffic and landscaping done as part of an urban renewal project have made the circle into a pleasant pedestrian environment.

1. Plymouth Congregational Church, 1859, 1871

(see also No. 2, Downtown Abolition Sites tour)
232 East Onondaga Street
Architect: Horatio Nelson White, Syracuse
Parish house addition: 1930, Charles H. Carpenter, Rochester
CSPS

The Plymouth congregation was in the forefront of the local antislavery movement and was named after Plymouth Church in Brooklyn, whose one-time parson, Henry Ward Beecher, was a leading abolitionist. In the 1870s, Plymouth was the largest Protestant church in Syracuse. Originally, a wooden chapel served the congregation (1855; Horatio Nelson White), which four years later was replaced by a brick church. Within little more than a decade, this building became too small for the growing congregation, and a new church was built around the old. The result is a structure of picturesque massing on a limited triangular site.

In mid-nineteenth century, architects tended to employ a variety of

1. Plymouth Congregational Church

revived architectural styles and sometimes combined their elements. Horatio Nelson White followed these trends, and Plymouth stands as an example of this eclecticism. Its round-arched openings and corbel tables along the cornice line are Romanesque Revival features. The large ogee arch—a Gothic Revival element—is flanked by two small circular windows, giving the main facade a distinctive appearance. According to Jean Henderson, the present church historian, functional metal turrets, later removed, were originally placed along the roofline. They collected water that was led into a basement cistern, setting a waterwheel in motion, which in turn provided air to pump the church organ. (This device was not designed by Rube Goldberg!)

Besides the addition of a parish house, other alterations have been made over the years. A steeple that swayed in the wind too precariously was removed in 1923, an indication that nineteenth-century church steeples were not free of problems. To give churches visibility from afar, tall steeples rose heavenward. But there were some who felt that the very idea of steeples was blasphemous and so prayed for their downfall. In the end, poor building practices, not prayers, caused many to fall or to be taken down for reasons of safety.

2. Onondaga County Korea-Vietnam Veterans Memorial, 1984
Intersection of South Warren, Madison, and East Onondaga streets
Design: Kevan Kane, Syracuse

The abstract sculpture of polished red granite has a five-stepped base symbolizing the five branches of military service. Two triangular forms, representing the two wars, rise from the base and face each other. The abrupt termination of each triangle reflects the lack of resolution of both wars; the beveled vertical edges represent conflict.

Walk northeast on East Onondaga Street to Columbus Circle. In the 1970s, a number of changes were made in this street to encourage pedestrian traffic. The sidewalk was widened, new pavement was laid, trees were planted, and a parking lot was hidden from view by a brick wall. Columbus Circle is one of the city's most attractive and heavily used open spaces.

3. Columbus Monument, 1934
Columbus Circle
Design: Dwight James Baum, New York
Sculpture: V. Renzo Baldi, Florence
Landscaping of circle: 1972, Schleicher-Soper, Syracuse
Restoration of monument: 1991–92, David W. Tessier,
City of Syracuse Department of Parks and Recreation

The monument is the focal point of the circle. As early as 1909, Torquato de Felice, professor of fine arts at Syracuse University, had proposed a Columbus monument. Years later, the Florentine sculptor V. Renzo Baldi was commissioned to create the bronze figure, and the architect Dwight James Baum was asked to design the monument. Syracusans of Italian descent raised money for its realization, and various city parks were suggested for its placement. Finally, the Depression made it difficult, if not impossible, to pay for shipment of the bronze figure and the massive granite stones cut from Italian mountains. None other than Benito Mussolini came to the rescue by paying the shipping costs from Italy to New York, and the inscription, "Christoforo Colombo, Discoverer of America," is there at his request. Thousands came to the unveiling in 1934; speeches were made; Baldi, who had been made an honorary tribal brother by the Onondaga, spoke in Italian and all rejoiced.

The explorer is depicted as a young man. Chart in one hand, he points with the other to the land he hopes to reach by a new route. The figure faces west, the direction in which Columbus sailed. The stone pedestal is ornamented with four bas-reliefs depicting Columbus's voyage: Columbus at Queen Isabella's court, the departure of his fleet, the vessels at sea, and the arrival in the "New World." Stone figures on the north and south sides of the shaft represent prows of ancient ships. Bronze turtles are at the base of the monument and signify the connection to Native Americans: for the Iroquois, the turtle symbolizes the island of the North American continent, and the Turtle Clan is an important clan of the Iroquois nations. Dick Case wrote in the *Herald-Journal* that four Indian bronze heads originally placed around the top of the shaft were taken down at one time and placed into storage, but then were stolen. Rediscovered in Florida and brought back to Syracuse, they have regained their rightful place.

Dwight James Baum wanted the immediate surrounding to have a "Roman feeling," and he designed the city's largest fountain within a pool that has the shape of a mariner's compass. It has been said that the stones in the mosaic on the bottom of the pool were laid in the manner of the stones that paved the Roman Appian Way.

4. Cathedral of the Immaculate Conception, 1886
259 East Onondaga Street
Architect: Michael O'Connor, New York
Sanctuary and tower additions: 1903, 1906, Archimedes Russell,
Syracuse
Renovations of the interior: 1958, 1985, James D. Curtin,
Syracuse
NRHD CSPD

The growing Irish-Catholic population of the city needed a new centrally located church. After $35,000 for the building site had been raised, an amount many considered excessive, the construction of a Gothic Revival building of Onondaga limestone began. It was a task not free of difficulties. St. Mary's, as it was then known, could not be completed because LaConcha, a Turkish bath establishment of ill-repute located directly behind the church, was in the way. Only when it went bankrupt and its building was torn down could construction be resumed. Considering the reputation of LaConcha, however, some felt strongly that the building of a sanctuary on this site was inappropriate. But, according to a history published by the church, Bishop Ludden dismissed his critics by saying that "cleanliness was next to godliness," commissioned Archimedes Russell to finish the sanctuary, and celebrated its completion in 1903. Within the next three years, the two towers flanking the main entrance were also completed. During construction of the square tower marking the corner at Jefferson Street, it was discovered that the foundation would not support the weight of a cast-bronze bell. For this reason a set of Flemish carillons was installed. In 1904, the building became the Cathedral of the Roman Catholic Diocese and was consecrated six years later.

Notice the handsomely carved main portal with sculpture in its tympanum and the rose window above it. Gothic pointed-arch and lancet windows pierce the walls. If you would like to go inside, enter through the main portal. The interior features fine stained-glass windows as well as carvings and moldings reminiscent of medieval craftsmanship. The windows came from the Meyer Studios in Munich, Germany. Five teaching windows in the apse depict biblical scenes from the Annunciation to the Crucifixion. A quiet color scheme throughout, repeating the shades of the Botticino marble, conveys a feeling of spaciousness. Features such as ornamented ceiling trusses, the ribbed sanctuary ceiling, and openings with pointed arches are characteristic of nineteenth-century Gothic Revival churches. The crypt is the burial place of three bishops and a former rector of the church.

5. Chapel Dedicated to the Holy Mother, 1958
259 East Onondaga Street (use entrance on south side of building)
Architect: James D. Curtin, Syracuse
Mosaics: Nicholas Vergette
Sculpture: Jaqueline Belfort Challat

The interior of this small chapel (it is part of the main building and adjoins the south side) was originally designed as the baptistry and is a quiet retreat from noisy street life. It is a work of art: interior walls are covered with fine ceramic mosaics depicting the sacrament of baptism. A bonded bronze statue underlines the building's new function, as does a large green plant symbolizing the Tree of Jesse, of whom Mary is a descendant.

6. Cathedral Rectory, Bishop's Residence, 1914
239 East Onondaga Street
Architect: James A. Randall, Syracuse
Landscape architect: Noreda Rotunno
NRHD CSPD

The building is adjacent to the cathedral and faces Onondaga Street. It was designed to harmonize in style and materials with the cathedral, a good early example of contextual design. The small landscaped green space

7. Columbus Center (r) with Cathedral of the Immaculate Conception (l) and Columbus Monument

between the two buildings was the first of its kind in downtown and was designed by Noreda Rotunno (1899–1978).

James A. Randall (1861–1940) also designed the Cathedral School (1916) at Madison and Montgomery streets and the Cathedral Convent (1926) at 422 Montgomery Street. He apprenticed in the office of James H. Kirby, whose partner he became. The firm was later reorganized as Randall & Vedder (James R.) and was responsible for a great number of school buildings and other types of structures in and around Syracuse.

7. Columbus Center, 1914 (former First Baptist Church)
215 East Jefferson Street
Architect: Gordon A. Wright, Syracuse
Renovation: 1989–, Schopfer Architects, Syracuse
NRHD CSPD

The emphasis on verticality in this building—a good example of the Late Gothic Revival style—stands in contrast to the cathedral's earlier Gothic Revival style building across the street, where rough-cut stone walls convey a sense of weight and down-to-earthness. First Baptist replaced the Central Baptist Church designed by Horatio Nelson White in 1868. Looking at the building, the viewer does not realize how unusual it was for its day. The architect not only combined religious and commercial functions under one roof—it was listed in *Ripley's "Believe It or Not"* as an oddity—but also employed building techniques innovative for their time.

Often referred to as "the church with the hotel over it," the building's upper stories (at one time furnished with Stickley furniture) were originally connected with the adjacent YMCA building to take care of its overflow. In the 1940s, the connection was closed and the space converted into a regular hotel. Twenty years later, the church took over management, and the Mizpah Tower functioned as apartments and rooms for single women. In 1969, it was named Mizpah, which is said to mean "temporary rest under the tower." Mizpah also stands as a symbol of the faithfulness of the daughters of Israel (Judges 11.34). At one time, a five-room penthouse on the roof was occupied by one of the ministers and his family, and was surrounded by a victory garden. Now the YWCA occupies part of the upper stories and the penthouse for residential and administrative purposes.

Below the level of the third floor is the large open space of a semicircular auditorium, expressed on the exterior by its tall pointed-arch windows. With the exception of the window above the pulpit, all windows of the auditorium are of light gray grisaille glass designed by the Pike Studios of Rochester. These windows allow daylight to enter and give it a soft silvery quality. The former sanctuary is used for theater performances and for concerts.

A different plan on various levels presented difficulties in construction. Therefore, and for reasons of safety and economy, the architect decided to use reinforced concrete, an early example of reinforced concrete construction in Syracuse. Granite covers the exterior of the basement, and the upper levels and towers are faced with a skin of nonabsorbing terra cotta tiles. Designs in terra cotta that could be easily duplicated, since thousands of pieces could be cast from the same mold, embellish facades and rooflines. According to a church history, Canterbury Cathedral was the inspiration for the exterior ornamentation of the main tower, which lost its upper cresting of finials during an electrical storm in the 1980s.

Gordon A. Wright (1866–1950) graduated from the Department of Architecture at Syracuse University, where he also taught. He set up his architectural office in Syracuse in 1892 and was in partnership with Charles R. Ellis and later with his daughter Marjorie Wright. The firm designed residences, churches, and public buildings, among them the Onondaga Orphans' Home (1924) at 960 Salt Springs Road, now occupied by the Elmcrest Children's Center.

8. Former Syracuse Public Library Building, 1902–5
335 Montgomery Street
Architect: James A. Randall, Syracuse
NRHD CSPD

The Central Library (founded in 1852) was under the jurisdiction of the board of education. Housed in the old City Hall, it consisted of a "a large and convenient book case which will accommodate the Central Library for years to come." This hope was in vain. Soon more than one bookcase was needed, and an ever-increasing number of books were moved to the high school on West Genesee Street and from there to the Putnam School, which stood on the site of the new library building. In 1893, the library was granted a charter with a board of trustees and a few years later changed its name to Syracuse Public Library. A growing number of books and readers demanded more space. Andrew Carnegie, whose money helped to built a great number of libraries throughout the country, gave $200,000 for a new structure that was to be the city's first public library building. He did not attend the opening ceremonies in 1905, and even blamed the city and the trustees for "uselessly dissipating funds" because there was not money left to buy books or furniture. This marred the enjoyment of the new library somewhat, but the building did not remain an empty shell for too long. Some eighty years later another change became imminent, and the Onondaga County Public Library, which it had officially become in 1975, moved to larger quarters in the Galleries of Syracuse on Warren Street.

The building's Beaux-Arts form and exterior are elegant additions to Columbus Circle. The steel-frame structure is faced with Indiana limestone and light-colored brick. An imposing round-arched entrance on Montgomery Street is flanked by coupled columns, a common Beaux-Arts feature. They are crowned by composite capitals and rise from the ground through two stories, carrying an ornate parapet. The exterior displays an exuberance of classical detail, such as sculpted medallions and heavy keystones above windows. A grand staircase and oak-trimmed marble wainscoting are

8. Former Syracuse Public Library Building, detail

notable interior features. The shape and placement of windows allow an abundance of natural light to enter the interior. From within, one has a fine view of the immediate outside space, thus making Columbus Circle an intimate part of the building.

9. Monroe Building, 1968
333 East Onondaga Street
Architect: Schopfer Architects, Syracuse

The designer took style and forms of the adjacent building into consideration when designing this new office building with a setback facade and a zigzag roofline. Enhancing the streetscape, the building is a good example of contextual design, demonstrating that old and new can coexist comfortably. The building was built for and is named after the Monroe Abstract and Tile Corporation.

10. Former Wesleyan Methodist Church, 1845
(see also No. 3, Downtown Abolition Sites tour)
304 East Onondaga Street
Renovation: 1991–, Vaughn Lang, Syracuse
NRHD

In the mid-1840s, the lot now occupied by the church building was bought for $400. According to files at the Onondaga Historical Association, construction of the building began in 1845. The church became First Gospel Church in 1936 when the organization absorbed the membership of the Syracuse Gospel Tabernacle. Until 1989, it was the oldest building in Syracuse in continuous operation as a church; it is at present adaptively reused. The small brick building, now dwarfed by its neighbors, reminds us of an earlier, smaller-scale assemblage of buildings around Columbus Circle. The "old village church," as it was once called, was originally built in the style of a vernacular Greek Revival meetinghouse. Corner pilasters, a low-pitched pediment, and rectangular openings attest to this. The tower, with its round-arched openings and recessed arches, the rear portion, and the stained-glass windows are later additions. It is said that the congregation took an active part in underground railroad activities during pre–Civil War days.

11. First United Methodist Church of Syracuse, 1959
317 East Jefferson Street
Architects: Clark Clark Millis & Gilson, Syracuse

The church is built, in part, on the site formerly occupied by the First Methodist Episcopal Church, a fine Gothic Revival edifice designed by Archimedes Russell in 1904 and destroyed fifty years later by a spectacular fire. An old congregation, the First Methodists have existed in Syracuse since 1824. Mergers with Centenary Methodist Episcopal Church and with the Furman Street United Methodists led to the present First United Methodist Church. The location in the heart of an area that was being considered as the future site of the Civic Center, posed some difficulties, and the architects decided on a "contemporary design, without being radical." The result is a modern building that rounds the corner at the intersection of Jefferson and State streets. It is organized around a small atrium that separates the rounded oblong sanctuary of the church from the church school. (The main entrance is on Jefferson Street.) The exterior is faced with pink granite, buff brick, and limestone. A decorative band running around the structure symbolizes Christian community. Stained-glass windows are framed in bronze.

The senior partner of the firm that built the present church, Carl W. Clark (1893–1985), studied architecture at the University of Pennsylvania, set up office in Cortland in 1914, and in 1947 moved to Syracuse. His son Robert, architect and engineer, became his partner two years later, and in 1963 the firm became Clark Clark Millis & Gilson.

12. Fourth Onondaga County Courthouse, 1904–6

401 Montgomery Street
Architects: Archimedes Russell, and Melvin L. King, Syracuse
Interior: Allewelt & Brothers, Syracuse
Murals: William De L. Dodge, New York; Gustave Gutgemon, New York
NRHD CSPD

Four residences were razed to make room for the imposing Beaux-Arts building that replaced the third Onondaga County Courthouse on Clinton Square. Its design was inspired by the Rhode Island State Capitol in Providence, designed by McKim, Mead and White, at that time the leading architectural firm on the East Coast. When the building was ready for occupancy, Syracusans rejoiced in their "Great Marble Temple of Justice." But marble it was not. Since conservatism in spending public money was still a concern, the steel-frame structure was faced with Indiana limestone, a material that could easily be worked with machines, making it less expensive than marble. Because of the swampy ground, the structure floats on a concrete raft. The form—three symmetrically arranged "hyphenated" blocks—is representative of Beaux-Arts. The central block of the west facade is emphasized by a second-level porch with a pedimented temple front, a central staircase, and a crowning dome. The large copper-covered dome is anchored by four small ones, thus forming a square for the circle of the large dome base. A rusticated granite base, conveying a sense of solidity, a combination of round-arched and rectangular windows, some crowned with pediments, and pilasters framing window bays in the upper stories are features used in Renaissance architecture.

According to Beaux-Arts design principles, the center of the courthouse is occupied by a light court (open interior court) that organizes the design of the interior. Compartmentalized spaces are arranged around the court and open into the encircling corridor. Apart from the ornate third floor court-

12. Fourth Onondaga County Courthouse

rooms with richly carved and ornamented judges' benches, the main lobby (atrium), from which a wide staircase leads to upper floors, is the visual focal point of the building. The textural richness of marble floors, wainscot, and columns, of an ornate plaster ceiling in gold and blue, and of doors and windows with leaded glass is impressive.

The design of the fourth Onondaga County Courthouse exemplifies the practices of the American Renaissance, when architects and artists, following the example of the Renaissance, worked together to create a building that combined all the arts (with the exception of sculpture in this case). The local interior design firm of Allewelt & Brothers commissioned two painters, both working in New York, to paint historical and allegorical murals. William De L. Dodge painted four canvases, cemented on the wall above the wainscot in the atrium, that depict historical and legendary episodes of the area that is now Onondaga County. The artist, who followed a national trend in relating murals in public buildings to local history, had previously done mural work for the Library of Congress and for Richard Morris Hunt's Administration Building at Chicago's Columbian Exposition. Murals on the stair landing of the third floor, painted by Gustave Gutgemon, symbolize law and justice.

In 1915, the courthouse was the site of "the Trial of the Century," as it was hailed by the local press. William Barnes, once Chairman of the National Republican Committee, brought a libel suit against former President Theodore Roosevelt and lost. It seems, however, that both men lost because each suffered irreparable damage to his reputation.

13. Bryant & Stratton Business Institute, 1970
400 Montgomery Street
Architects: Finnegan Lyon & Colburn, Syracuse
CSPD

The modern structure was hailed as "the latest step in the renewal of Columbus Circle." Its vertical accent and its brick and glass curtain wall correspond to the towers of MONY Plaza directly behind, while the building's scale is appropriate to the circle. Built and originally occupied by the Powelson Institute, the building was later occupied by the Bryant & Stratton Business Institute. The structure replaced the Ely Block apartments, which at one time housed the Syracuse University College of Law.

14. Trompe-l'Oeil ("Fool the Eye") Mural, 1979
240 East Onondaga Street
Design and artwork: Syracuse Art Squad

This handsome mural presents us with historic connections on an otherwise dull facade and enlivens the small space that is used as a playground.

15. John H. Mulroy Civic Center, 1975
421 Montgomery Street
Architects: McAfee Malo Lebensold Affleck Nichol, Syracuse and Montreal
Sculpture in interior facing Montgomery Street: 1989, Larry Morris

The Civic Center underlines the civic and cultural importance of Columbus Circle. The form of the building not only reflects the diversity of scale in this downtown area but also expresses the building's various functions: the sixteen-story tower houses county offices, while its lower wings contain two theaters and an 1,800-seat concert hall. Great care has been taken to open interior spaces to exterior surroundings. Large second-story windows present the visitor with a fine view of Columbus Circle, and the landscaped area between the Civic Center and the courthouse was designed for the enjoyment of a quiet urban space in a busy downtown area. The building has been referred to as "the Lincoln Center of Upstate New York." It is the home of the Cultural Resources Council, the Syracuse Symphony Orchestra, as well as a variety of other organizations devoted to opera, dance, drama, and film. A whimsical sculpture named *For the Love of Mike* is placed in a window facing Montgomery Street to welcome the many children who come here to enjoy youth theater productions. The painted steel sculpture was given to the Cultural Resources Council by Beverly Harms in memory of her son.

15. Columbus Circle with Fourth Onondaga County Courthouse, John H. Mulroy Civic Center, Bryant & Stratton Business Institute, and MONY (l to r), looking south

16. County Office Building, 1955
600 South State Street
Architects: King & King Architects, Syracuse

Adjacent to the Civic Center, facing State Street, the building was the first in central New York to be built with a glass curtain wall. In accordance with the design principles of architecture in the Modern style, the building is unadorned; aquamarine-colored glass panels, a black granite base, and white marble facing make the building visually interesting and give color and texture to the main facade. Green marble lends elegance to a small lobby.

17. Onondaga County War Memorial, 1951
515 Montgomery Street
Architects: Edgarton & Edgarton Architects and Engineers
Associates, Syracuse; consulting engineers, Ammann and Whitney.
Renovation of the Interior: 1992-, King & King Architects,
Manlius, N.Y.
Murals: G. Lee Trimm
NRHP

The Onondaga County War Memorial is dedicated to the U.S. veterans of the two world wars and to the Korean and Vietnam wars. Its design is the result of a countywide competition sponsored by the American Institute of Architects. When completed, the War Memorial was considered to be an engineering feat and its roof was hailed as the "most advanced form of shell vaulting" in the country at the time. The structure rests on concrete-filled steel pipe piles. The main hall—the nucleus of the structure: 250 feet long, 138 feet wide, and 60 feet high at the apex—is spanned by a roof of poured concrete-shell construction that does not require interior support. The roof that covers the War Memorial auditorium is a single span-rib-and-shell vault, three to five inches deep and with a clear span of 160 feet. The designers of the War Memorial expanded on thin-shell construction by adapting the form to suit the function of the multipurpose auditorium space and to accommodate the seating areas on the balcony level. They supported the end of each rib with cantilevered brackets, thus making it possible to have a two-story space under the shallow arch of the barrel vault. There were also structural and economical advantages of shell construction: a single wooden framework could be used repeatedly to form the contiguous concrete sections of the vault, thus avoiding time and expense in building and breaking down several frames. The barrel-vaulted auditorium is surrounded by two-story rectangular blocks whose facades are covered with limestone panels at the foundation and with tan bricks above. A band of raised letters depicting the names of fifty-five battles of both world wars in which Onondaga County residents fought terminates the limestone-covered foundation. The large block facing Harrison Street contains the auditorium stage. Here the walls are of concrete, finished and scored to simulate the limestone of the foundation. At the north end of the building is another distinct block containing Memorial Hall. The austerity of this vaulted room with its heraldic ornamentation and murals symbolizing both world wars, together with the massive form of the building, convey the idea of commemoration. An exhibit, in an extension to Memorial Hall, and open to the public, commemorates the deeds of American veterans. But in contrast to a purely commemorative memorial, this building is a "living memorial," because it also serves many community purposes. Sports events and concerts, industrial exhibitions and the annual "Festival of Nations" are some examples.

18. Everson Museum of Art of Syracuse and Onondaga County, 1968

Corner of South State and Harrison streets
Architects: I. M. Pei Associates, New York, and Pederson Hueber
Hares & Glavin, Syracuse

The Everson began as the Syracuse Museum of Fine Arts in 1896. It was founded by George Fisk Comfort, who also helped organize the Metropolitan Museum of Art and for twenty years served as the first dean of the College of Fine Arts at Syracuse University. The museum's first quarters were a few rented rooms in the Onondaga County Savings Bank. From there it moved to the Syracuse Public Library Building, where it remained for about thirty years until the Lynch Mansion (now demolished) at James and North State streets became its home for another three decades. The financial legacy of the museum's long-time patron, Helen Everson, and a newly chartered Everson Museum of Art, consolidating with the Syracuse Museum of Fine Arts, made the creation of the present museum possible. The Everson Museum of Art of Syracuse and Onondaga County was chartered in 1959 to erect a new art museum on the condition that the city provide the site.

After eight years of planning and fund raising, the new Everson Museum, an "object lesson in art and museology," to quote Ada Louise Huxtable of the *New York Times*, had become reality. It was built on an urban renewal site, part of which was occupied by the bus station. The architect, chosen by then-Director Max Sullivan and the museum trustees' building committee, was the firm of I. M. Pei Associates, which was to work in collaboration with Pederson Hueber Hares & Glavin. Except for a student exercise at MIT, Pei had never designed a museum before he received this 1961 commission. Five years later, he said that "it is one of my favorite commissions … it pleased me very, very much." Its influence can be clearly seen in the East Building of the National Gallery of Art (1978) in Washington, D.C., and it did earn him the prize commission for the John F. Kennedy Library in Boston (1979).

The form of the building is that of an abstract sculpture: massive windowless gallery blocks are cantilevered over a base, hovering above a large paved plaza complete with reflecting pool. The curvaceous lines of a Henry Moore sculpture, *Two Piece Reclining Figure*, Lila Katzen's *Delphi*, and Arne Zimmerman's ceramic vessels near the Harrison Street entrance serve as counterpoint to the stark rectangular forms of the building. The structure seems to change shape constantly as one walks past it and around it. Reinforced concrete used for its construction was cast in place and was given a rough bushhammered finish on the exterior and on most of the interior walls on the site. This "purist" approach, as Pei called it, brings out the warm red granite aggregate in the concrete, its components having been carefully selected. Said Pei, "not just any old piece of sidewalk was used." The interior provides maximum flexibility: there are nine galleries in the interior, each different from the other in size and shape. The central element of the building is the sculpture court. The largest space in the museum, it is two stories high and is dominated by a spiral concrete staircase, the museum's "most extravagant piece of sculpture." Natural light comes through narrow strips of clear glass in the waffle-grid ceiling through two floor-to-

Everson Museum of Art of Syracuse and Onondaga County, interior sculpture court

ceiling window strips that also offer glimpses of the outside. Below ground are storerooms, administrative offices, a lecture hall seating 320 people, and a ceramics study center that opened in 1986. The latter, planned by Director Ronald A. Kuchta for several years, was made possible by a generous donation from Syracuse China, a firm established in Syracuse in the 1870s. The Everson has an impressive collection of contemporary ceramics and ceramic art from all cultures of the world through the ages. The study center exhibits the entire collection of 2,500 ceramic artworks.

A walk through the museum provides the visitor with views not only of art but of the building itself, which is as much on exhibit as is the artwork. To quote Ada Louise Huxtable once more, "the building demonstrates a dramatic oneness of contemporary art and architecture. ... Not since the age of fresco have art and architecture provided such an esthetic and environmental whole."

19. ONCENTER (Onondaga County Convention Center), 1991–
800 South State Street
Architects: Mitchell/Giurgola, New York

Because of its central location in the state, Syracuse traditionally has been a convention city. Until now, however, the city could accommodate only small- and medium-sized groups.

With the spacious Post-Modern convention center, the city hopes to attract large conventions.

20. Greystone Square, 1903
(former Central Technical High School)
701–745 South Warren Street
Architect: Archimedes Russell, Syracuse
Addition: 1928, Albert L. Brockway, Syracuse
Renovation: 1984–86, Gregory Ferentino and Associates,
Syracuse; interior in part: 1984, Modern Times Interiors, Syracuse
NRHP

In 1900, Archimedes Russell submitted plans for a new high school to replace the old one on West Genesee Street (1869; Horatio Nelson White), which had become a health hazard. The separation of study and recitation rooms seemed then to be the latest trend in school construction, and the architect was quick to embody this in his plans for Central Technical High School. The building was originally U-shaped in plan, assuring the classrooms had plenty of light. A large assembly hall on the first floor was the core of the building, and study, class, and recitation rooms were arranged around it. The Beaux-Arts building consisting of "hyphenated" blocks with a pedimented central section and rich exterior ornamentation seems like a smaller, simpler version of the fourth Onondaga County Courthouse (**No. 12**), which Russell was to design within another year. The three-story brick building could accommodate 1,500 students. It was of slow-burning rather than fireproof construction; metal and concrete were placed under the wood floor system supported by iron columns, and iron stairways were used, with wrought iron and wooden balustrades. The entrance for teachers and visitors on Billings Park was placed in the central section that was ornamented with paired Ionic columns and a richly decorated pediment. Students had to use the less ornate side entrance on Adams Street. In 1928, Albert L. Brockway enlarged the assembly room and created Lincoln Auditorium, a multipurpose hall with fine acoustics, where for many years music lovers enjoyed concerts. The Syracuse Symphony performed there until the construction of the Civic Center (**No. 15**). The building functioned as a school until 1975 and is now, in part, adaptively reused.

21. Billings Park
Warren and Salina streets
Sculptures: 1920, Roland Hinton Perry and Frederick R. Lear (architect); 1924, Alice Ruggles Kitson

The small park is named after Roger Billings, who in the mid-nineteenth century owned a wagon shop across the street. A public-spirited man, he offered to take care of the landscaping of the park and was authorized to do just that. Two statues adorn the park. Although *The Hiker* (Alice Ruggles Kitson) commemorates all military ventures between 1898 and 1902, it is generally considered to be a memorial to the Spanish-American War. While its bronze soldier on a granite base is characteristic of the sculptural style of the 1930s, the design of *Rock of the Marne* (Roland Hinton Perry and Frederick R. Lear) is Renaissance inspired. The single figure of a defiant soldier indicates his unwillingness to retreat and honors the special valor of an infantry regiment formed in Syracuse that distinguished itself in the second battle of the Marne during World War I. Enlisted men of the Thirty-eighth Infantry gave the sculpture to the city in appreciation of the hospitality they received while training at Camp Syracuse during World War I.

22. MONY (Mutual of New York), 1966, 1970
1 MONY Plaza
Architects: John Graham Kahn & Jacobs, New York
Sculpture: 1975, Dorothy Riester

In addition to office space, this modern building complex houses banking and commercial facilities. MONY Plaza, along with Lincoln Plaza on South Salina Street and Presidential Plaza on East Genesee Street, belongs to the phase of skyscraper development that started in the 1930s with Rockefeller Center in New York. Similar to pieces of sculpture placed on pedestals, the buildings are set back and apart from the street on a platform that is raised above the sidewalk. These rectangular forms—two twenty-story towers flanking a five-story wing—are connected with each other and cover a city block. The steel, glass, and concrete towers are stark sculptural forms, devoid of ornamentation. They stand in contrast to the rounded, striated facade of the parking garage, which has an underground connection with the Hotel Syracuse.

In the interior of the Chase Lincoln First Bank branch stands a figure entitled *Young Lincoln*. Constructed of welded and forged iron, the elongated figure of nearly ten feet corresponds well to the tall buildings around it.

23. Hotel Syracuse, 1924
500 South Warren Street
Architects: George B. Post & Sons, New York
Addition (Hilton Tower): 1980, William Taber, New York, and
Gregory Ferentino and Associates, Syracuse

The Truax Building was moved across Harrison Street when this steel-frame structure was built on its site, designed by the architectural firm George B. Post (1837–1913) & Sons, which specialized in hotel construction. The original design of Hotel Syracuse provided for retail stores, an emergency hospital, and 612 rooms with baths. Tennis, squash, and handball courts were on the hotel roof. In contrast to MONY Plaza, the structure represents an earlier phase of skyscraper development. It is built to the edge of the sidewalk, thus emphasizing the building's connection to the street. The three hotel towers connected by lower wings resemble classical columns. The vertical three-part division into base, shaft, and capital is brought about by the use of different materials and ornamentation. Red brick is used to face the shaft, and light sandstone is the facing material for the base. Sandstone is also used to frame windows in the uppermost stories, the capital. On the ground level, quoins and Ionic columns surround tall round-arched windows ornamented with pictorial keystones and garlands, fluted pilasters carry balustrades, and blind window niches are surmounted by classical pediments. This use of classical and Renaissance motifs enlivens the facade and provides the pedestrian with interesting features to look at.

In the interior, the Persian Terrace was an elegant space for festive occasions. The Rainbow Room (1937; Paul Hueber), not installed until the end of Prohibition, was named for the changing colors of the tubular lighting within the glass-block entrance. In recent years, the interior of the hotel has been remodeled. Unfortunately, Carl Roters' forty-foot mural in the lobby, commissioned in 1948 and depicting people and events of Syracuse's early years, was covered over. Four murals painted on walnut panels, also by Carl Roters, were taken off the walls in the Cavalier Room. In 1980, the Hotel Syracuse expanded with the construction of the Hilton Tower, and the complex is now called the Hotels at Syracuse Square.

Montgomery Street Area

NRHD

Estimated walking time: 1 hour (Nos. 24–37)

Residences shaded by trees lined the street during most of the nineteenth century. Montgomery was also one of the first city streets to have street lighting, but the gas lights were not used on moonlit nights. The street forms an axis between City Hall to the north and Columbus Circle to the south and is visually terminated by both.

East side of Montgomery Street, between Fayette and Jefferson streets, ca. 1880. Courtesy Onondaga Historical Association, Syracuse

24. Onondaga Historical Association Building, 1895
311 Montgomery Street
Architect: Henry W. Wilkinson, Syracuse and New York
NRHP NRHD

The building was the first in central New York to be erected for the use of a telephone company, in this case the Central New York Telephone and Telegraph Company. It was built to carry heavy loads, and its basement and five stories were divided into offices and equipment and operating rooms. The stairs are of cast steel with slate treads, and the open stairwell is occupied by a cast-iron conduit that carried the telephone wires from the basement to the fifth floor. A bicycle room addition to the rear of the first floor tells us that this was a favorite mode of transportation at the time.

The finely detailed composition of this building front is representative of commercial structures in large Eastern cities of the United States of the

1890s. Their designers looked at northern Italian Renaissance buildings for inspiration and created the Second Renaissance Revival, of which this building is a good example. Between the second and third stories, terra cotta ornamentation and molded brick, flanked by terra cotta cartouches, embellish the main facade. Molded belt courses mark the floor levels, and a Corinthian cornice terminates the building. A charming detail is the engraved bell on the silver-plated door handle of the entrance, a reminder of the structure's original function. When Syracuse University Chancellor James Roscoe Day was shown through the new building he was impressed: "It is magnificent and astounding," he said. "I confess having very little idea of a telephone system, except that part contained in the little box on the wall, before which I frequently get angry."

After the telephone company moved into its new building at 321 Montgomery Street in 1906, the earlier one became the home of the Onondaga Historical Association (OHA) and is now used as its research center. A bequest from local salt manufacturer William Kirkpatrick made the purchase of the building possible. From its beginnings in 1862 as "an institution for the preservation and care for the curiosities and relics of the county," the Onondaga Historical Association, one of the oldest in the nation, has grown into an important research center. (Without it, this book could not have been written.)

The building's architect, Henry W. Wilkinson (1870–1931), graduated from the Cornell University School of Architecture, worked in Boston, and practiced in Syracuse for several years, designing several residences on James Street, before he moved to New York.

The building is flanked by two late nineteenth-century bow-fronted commercial structures at 317 and 305 Montgomery Street. 317 Montgomery Street is being renovated by Manuel Barbas (1989–). The basement and first floor of the building houses a restaurant, and there will be offices upstairs. Both 317 and 305 are part of the National Register Historic District.

24. Onondaga Historical Association Building

25. Onondaga Historical Association Museum, 1906
(former New York Telephone Company Building)
321 Montgomery Street
Architect: Elmlitz & McKenzie, New York
NRHD

Several residences were razed to make room for this structure (including one that Horatio Nelson White had designed and lived in). Within a short time of having occupied the building at 311 Montgomery Street, the telephone company needed a larger structure and moved into another five-story Second Renaissance Revival building. The OHA Museum was set up here in 1983 to display and store OHA's vast collection.

The building's light-colored brick facade is embellished with fine stonework; windows have heavy keystones; and a distinctive feature is a bold cornice with dentils, modillion blocks and a series of lions' heads. In Renaissance architecture, lions symbolized the sun and its powers. A photograph at the OHA's research center shows a group of female operators enjoying themselves on top of the building after completing a class on the "new-fangled contraption," the dial telephone, that had arrived in Syracuse in the 1920s. The Museum exhibits feature many interesting objects from Onondaga County's past.

25. Onondaga Historical Association Museum, detail

26. Metropolitan School for the Arts, 1917
(former Masonic Temple)
318–322 Montgomery Street
Architects: Gaggin & Gaggin, Syracuse
Ceramic Artist: 1988, Tammy Tarbell
NRHD

This Second Renaissance Revival building is of concrete and veneered in brick. Arched windows are surrounded with limestone trim, which is also used for the pedimented entrances. The five-bay facade is ornamented with copper spandrels and a decorative cornice. The Masons occupied the building until 1985 when it was purchased by the Metropolitan School for the Arts. The original lodge, drill halls, and men's club facilities were converted into theater and recital halls as well as into studios, a gallery, and administrative offices. The Metropolitan School for the Arts is a professional art school with programs in music, drama, dance, and art for children and adults. A ceramic panel in the theater lobby on the third floor depicts the creation myth of the Iroquois.

The building's architects, T. Walter Gaggin (1871–1945) and Edwin H. Gaggin (1866–1955) graduated from the School of Architecture at Syracuse University. The latter also studied at the École des Beaux-Arts in Paris and the former at Columbia University. Their firm, Gaggin & Gaggin, was responsible for the design of various buildings at Syracuse University, the YMCA, additions to St. Joseph's Hospital, and the Crouse-Hinds factory building, among others.

27. St. Paul's Episcopal Cathedral, 1885
310 Montgomery Street
Architect: Henry Dudley, New York
Interior renovation: 1971, D. Kenneth Sargent, Syracuse
and
Lockwood Memorial Parish House, 1909
Architect: Alfred C. Taylor, Syracuse
Both buildings: NRHP NRHD CSPS

The history of Syracuse is closely connected with that of the local Episcopal Protestant church, founded in 1803 on Onondaga Hill. After having bought a site from the Syracuse Company for a dollar, the congregation erected its first building in 1827, on the present site of thè S. A. & K. Building on Hanover Square. Soon the white frame church became too small for its ever-growing congregation and was replaced in 1842 by a larger stone edifice on the present site of Merchants Bank. The congregation's present home, the third St. Paul's church, anchors the southwest corner of East Fayette and Montgomery streets. Adjacent to it is the Lockwood Memorial Parish House, a three-story brick structure with pointed-arch windows. The Hadley Chapel (between the two buildings and attached to both) was finished a year before the church could be occupied. One of the stained-glass windows of the previous St. Paul's church has been incorporated in its

27. St. Paul's Episcopal Cathedral, detail

interior. The chapel was later named after one of the ministers, Henry Harrison Hadley.

St. Paul's Episcopal Cathedral was designed by English-born Henry Dudley (1813–1894), who was in partnership with Frank Wills in New York. Dudley designed the church in the Gothic Revival style and in accordance with ecclesiological guidelines for church architecture that had been developed in England to revive thirteenth- and fourteenth-century village church forms and motifs. Ecclesiologists in the United States were not quite as strict as their English counterparts, but an adherence to the principle that the building be "without ostentation and open to all" was followed in St. Paul's. Therefore, some free pews were installed, although pew rentals provided additional income for the church. The nave has a barrel roof of stained pine, and side aisles are separated from it by arches supported by pillars of Nova Scotia granite. All walls are finished with brick and terra cotta. Above the chancel on the east end is a fine stained-glass window depicting Paul preaching to the Athenians. There is a south aisle window designed by the Tiffany Stained Glass Studio, and another came from the local Henry Keck Stained Glass Studio, which also did extensive restoration work. Some of the original decorative elements were removed, and the interior, which can seat about 900 people, was renovated in the early 1970s. Local architect D. Kenneth Sargent designed the chancel furniture and the tablet that commemorates St. Paul's becoming a cathedral.

Limestone for the structure came in part from the old church and in part from the Onondaga Nation's land. Its rock-faced walls are pierced with pointed-arch windows and are supported by buttresses. The simplicity of the design, its massing, and a magnificent tower crowned with an octagonal spire are impressive and speak for the skill of the architect. The weight of the 205-foot tower, built on swampy soil, is carried by inverted stone arches. The spire topped with a stone cross was a gift of the brothers Andrew D. and Horace K. White, and it is dedicated to their mother Clara Dickson White.

28. Hills Building, 1928
217 Montgomery Street
Architect: Melvin L. King, Syracuse
NRHD

"The Hills Building is the best example of Gothic styling to Art Deco forms," remarked a commentator in the local paper. The design of the building follows a 1916 zoning law controlling the profile of tall buildings in New York City, stipulating that the bulk of the building had to be set back to allow enough sunlight to reach the street level. It shares this setback skyscraper form with the New York Telephone Company Building on Fayette Park, the Niagara Mohawk Building on Erie Boulevard West and the State Tower Building on South Warren Street. Architects at that time tried various ways to articulate and ornament tall buildings. Here a gargoyle, about to swoop down from the building's south facade, is a stylistic nod toward Gothic structures with which the early twentieth-century tall buildings were sometimes associated. The gargoyle is heading in the direction of St. Paul's, where it might feel more at home. Another interesting exterior feature is a decorative band of small shields above the second story, depicting the signs of the zodiac. The twelve-story office building is of steel-frame construction and clad with stone and brick. It was named after the original owner, Clarence A. Hills, who in 1910 formed one of the largest real estate firms in Syracuse.

28. Hills Building, detail

The architect of the Hills Building, Melvin L. King (1868–

1946), worked in the architectural office of James H. Kirby and later for Archimedes Russell, whose partner he became in 1906. After Russell's death in 1915, Melvin King practiced under his own name until 1932, when his son, Harry A. King (1900–1976), became his partner. They were later joined by Melvin's nephew, F. Curtis King (1900–1975). Both graduated from the School of Architecture at Syracuse University. The firm still exists as King & King Architects in Manlius, New York, and is the oldest continuous architectural firm in New York State and the fourth oldest in the country.

29. City Hall, 1892

233 East Washington Street
Architect: Charles E. Colton, Syracuse
Renovation and restoration: 1977, Quinlivan Pierik & Krause, Syracuse
NRHP CSPS

When City Hall opened in 1892, Syracusans were presented with a Richardsonian Romanesque fortresslike building of rough-faced limestone that covered a small city block. Commentators in local papers praised the new building as "solid without being heavy, durable, useful and ornamental." A 165-foot tower, reminiscent of medieval European town halls, complete with corner turrets and a vertical band of windows, anchors the structure to the intersection of Washington and Montgomery streets. Small towers on the north elevation, a hipped roof with steeply pitched dormers, windows divided by heavy stone bars, and an arcaded entrance porch are distinguishing features of the Richardson Romanesque style, which was often used for city halls.

City Hall's architect, Charles E. Colton, may have been inspired by Richardson's granite Albany City Hall (1882), but for economic reasons Onondaga limestone was chosen for the Syracuse building. Oak, marble, and encaustic tiles were used in the interior. Originally the Syracuse Police Department occupied the rear of the building, which contained prisoners' cells, offices, a courtroom, and even an armory where rifles and ammunition could be stored "in case of emergency." To the amusement of many, bunting and "Welcome to Syracuse" signs would occasionally appear on the north facade with its entrance to the Police Department. When in 1905 that space was converted into municipal offices, the Water Street entrance was closed and replaced by a window. Once a two-story high, 1,200-seat assembly room, complete with stage, skylight, and stained-glass windows, occupied the front portion of the fourth floor. Soft yellow walls were ornamented with a frieze of festooned lilies. "This beautiful apartment, that will constitute a study for an artist," was used as a public hall. It was subdivided into two floors in 1919, providing room for the city engineers on the fourth floor and for mechanical equipment on the fifth.

The original city seal is represented in a bronze tablet to the east of the double-leafed, oak entrance door. It tells the story of the city's economic

29. City Hall

development and emphasizes the symbolic importance of the building's location: salt sheds line the shores of the Oswego and Erie canals directly to the north, and a train and salt boiling blocks are silhouetted against the horizon. At one time trains ran along Washington Street, passing City Hall to the south. A bronze plaque containing a rail section is embedded in the sidewalk in front of the building. It commemorates the removal of trains from the city center in 1936.

At one time, the site now occupied by City Hall was covered with water and was called the south basin, which served as a parking lot for canal boats. The stagnant waters became a health hazard; the basin was filled and Market Hall (1845; Luther Gifford) was built on that site. It housed market stalls (downstairs) and a jail with municipal offices and a public hall (upstairs), which was crowded with participants of the Women's Rights Convention in 1861, presided over by Lucretia Mott. After Syracuse became a city in 1848, Market Hall was renamed City Hall and served this purpose until 1892. A bell tower was installed in 1857, and one year later it was fitted with a bell that became an important feature in city life. It tolled for many occasions, happy and sad. It also functioned as a fire bell. In the days of volunteer firefighting, a dollar reward was paid to the first person to spot the fire and ring the bell—a custom that was sometimes abused. During construction of the present City Hall, the bell was temporarily placed in a makeshift tower erected on Columbus Circle. When it came time for the bell to be placed into the tower of the new City Hall, a controversy arose that allegedly cost both Mayor Kirk and Charles Colton their jobs. The architect did not want his tower defiled by mechanical equipment. He was replaced by his assistant Frederick A. Whelan before construction was completed, because there were others who felt strongly about the bell's rightful place in the tower. The tower issue, considered to be an extravagance by some, is believed to have contributed to Mayor Kirk's defeat by William Cowie in 1891. The bell did go into the tower, but it sounded for the last time on Armistice Day in 1939 and was melted down for use by Allied troops in World War II. The tower remained silent until 1987 when the Rotary Club donated electronic carillons and—for sentimental reasons—a bronze-plated aluminum bell.

30. Courier Building, ca. 1844
(see also No. 5, Downtown Abolition Sites tour)
Northwest corner of East Washington and Montgomery streets

The brick building with a rounded corner facing the corner of East Washington and Montgomery streets is named after the *Courier*, an early newspaper that was once published here. Before then, it was used by the Sons of Temperance and known as Temperance Hall. At some time, it housed Frazee Hall, a well-known public gathering place. And in 1918 it was dedicated as Moose Building by Lodge No. 625 of the Loyal Order of Moose. It is one of the oldest remaining structures in this downtown area. Alterations have been made over the years; Chicago windows (a fixed central plate glass, flanked by narrower window panes) replaced earlier openings, and a metal cornice was added. To the rear, on the Montgomery Street side, straight sandstone lintels above rectangular sash windows give us an idea how the building may have looked originally. The Courier Building's most famous feature is the small iron balcony on Montgomery Street. From there Daniel Webster addressed Syracuse abolitionists and tried to show them the "error of their ways."

31. Former Fire Barn or Engine House No. 1, 1915
118–120 Montgomery Street
Architect: James A. Randall, Syracuse

This is one of several firehouses that James A. Randall designed in the city. The three-story, three-bay brick structure is embellished with modest Neo-classical elements. The building served the Fire Department until the 1970s when it was evacuated because of limitations the site imposed on heavy engines. It has been adaptively reused since then.

32. Erie Canal Museum, 1849–50
318 Erie Boulevard East
Builders: Edward Fuller (carpenter); William D. Champlain and
James Thorne (masons)
Weighing lock: Kasson and Lewis
Restoration in part: 1985, Schleicher-Soper, Syracuse
NRHP

The two-story Greek Revival building served as a weighlock, weighing canal boats and their cargo, which is to some extent comparable to today's truck-weighing stations. In the building structure inventory form, Harley McKee writes of its operation: "After the boat was drawn into the lock, gates were closed at each end. The water was drained out and the boat settled into a massive cradle suspended from the balance beam overhead. The gross weight of the boat and its load was recorded in the scale room and the registered or empty weight of the boat was subtracted from the total. The net weight of the load was the basis on which tolls were assessed."

The brick building was the third weighlock building to be erected on the site and was the most substantial of the three, designed to accommodate the larger, heavier boats used by midcentury. Each facade has a pediment and brick corbels along the cornice. Unlike other buildings along the canal, the ornamented facade of the weighlock building faces the canal (now Erie Boulevard) while the facade facing the street is plain. More than half of the first floor along the canal was originally taken up by the lock, which was sheltered by a portico of eleven square piers with Doric capitals. There was space on the ground floor for the weighmaster and the toll collector and sleeping room for the men who were on night duty. On the second floor were offices for the engineers and superintendents of repairs. When tolls on all New York State canals were abolished in 1883, the Syracuse weighlock was retained to weigh cargo for the information of shippers and to provide a dry dock for repairs. In 1906, the scales were removed, and the space above the lock became part of the second story. Thirty years later, the portico that housed the lock was enclosed, and the building continued to be occupied by offices of the state Department of Public Works until it was vacated in 1957. A group of public-spirited local citizens saved it from demolition, and this only surviving weighlock building in the Western Hemisphere now functions as the Erie Canal Museum. In 1985, the ground floor was restored to its 1906 condition. The lock was reopened, but transparent glazing was installed between the piers.

32. Erie Canal Museum

33. Urban Cultural Parks Visitor Center
at the Erie Canal Museum, 1992
318 Erie Boulevard East
Architects: Quinlivan Pierik & Krause, Syracuse
Mural: 1990, Corky Goss

The Urban Cultural Parks Visitor Center, connected to the Erie Canal Museum, houses an information area and a small orientation theater to acquaint visitors with Syracuse's Urban Cultural Parks. The window arrangement of the two-story, brick-veneered building and the replica of a storefront on its south elevation refer to the design of warehouses built along the canal in the early 1800s. To the north, part of the canal bed has been excavated.

A trompe-l'oeil ("fool the eye") mural, *A Moment on the Erie Canal*, depicting a commercial scene during canal days, enhances the facade of the building to the east of the museum and is part of the entrance plaza. The Syracuse artist also painted the mural showing salt crystals arising from Onondaga Lake on the north side of the building at 100 Clinton Street.

34. 323–325 East Water Street, ca. 1840

To the east of the Erie Canal Museum, most of the warehouses that once served canal traffic were torn down. These two brick buildings distinguished by stepped gables and straight stone lintels are the exceptions.

35. Man and Mule Monument, 1990
North side Erie Boulevard East
Sculpture: Tom Tischler

Nearby is a charming bronze sculpture of a mule being led by a young mule driver, a "hoggee." Mules and hoggees worked on the canal pulling boats. The two figures are life-size and do not stand on a pedestal, thus conveying a feeling of immediacy and lifelikeness.

36. Tablet at Northwest Corner of Erie Boulevard
East and Oswego Boulevard
A boulder with a tablet commemorates the help given by the Native Americans and a few European settlers when, in 1793, thirty out of thirty-three inhabitants of the village of Salina were sick with "the fever."

37. Collela Galleries, 1879
(former Howard and Jennings Pump Factory)
123 East Willow Street
Architect: Charles E. Colton, Syracuse
Renovation: 1973, 1974, Collela Galleries

It is believed that this building was Colton's first design. The building's fancy face belies its former function: it was constructed as a pump factory. The ornamental front built of Trenton pressed brick laid in black mortar, complete with gargoyles, is of High Victorian Gothic design. In many ways similar to the earlier Gothic Revival, the High Victorian Gothic called for color in architecture, meaning color that was inherent in the material rather than applied. Sunflowers that grow from the apex of the two gables foreshadow the Queen Anne style, in which the sunflower played an important role.

A look at some structural components gives credence to this statement of a city engineer: it is "one of the strongest structures in Syracuse." Thirty-inch vertical supports, heavy supporting beams ten inches on center, and eighteen-inch exterior brick walls assure the structure's solidity. When Collela Galleries bought the building, the interior was gutted, and lower-level wooden floors under which inches of silt had collected were replaced with concrete slabs. In 1974, fire damage, which destroyed the adjacent building, led to further renovations. The fourth floor was removed; in back, underneath the third floor, a Roman garden with a six-foot wall was created. The second level became a townhouse, and the rest of the building is occupied by gallery and storage space.

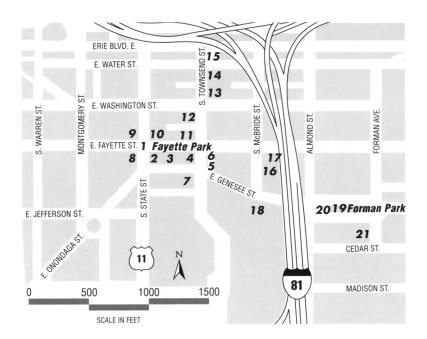

ERIE BLVD. E.

E. WATER ST.

S. TOWNSEND ST.

15

14

13

E. WASHINGTON ST.

MONTGOMERY ST.

S. WARREN ST.

S. McBRIDE ST.

ALMOND ST.

FORMAN AVE.

12

9   **10**   **11**

E. FAYETTE ST.   **1** *Fayette Park*

8   **2 3 4**   **6**
                  5

17

16

E. GENESEE ST.

S. STATE ST.

7

E. JEFFERSON ST.

18

20 19 *Forman Park*

E. ONONDAGA ST.

21

CEDAR ST.

US 11

N

81

MADISON ST.

0   500   1000   1500

SCALE IN FEET

Fayette Park and Forman Park

*Estimated walking times: 45 minutes (**Nos. 1–15**); 35 minutes (**Nos. 16–21**). To walk from **No. 15** to **No. 16** requires about five minutes.*

1. Fayette Park (see also No. 1, Downtown Abolition Sites tour)

At one time, Fayette Park was a cedar swamp where animals, wild and domestic, found refuge. When Onondaga Lake was lowered, most of the land then occupied by the small village of Syracuse, which included the park, was drained. A section of East Genesee Street ran diagonally through the area of the park, leaving open triangular spaces that were used for parades and military drills. In the late 1830s, the road through the park was discontinued, and the area slowly became residential. Originally called Centre Square, it was later renamed in honor of the popular Marquis de Lafayette.

The park witnessed local history from the noble to the mundane. Before the Civil War, antislavery leaders rallied their forces here and listened to Frederick Douglass, whose eloquence convinced them of the evils of slavery. The roaming of cows, pigs, and horses, as well as the shaking and beating of rugs within the park's enclosure, became an annoyance, and city ordinances were passed to end all this. A slaughterhouse operator had to be restrained from hanging animal hides on the then-dilapidated fence. And controversy focused on whether boys should be allowed to play ball in the

Fayette Park with fountain, early 1900s. Courtesy Onondaga Historical Association, Syracuse

117

park. When in the late 1860s a number of dead chickens were found within its confines, the neighboring residents decided to take action: they donated money to build a cast-iron fence around the green space and employed the services of "Mr. Hastings, the celebrated landscape gardener of New York." Soon the park, with its curving flagstone walks and benches shaded by stately trees, became the appropriate front yard for fine Greek Revival and Italianate houses of many well-to-do Syracusans. Here architectural critic Montgomery Schuyler found "an oasis" in a city that he found to be "particularly unfortunate ... in its architecture." John Crouse, whose house bordered the north side of the park, donated two bronze statues and a fountain graced with Neptune and his mermaids. Until the City of Syracuse Department of Parks and Recreation was created in 1917, the residents paid for maintenance, a gardener, and a guard.

During the early decades of the twentieth century, the residential character of the area surrounding the park changed, and it became commercial. One by one houses were converted for uses other than residential and then torn down and replaced by larger commercial structures. The park deteriorated; only images on old postcards told of its one-time splendor. A revival came in the 1970s when the Department of Parks and Recreation came to its rescue, rebuilt the fence, landscaped the park, and installed a fountain and benches. The park has become once again a pleasant place to visit. Various monuments relating to firefighting have been erected in the park, and in 1972 its official name became Fayette-Firefighters' Memorial Park.

2. Memorial to Hamilton S. White, 1905

Design: Harvey Wiley Corbett
Sculpture: Gail Sherman Corbett

In 1899, Hamilton S. White, wealthy Syracusan, dedicated firefighter, and one of the first presidents of the Board of Fire Commissioners, lost his life fighting a fire. The memorial dedicated to him is located on the west end of the park. The bust of White in the center of the granite monument is flanked by two figures, a fireman on one side and a woman holding a child clutching a toy fire truck on the other. The monument was paid for by public contributions of 10 cents to large sums, and Syracuse school children donated their lunch money.

2. Memorial to Hamilton S. White

Before the city Fire Department employed salaried firefighters in the 1870s, firefighting was done by volunteer companies. White built and maintained his own firehouse (now demolished) near the park, where he kept his small army of firefighters in comfort. White's company not only was equipped with the latest in machinery but was also very efficient, thanks to White's inventiveness. To speed the dressing process and to make sure the men got to the fire in record time, he invented the one-unit boots and trousers combination. Moreover, a contrivance that snatched the bed covers from the sleeping men and that propelled them out of bed as soon as the alarm was sounded ensured that no time was wasted in getting to the fire.

3. Philip Eckel Memorial, 1900
Design: Carrick Brothers

Carved in Vermont from granite, the monument was designed by a Vermont-based monument firm that established a branch office in Syracuse in the 1890s. The monument, paid for with contributions solicited by the city's firefighters and police, commemorates Syracuse's second fire chief, who also lost his life in the line of duty. The figure holds a trumpet, which was used as a megaphone during fires. Trumpets placed bells down, a cross of five trumpets within a circular band, and fire hydrants around the base further underline the theme. The sculpture was moved here from a location on the North Side, as was the nearby fire bell.

4. Firemen's Memorial, 1939
Stone relief work: William Cowie

The monument is dedicated to those who lost their lives fighting fires. Located on the east end of the park, it was erected by the city after the Collins Block fire, in which nine firemen were killed. Their names are inscribed in the wings of the monument.

5. Hamilton White House, ca. 1842
1 Fayette Park
Renovation and restoration in part: 1978, Crawford & Stearns, Syracuse
NRIIP CSPS

Of the many beautiful homes that once surrounded the park, only the Hamilton White House remains. It was built by Hamilton White, a successful entrepreneur engaged in salt and railroad businesses, and father of the firefighter Hamilton S. White. The family occupied the house until 1896. Converted to various other uses since then (at present serving as an office building), it survives today as one of the oldest houses in downtown Syracuse. The white picket fence is a reproduction of the initial one that once enclosed a fine garden. A greenhouse at the rear of the building recalls the original greenhouse on the property.

The Whites have been a prominent Syracuse family. Andrew Dickson White, who served as the first president of Cornell University, at one time championed a Syracuse location for Cornell University. His extensive collection of architectural books became the nucleus of the library for the newly established School of Architecture at Cornell, which, together with Syracuse University, was among the first schools in the country to teach architecture.

The Hamilton White House is a brick structure with sandstone sills and lintels, and a crowning cupola. Small attic windows in the frieze have iron grills with anthemion designs. The side wing with bay connecting the building to the church is a later nineteenth-century addition that once housed a billiard room. A fine porticoed entrance with Ionic columns supporting an entablature welcomes the visitor to a marbleized main hallway with a winding staircase. Each of the original rooms has a size and shape different from the rest, and some have hand-painted ceiling and wall decorations.

Although not a temple-front house, the Hamilton White House is a good example of the Greek Revival style, a style popular during the early part of the nineteenth century, when upstate New York was settled. At one time, many Syracuse streets were lined with temple-front houses, but progress and prosperity destroyed most of them.

5. Hamilton White House

6. Park Central Presbyterian Church, 1875

504 East Fayette Street
Architect: Archimedes Russell, Syracuse
Addition of west porch and interior renovation: 1960s,
Sargent Webster Crenshaw & Folley, Syracuse

Park Central Presbyterian Church was founded by former, more conservative members of the First Congregational Church of Syracuse who were in favor of compromise on the abolition issue. The Gothic Revival style building of red brick with sandstone trim has buttressed towers of uneven height that flank the gabled structure. Its pointed-arch openings are surrounded with heavy hood molds. The main facade is embellished by a rose window; stained-glass windows came from the Willet Studio in Philadelphia. Contemporary newspaper accounts delighted in the church being properly heated—an important condition, it would seem, considering the climate and the many hours spent in church in those days. Some later changes include the renovation of the interior and the addition of the west porch. The metal sculpture in the tympanum of the porch depicts Jesus' invitation, "Come unto me."

The church replaced the congregation's first building on the west side of the park, a Greek Revival structure (1847) whose architects had been Elijah T. Hayden (1809–1901), an abolitionist, and Luther Gifford (1811–47), a volunteer firefighter who was seriously injured in the great gunfire explosion of 20 August 1841. It was typical in Syracuse that early nineteenth-century wooden structures, which often showed classical design elements, were replaced by churches of brick or stone having a simple rectangular or cruciform plan. Variety was achieved by the placement of towers, either in the center or flanking the basic box, as well as by the shape of openings and type of ornamentation. In general—and there were always exceptions Catholic and Episcopal churches tended to favor the Gothic Revival style, while most Protestant denominations liked to construct their buildings in the round-arched or Romanesque Revival style, which was less expensive to build than the pointed-arch Gothic.

7. 430 East Genesee Street, 1922 (former Syracuse Boys' Club)

Architect: Melvin L. King Syracuse
Addition: 1982

Financed with money from voluntary contributions, this building was originally designed to house the Syracuse Boys' Club. Syracuse was one of the first cities in the United States to have a Boys' Club. The structure, of steel-frame construction faced with brick and terra cotta, has ornamental copper panels between stories and clustered pilasters separating window bays. A Tudor-arch entrance, pointed-arch windows, and quatrefoil and tile ornamentation are Gothic Revival elements and were often employed for clubhouses. The design seemed to be the urban counterpart to the suburban Tudor Revival house. Based on the English medieval manor house, the style was an alternative to the classical buildings of the time. The building served as home of the Boys' Club until 1982 when it was altered to be adaptively reused. The attic story was added at that time.

8. One Park Place, 1983
Architects: Quinlivan Pierik & Krause, Syracuse
Sculpture in lobby: Arlene Abend

This is the most recent structure in Fayette Park. Built as an office building, it encloses the park on its west end; the central axis of the park is aligned with the building's lobby. In scale and size, the structure is consistent with its neighbors to the north. Its brick cladding refers to the two brick buildings on the east side of the park. The main facade has a bay window that projects toward the park and reflects its neighbors like a fun-house mirror, provided you catch it from the right angle. Designed with energy efficiency and durability of material in mind, the building received a design award from the Central New York Chapter of the American Institute of Architects.

A steel sculpture entitled *Process* extends from the walls of the main lobby to the lower level of the building. It symbolizes the development of the city and was commissioned by Pioneer Group, the owners of the building.

8. One Park Place

9. New York Telephone Company Building, 1972
300 East Washington Street
Architects: Kahn & Jacobs, New York

A four-story structure faced with bronze-colored brick serves as the base for a six-story, steel and glass tower. Bronze-tinted glass is used in all windows, and the structure is set back from the curb to provide space for landscaping. The stark rectangular form and the modular surface pattern are representative of modern architecture. With its construction, the visual historic link between Fayette Park and Clinton Square was destroyed.

The building occupies the site of the city's first urban renewal project and interrupts Genesee Street. In the late 1950s, the Triangle Block, consisting of an odd assortment of about twenty buildings of 1870s and 1880s vintage, was razed to make room for a parking lot. In 1877, Fred Brower had strung the first telephone line in Syracuse from his shop in the Triangle Block to his house on Armory Square. During excavation for the telephone building, a small granite marker was found pointing west and inscribed were the names of two streets, Genesee Street and Second South Street (now East Washington Street). The inscription on top of the granite slab reads "Walton Tract."

10. New York Telephone Company Building, 1928
201 State Street
Architect: Voorhees Gmelin & Walker, New York
Additions: 1940s; 1969, Haines Lundberg Waehler, New York

Two years before designing the Syracuse building, Ralph Walker (1889–1973) of MacKenzie Voorhees & Gmelin was the architect in charge of the New York Telephone Company headquarters in New York (sometimes called the Barcley Vesey Building), which for its time had been considered to be "shockingly modern." Walker is best known for his design of "Manhattan's Deco Mountains," in which he responded to the 1916 zoning regulation by employing the setback design for tall buildings. This he also did in the Syracuse building, which is embellished with Art Deco ornamentation. Notice the naturalistic floral metalwork above the former entrance on State Street and the ornamental design in low relief that grows like a rock garden on the facade facing the park. The verticality of the building is underlined by the absence of a cornice and by pilasters that reach the roofline uninterruptedly. An addition to the east was built in the 1940s; in 1969, additions to the north were made, and the original skeleton steel tower was replaced by an enclosed microwave tower, an alteration of which Ralph Walker did not approve.

The building occupies the site of John Crouse's Italianate villa—later occupied by the Syracuse University law school—with the famous Crouse Stables (1888; Archimedes Russell directly behind it. The owner, D. Edgar Crouse, one of the wealthiest men in the city, became the stuff of local legend. A bachelor, he lived here with his horses and carriages in oriental splendor. The horses drank from Delft bowls, and their feet rested on Brussels carpet. Every afternoon, a crowd would gather to watch D. Edgar being helped into one of his elegant carriages to be taken for a drive. His love for his horses did not extend to women. It therefore seemed surprising that after his death a woman appeared in Syracuse, accompanied by her daughter. The woman claimed that she had been secretly married to D. Edgar, that the child had been fathered by him, and that she named her Dorothy Edgarita after her father. To avoid a court case the family gave her $2 million.

Archimedes Russell designed the building in the then-popular Queen Anne style, and Herter Brothers of New York furnished the interior. Some time after D. Edgar Crouse's death, Gustav Stickley occupied the structure, then called the Craftsman Building.

11. Skaneateles Bank, 1917 (former University Club)
431 East Fayette Street
Architects: Taylor & Bonta, Syracuse
Addition: ca. 1950
Interior changes: 1988, King & King Architects, Manlius, N.Y.

The structure was originally built to house the University Club, founded by Princeton graduates in the later 1890s. The red brick building with white trim was designed in the Georgian Revival style, popular during the early years of the twentieth century, and was then consistent in scale and size with the neighboring residences. A symmetrical facade, dormer windows, bays, paired columns on the second-story porch supporting the roof, as well as dentils and an open-topped pediment above the entrance, are some of the characteristic elements of the style. The building received an addition in mid-twentieth century. Sold in 1986, it is now occupied by the Skaneateles Bank.

The Syracuse city directory lists the architectural firm of Taylor & Bonta as practicing between 1908 and 1924. Alfred C. Taylor (1862–1944) studied at MIT and was associated with architectural firms in New York before he established his office in Syracuse in 1902. For five years, Taylor was in partnership with Albert L. Brockway. Edwin W. Bonta (1886–1959) graduated from MIT, and in 1920 worked with a firm of Japanese and American architects in Japan who designed American-style hospitals and commercial buildings near Kyoto.

12. One Landmark Place, ca. 1860
Renovation: 1978, Benjamin Harrington Holmes, Syracuse

The small brick structure, now adaptively reused, is the only remaining example of a number of carriage houses that lined Crouse Place (now Landmark Place) as far as State Street. The throughway to State Street was closed off by the addition of the New York Telephone Company Building. Fine brickwork in the cornice of the main facade and the keystones in the round-arched windows of the second story show that attention was paid to detail even for service buildings. It once served the William Teall House, which stood on the site of the former University Club. The bay window has been added, but the loft windows and doors are original to the building. A carriage used for special occasions was lifted by pulley to the second floor for storage, with grain and hay brought into the second story through the smaller windows. A wrought-iron stairway leads to the loft. The ground floor was occupied by quarters for the grooms, horse stables, and the everyday carriage.

12. One Landmark Place

13. Brown's Place, 1880s
501–505 East Washington Street
Renovation: first floor, 1969, Oot & Fallon, Syracuse; second
floor, 1973, Reimann Buechner Partnership, Syracuse
CSPS

The four-story brick building exhibits some Queen Anne features in the texture of its facades. Notice the brick "diaperwork" consisting of small repeated and connected patterns in the corner gable and between third- and fourth-story windows. The round arches of the second-story windows are embellished with a flower motif, a favorite among architects who built in the Queen Anne style. Its location near the Erie Canal and the railroad that ran along Washington Street made it most convenient for travelers. It was used as a tavern, a rooming house, a house of prostitution, and a gambling hall, one of many in this city (especially along Washington Street). A good example of twentieth-century adaptive reuse, the structure now serves as an office building.

The railroad and the Erie Canal promoted building in this area. Foundries, factories—the Brennan Motor Manufacturing Company was located here—and a variety of industrial buildings lined the streets. Of these only a few remain.

14. 500 East Water Street, 1882
Renovation in part: 1966

The sturdy brick structure is the remaining part of a foundry that once occupied the block. Since 1966, it has been used by Janitorial Services as office space on the first level with storage above. The building is crowned by a cupola. Round-arched windows and brick ornamentation below the metal cornice ornamented with brackets, as well as the rounded corner that takes the street corner into consideration, make this building an asset to the streetscape.

15. 500 Erie Boulevard East, ca. 1890
Renovation in part: 1946

Originally these two connecting structures were of the same height. Fire damage made it necessary to remove three stories from the part of the building that now serves as storerooms for Smith Restaurant Supply. The six-story section is used as storage space. According to the present owner, Elison Kuppermann, this is a canal building, without basement, that was once home to the manufacture of pianos as well as of bicycles. The original main entry on Townsend Street was closed, and the building was opened on the Water Street side when Interstates 690 and 81 were constructed and Townsend Street was widened. Smith Crockery, a small business that started in Syracuse in 1894, grew into Smith Restaurant Supply, thanks to the business acumen of Lester Serling, who married into the Smith family.

16. Peck Hall, 1896
Southeast corner of East Fayette and McBride streets
Architect: Albert L. Brockway, Syracuse
Renovation: 1950

The bichrome, four-story brick building is modestly Beaux-Arts. When it opened in 1896 as the new home of the Syracuse University College of Medicine,, it replaced a remodeled carriage factory that had housed the Medical College since 1875. (The remodeling and additions of the demolished carriage factory had been the work of Joseph Lyman Silsbee.) One of the outstanding features of the new building was a physiological laboratory for students, the first of its kind in the country. When the State University of New York purchased the College of Medicine, the building was remodeled to be used by University College, the continuing education branch of Syracuse University. The classically inspired main entrance, originally on McBride Street, was changed to face East Genesee Street. The small green space in front of the building and the adjacent parking lot were formerly occupied by Greek Revival residences. The building was named after a founder and trustee of Syracuse University.

17. Reid Hall, 1914
610 East Fayette Street
Architect: Earl Hallenbeck, Syracuse
Renovation: 1957

The design of this three-story brick structure complements its slightly older neighbor, to which it was joined by an underground tunnel. A classically inspired main entrance faces East Fayette Street. The building was originally built as a dispensary, and the upper two floors were used for teaching purposes. Since 1958, it has been occupied by classrooms and offices used by University College. The building is named after a Syracuse University trustee.

The Syracuse Free Dispensary was founded in 1888 by a group of local businesses and physicians under the leadership of Dr. John Van Duyn. For thirty years, patients were able to buy their medicine for approximately a dime per prescription. In 1917, the dispensary began its formal association with the Syracuse University College of Medicine and later served as the Upstate Medical Center's outpatient department. That the institution had four homes before it moved into the State University Hospital reflects its importance in the community.

Hamilton White firehouse, late 1800s. Courtesy Onondaga Historical Association, Syracuse

18. Presidential Plaza, 1968–75

600 East Genesee Street
Architects: Keyes Lethbridge & Condon, Washington, D.C., and Pederson Hueber Hares & Glavin, Syracuse

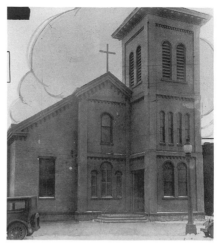

St. Joseph's French Catholic Church, early 1900s. Courtesy Onondaga Historical Association, Syracuse

Hailed as a "milestone of progress," the complex was the first residential development in downtown's near east side urban renewal area. When built, the twenty-three-story apartment towers were considered to be the highest residential structures in central New York. They replaced a number of Greek Revival residences and Hamilton White's elegant but functional firehouse (1878; Archimedes Russell), home to his seventeen firemen and the latest in firefighting equipment. Now the Presidential Plaza Medical Building is located on that site. Further west was St. Joseph's French Catholic Church, the "little French church", originally built in mid-nineteenth century as a Baptist church. A bank building now occupies its site.

19. Forman Park, 1839

Crossed by Yellow Brook as well as by a corduroy road (later East Genesee Street), Forman Park began as a cedar swamp and evolved into Daniel Comstock's meadow. The land was owned by Lewis H. Redfield, other entrepreneurs, and the Syracuse Company. They gave it to the village for use as a park, and it was dedicated in 1839. The brook bed was filled in, the street was rerouted, and trees and flowers were planted. The little park had its ups and downs, and by 1870 it was termed an eyesore. To counteract the neglect, an improvement association was formed, the space was landscaped, and an iron fence and a fountain were installed, to which Alonzo Chester Yates, owner of the famed Yates Castle, contributed generously. Landscaping and artifacts disappeared over the years. At the turn of the century, the park received some short-lived attention with the placement of the Redfield Monument there. The nearness of Interstate 81, which presents a strong barrier by cutting the downtown area into east and west, did not help the struggling park to flourish. In 1983, the City of Syracuse Department of Parks and Recreation made noticeable improvements to its landscape.

Forman Park, 1894. Courtesy Onondaga Historical Association, Syracuse

20. Redfield Monument, 1908
Design: Nehemiah C. Hinsdale
Sculpture: Fidardo Landi

The monument is dedicated to pioneer history and was a gift by Lewis H. Redfield's daughter, Margaret T. Smith. The designer, Nehemiah C. Hinsdale, was a former stone and marble dealer in Syracuse. The three bronze figures were cast in Florence. The figure in front of the pedimented Neoclassical stone base represents Hiawatha, the legendary founder of the Iroquois Nation. He holds five bound sticks in his hand, symbolizing the unification of five nations. Joshua Forman is seated in a chair on top of the base. Lawyer, champion of the Erie Canal, and promoter of the solar method of producing salt in this city, Forman has been credited with being the founder of Syracuse. Next to him stands Lewis H. Redfield, who, like Forman, lived at one time in Onondaga Hollow, where he published the *Onondaga Register*. Forman's articles advocating a canal from Lake Erie to the Hudson had appeared in the *Register* and were no doubt influential. In 1829, Redfield set up his business on the banks of the canal opposite the Syracuse House on the site of the present Gridley Building, where he published his paper until he retired from the newspaper business in 1832.

20. Redfield Monument

21. First Church of Christ Scientist, 1923
728 East Genesee Street
Architect: Gordon A. Wright, Syracuse
Addition: 1949, Pederson and Hueber, Syracuse

The Academy of Christian Science was incorporated in Syracuse in 1887 and was housed at various locations in the city. In 1898, the name was changed to First Church, and the church was incorporated in the following year. This Neoclassical Revival building has been occupied by the congregation since 1923. It has a circular plan and an auditorium ornamented with Neoclassical detailing. Its temple-front entrance faces Forman Park. Besides a fine interior, distinguishing features include a copper roof with lantern and metal ornamentation based on the anthemion design along the roofline.

21. First Church of Christ Scientist

Other buildings of interest in the area but not on the tour are

Pioneer Homes, 1938–40
East Adams Street
Architects: Randall King Vedder & King, Syracuse

On the north side of East Adams Street is the Syracuse Housing Project (USHA Project N.Y. 1–1). Three hundred fifty United States Housing Authority projects were under construction by the end of 1940. Syracuse's was the first to be completed. The New Deal initiated several home building programs, which emphasized strong governmental control, rational planning, and modern design. None of them was officially called "public housing." With the passage of the Wagner-Steagall Housing Act of 1937, control tended to shift to local communities. Instead of owning and operating public housing, the U.S. Housing Authority provided guidelines and loaned money to local authorities. The Syracuse Housing Authority selected a site in an old section of the city. In an area of eight city blocks covering thirty-three acres, three-story apartment buildings, two-story buildings containing flats, and two-story group dwellings were constructed to house about 2,200 people. The Syracuse Housing Authority commissioned two local architectural firms to do the housing project. For this purpose the architects formed the partnership of Randall King Vedder & King. "Pioneer Homes," wrote one observer in the local paper, "is public housing as a reality, not as a hope or dream. ... It has been aided with unselfish devotion by numerous Syracusans who regard the attack on housing problems as the basic approach to the problem of the family and society." Some of the units were demolished in the 1960s when Interstate 81 was built through Syracuse.

The construction of Pioneer Homes foreshadowed the end to a neighborhood once called "the Ward." The Fifteenth Ward stretched roughly from East Washington to Monroe Street and from Almond to State Street. Although referred to as "Jew Town," it was an integrated neighborhood of Jewish, African, Irish, Italian, Polish, and Native Americans. The writer John A. Williams, who grew up here, described it eloquently: "The Ward was an entity into itself ... set in a lovely valley surrounded by green hills upon which sat the red brick and limestone buildings of Syracuse University. Looking up at them reminded us of what could be achieved. Securing an education was the primary drive of all our parents. ... In the Ward survival of the other fellow and his children meant survival for you. For me, the Ward was home and the rest of Syracuse radiated outward from it. ... It was a city within a city and at dusk the year around you could see men of all sizes shapes and colors returning to it from their jobs such as they were."

Former L. C. Smith Factory Building, 1903
700 East Water Street
Architect: Gordon A. Wright, Syracuse
Additions: 1911, 1937, 1945

An inventor from Cortland, New York, Alexander T. Brown, who had patented the breech-loading shot gun (among many other devices), came to Syracuse to work for L. C. Smith, at the time a manufacturer of guns. An easy-to-use typewriter that Brown developed in the Lipe Machine Shop prompted Smith to switch from guns to typewriters. The Smith Premier catalogue advertised the new machine as a "Declaration of Independence for Women," and for some decades Syracuse was known as "Typewriter City." One of the memorable events of the early 1890s was the visit to Syracuse and the Premier factory by the crown prince of Siam. Few were the notables who did not participate in the royal entertainment. When the prince left, he was presented with a Smith Premier typewriter. The Smith factory building replaced an elegant residence surrounded by extensive gardens. When the factory was vacated in mid-twentieth century, the building housed Onondaga Community College for a few years.

Christ Temple Pentecostal Church of the Apostolic Faith, 1910
711 East Fayette Street
Architect: Charles E. Colton, Syracuse
CSPS

This small brick church featuring pointed-arch openings and fine stained-glass windows was the second church building for the oldest African-American congregration in the city, the African Methodist Episcopal Zion Church, founded in 1837. An early minister of the church was the famous abolition leader Bishop Jermain Wesley Loguen.

Ignatius Fiesinger House, 1873
1010 East Washington Street
Renovation: 1976–1980s, Walda Metcalf, Ian Nitschke;
addition: Sheldon Williams
CSPS

The property once belonged to Harvey Baldwin, Aaron Burt, and Oliver Teall. Ignatius Fiesinger bought the land in 1864 and built the Italianate brick house with hipped roof nine years later. The exterior of the house has not been changed much except for the addition of a conservatory and passive solar collector recycled from discarded windows of Syracuse University's Hall of Languages. The interior still has its original oak and walnut woodwork, as well as a marbleized slate fireplace and ceiling medallion in the living room. Even one of the two bathrooms is original to the house. A plumber discovered wooden piping that hooked up to the city's sewer system.

Clinton Square
6

ERIE BLVD. E.

W. WATER ST.

4Hanover Square

E. WATER ST.

5

11

W. WASHINGTON ST.

E. WASHINGTON ST.

S. SALINA ST.

S. WARREN ST.

MONTGOMERY ST.

W. FAYETTE ST.

E. FAYETTE ST.
1
Fayette Park

S. CLINTON ST.

S. TOWNSEND ST.

McCARTHY AVE.

Armory

3

E. JEFFERSON ST.

Columbus
Circle

S. STATE ST.

E. ONONDAGA ST.

N

2

MADISON ST.

81

| 0 | 500 | 1000 | 1500 |

SCALE IN FEET

Downtown Abolition Sites

Estimated walking time: 1 hour, 20 minutes (Nos. 1–6)

> A handsome young woman arrived at the depot of the
> Underground Railroad in this city the night before last
> and was sent forward by the agent yesterday…a stout
> intelligent-looking young colored man arrived here
> last night from the south on his way to freedom.

Notices such as these would appear daily in the local newspapers during the decades before the Civil War. This Underground Railroad was not of steel and steam. It was a vast secret network of activists, called "agents" or "stationmasters," who helped fugitive slaves in their quest for freedom. The "depot," or "station," was a clandestine place where fugitives were able to rest and to obtain the necessary supplies for the remainder of their journey. These were dangerous activities, haunted by the specter of recapture and punishment and therefore veiled in secrecy; no one knows how many fled from bondage along those invisible tracks of the Underground Railroad nor how the term originated.

Long before the Underground Railroad had entered public and political consciousness, the hope of gaining freedom inspired numerous slaves to become runaways, despite great perils and hardships. Even before the American Revolution, slaves living in the northern provinces often sought asylum with the French in Canada. Although New York, a busy port city, provided hiding places as well as opportunities for passage on outgoing ships, the heavily forested upstate wilderness was a favorite refuge. Runaways were helped by the Iroquois, who refused to surrender them. As early as 1774, ten years before the first European settler came to this area, two black men, likely runaway slaves, were boiling salt in the Onondaga salines. Their only customers were the neighboring Indians. In 1810, 153 blacks lived in Onondaga County, 41 of whom were slaves. One Isaak Wales, who had come here as a slave, was able to get work digging the Erie Canal and made enough money to buy his freedom. He bought property and settled in the village of Salina as its first African-American resident. Others worked and lived in Onondaga Valley, where they had been brought by the first European settlers, and in nearby villages such as Jamesville and Pompey.

The abolition of slavery in New York State was joyously celebrated on July 4, 1827, two years after the completion of the Erie Canal and Syracuse's incorporation as a village. And within a few years, Syracuse became a stage on which the political drama of abolition was enacted. Gerrit Smith, a leading abolitionist and stationmaster from Peterboro, New York (his house, which was destroyed by fire in the twentieth century, was sometimes referred to as "the Grand Central Station of the Underground Railroad"), came to Syracuse in 1831 to meet with other like-minded folk to

135

form an abolitionist society. But at that time, Smith and his followers were in the minority. They were pelted with rotten eggs and driven out of Syracuse to nearby Fayetteville, where they reassembled and vowed to fight against the evil of slavery. In these early years, Fayetteville was the home of two leading abolitionists. One of them, C. L. Noble, had published a magazine, the *National Era*, in which Harriet Beecher Stowe's *Uncle Tom's Cabin* was first serialized. Noble's Greek Revival house on Genesee Street faces the former home of the other prominent Fayetteville abolitionist, Matilda Joslyn Gage, who was also a nationally known leader in the fight for women's suffrage. It is said that the cellar in the Gage house served not only as a meeting place for women's rights but as a hiding place for slaves as well. In Skaneateles, the houses of Quakers, staunch abolitionists, were stations on "the Road," as were the homes of other abolitionists in Syracuse, Baldwinsville, Clay, and Van Buren, to name only a few places in the immediate area.

One of the most famous agents of the Road was undoubtedly Harriet Tubman, who led hundreds of slaves through the wilderness to freedom. She brought her parents to Auburn, New York, where she herself returned after the Civil War. She raised money to help former slaves and in 1908 founded a home for disadvantaged African-Americans known as the Harriet Tubman House, which still exists in Auburn.

"The western part of the state was known as the 'Infected 8th'—the 8th judicial district—because it was infected with all sorts of social reform movements," retired Syracuse University Professor Robert Raybeck has been quoted as saying. Syracuse, centrally located in the state, accessible by canal and the railroad, and not too far away from Canada, became immersed in the struggle against this "sum of all villainies." American Anti-Slavery Society agents on lecture tour throughout New York State fanned the flames of pro- and antislavery sentiments. People listened. They took sides. They held meetings. Needing a forum, they founded churches.

The First Presbyterian Church, established in 1824, was the dominant church in the village of Syracuse. Its members were conservative, well-to-do citizens, and its pastor conformed to the wishes of the majority, who believed that the immediate abolition of slavery would be dangerous. Thirty-seven frustrated abolitionists, considered by many to be a raucous minority, split from First Presbyterian and in 1838 founded a new church, the First Congregational Church of Syracuse (site of Key Bank, downtown drive-in branch office, East Genesee Street). The architect was abolitionist and elder of the church, Elijah T. Hayden. Hayden had gone to Florida in 1854 and was eventually expelled for expressing his antislavery sentiments. Upon his return to Syracuse, he was invited to speak at City Hall to tell about his experiences. Mayor Lyman Stevens introduced him and welcomed him "back again, among his friends in Syracuse, which he hoped would always be the home of free speech, free labor, and free men."

The dissenters chose a Congregational form of government because it provided more flexibility for abolitionist action than the hierarchical and conservative Presbyterian system would allow. The First Congregational Church building, a small frame structure painted white and topped by a square tower, came to be known as the "Cradle of Liberty" or the "Faneuil Hall" of the upstate area. It served as an organizing center for the Liberty party, an antislavery political organization founded in 1840 by abolitionists, one of whom was Gerrit Smith. Well-known abolitionists delivered impassioned speeches from its pulpit. Most Syracusans, however, felt hostile to the church and its radical congregation. Meetings were interrupted, speakers were insulted, and once a cannon was set up next to the building and fired repeatedly to disturb an antislavery meeting inside.

Internal dissension finally caused the church to close its doors after twelve years, and the building was demolished in the 1850s. Some of its more moderate members returned to the Presbyterian fold and in 1847 founded Park Church, which stood on the west side of Fayette Park (now site of One Park Place). One of the designers of the church building was Elijah T. Hayden.

The Presbyterians of Park Church straddled the issue of slavery: slaveholding was a sin, but not all slaveholders should be expelled from the church. Prayers for the dissolution of evil seemed a good solution. In 1875, Park Church was replaced by Park Central Presbyterian Church, built on the east side of Fayette Park.

1. Fayette Park (see also No. 1, Fayette Park and Forman Park tour)

The park was named after General Lafayette, who was a member of the Philadelphia Abolition Society. Here the eloquent Frederick Douglass held forth on the evils of slavery in the 1850s. Douglass, a former slave and one

1. Fayette Park, 1894, looking northeast. Courtesy Onondaga Historical Association, Syracuse

of the most powerful antislavery orators, had lived in England and Ireland for several years. He returned to the United States in 1847 and established the *North Star* in Rochester, New York, which he edited in the abolitionist cause.

2. Plymouth Congregational Church, 1859, 1871
(see also No. 1, Columbus Circle and Montgomery Street Areas tour)
232 East Onondaga Street

Several of the orphans from the disbanded First Congregational Church were among those who founded yet another Congregational church in 1853. There was to be no compromise concerning slavery: there was to be neither slave nor master. To demonstrate this determination publicly, the church was named after Plymouth Church in Brooklyn, whose pastor, Henry Ward Beecher, was a leader in the antislavery cause. Dr. Strieby, the first pastor of Plymouth Congregational Church, was widely known as a reformer in temperance and abolition. A church history maintains that Plymouth Congregational Church was the very center of the antislavery movement in Syracuse, that Samuel J. May, Gerrit Smith, and Frederick Douglass spoke from its lectern, and that "the Underground Railroad passed many a fleeing slave to the haven of Canadian soil for this was a favorite way station." This implies that the church did function as a station, although it would have been the original wooden chapel of 1855 as well as the brick building of 1859 that replaced the chapel on this site rather than the present building, which was constructed in 1871 around the earlier structure.

2. Plymouth Congregational Church, late 1800s. Courtesy Onondaga Historical Association, Syracuse

3. Former Wesleyan Methodist Church, 1845

(see also No. 10, Columbus Circle and Montgomery Street tour)

304 East Onondaga Street

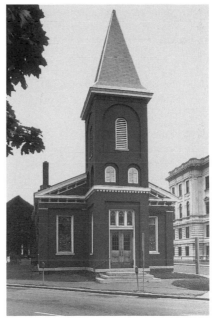

3. Former Wesleyan Methodist Church

The small church building, originally built by the Wesleyan Methodist congregation in 1845, and later known as First Gospel Church, still stands on Columbus Circle. The founders strongly declared themselves to be in opposition to slavery, and it is believed that the church took an active part in Underground Railroad activities. There are several faces carved in the earthen walls of the cellar, and legend has it that they were carved by runaway slaves while hiding there. Traditionally Wesleyans, like all good nonconformists, rejected sugar in protest against the trade in West Indian slaves.

The 1840s were important years in the history of abolition in Syracuse. With the arrival of three major figures, it became inevitable that increasing attention would be paid to the slavery issue. The first of these, Jermain Wesley Loguen, came here in 1841 as minister of Syracuse's first African-American church, the African Methodist Episcopal Zion Church, founded in 1837. The church building, located on South Crouse Avenue, no longer exists. Remembering his own past as slave and fugitive, Bishop Loguen devoted his life to freedom for black men and women. He served as president of the Syracuse Fugitive Aid Society, and his antislavery activities contributed to the distinction that Syracuse gained as "the Canada of the United States." His home at 293 East Genesee Street contained an apartment for fugitives. The house was demolished, and the site is at present occupied by a drugstore. The second church building of the oldest black congregation in Syracuse was erected in 1910 at 711 East Fayette Street (see also p. 133). It served the congregation until 1974 and still exists.

The second influential arrival, the general agent of the Fugitive Aid Society, was Unitarian Minister Samuel J. May. He came to Syracuse in 1845 and until 1868 headed the Unitarian Church of the Messiah on Burnet Avenue and State Street (1843; William B. Olmstead; demolished). Actively involved in improving social conditions, Dr. May is probably best known for his work in the antislavery movement and has been described as "Syra-

Unitarian Church of the Messiah, ca. 1885. Courtesy Onondaga Historical Association, Syracuse

cuse's public conscience on the slavery issue." His house on James Street Hill (now demolished) also served as a station on the Underground Railroad.

The third important figure, Samuel Ringgold Ward, a one-time agent for the American Anti-Slavery Society, moved in 1851 to Syracuse from Cortland Village, where he had served as minister of the Congregational church. Three years earlier, he began to publish *The Impartial Citizen* in Syracuse, which advocated not only abolition and the rights of African-Americans but also racial pride and self-help. His contemporaries viewed him as the "ablest and most eloquent black man alive." When Ward moved to Boston, he took the paper with him. In 1980, *The Impartial Citizen* was put back into circulation by Dr. Robert Pritchard of Baldwinsville, New York.

Between 1845 and 1850, Syracuse was host to twelve major antislavery meetings and twice as many smaller gatherings. A number of these meetings, as well as "donation parties" that were given for the purpose of raising money for the Underground Railroad, were held at the Convention Hall (East Genesee Street between Montgomery and Warren streets; now demolished). These events did not always proceed peacefully. "Radical" abolitionists were pitted against those residents who wanted to compromise with the South and uphold the Fugitive Slave Law signed by President Millard Fillmore in 1850. One of those many occasions was a two-day meeting scheduled by the American Anti-Slavery Society in Convention Hall in late January 1861. Abolitionists, among them Reverend Strieby, pastor of Plymouth Congregational Church, and Dr. May of the Unitarian church, tried to speak but were hooted down as "dangerous men and fanatical rebels," according to the local papers of the day. Eggs were thrown, benches broken, speakers interrupted. And at the end of the meeting, a crowd gathered in front of the Courier Building (**No. 5**). Led by a brass band and carrying signs with the inscriptions "Freedom of Speech, but Not Treason" and "Abolitionism No Longer in Syracuse," they paraded through downtown streets and marched to

4. Hanover Square (see also No. 1, Hanover Square and Clinton Square tour), where they burned two effigies, one labeled "Samuel J. May," the other "Susan B. Anthony." Ten years earlier, these same antiabolitionists had invited Daniel Webster to deliver an address to admonish Syracusans of the abolitionist persuasion about the "error of their ways." This he did, flamboyantly. And from the balcony of the

4. Hanover Square, 1887, looking southwest. Photograph by I. U. Doust, courtesy the Koolakian family

5. Courier Building, ca. 1844

(see also No. 30, Columbus Circle and Montgomery Street tour)
(northwest corner of Washington and Montgomery streets)

Webster accused all Syracusans who opposed the enforcement of the Fugitive Slave Law of being "traitors, traitors, traitors." The small cast-iron balcony on Frazee Hall, as the building was then called, from which Daniel Webster spoke, overlooked Market Hall (demolished, now site of City Hall), and it still exists.

Shortly after President Fillmore had signed the bill that enacted the Fugitive Slave Law on 18 September 1850, a mass meeting was held at Market Hall with the city's mayor, Alfred A. Hovey, presiding. Jermain Loguen spoke to the assembly. The local paper reported that all participants declared the Fugitive Slave Law "an outrage upon the inalienable rights of man" and that they vowed the "north would not be the slave catcher of the south." A series of thirteen resolutions was passed that called on people to oppose all attempts to enforce the law. It also provided for a vigilance committee, which included prominent citizens such as the Reverend Loguen and Charles B. Sedgwick, to see that "no person is deprived of his liberty without due process of law."

Syracuse's most famous antislavery event, the Jerry Rescue, was foreshadowed by another event, more than a decade before, in the 1830s. The place was the Syracuse House (demolished, now the site of OnBank), on the east side of Clinton Square. A slave, Harriet Powell, and her owners visited Syracuse from Mississippi and stayed at the popular hotel, where black employees plotted her flight to freedom with the help of two other Syracuse abolitionists. She escaped during a farewell party. Disguised, she was taken to a place near Marcellus, from there to the house of Gerrit Smith in Peterboro, and finally to Canada.

5. Balcony on
Courier Building

6. Jerry Rescue Monument, 1990
(see also No. 19, Hanover Square and Clinton Square tour)

The monument shows "Jerry," shackles broken, desperately trying to escape while being aided by two figures representing Bishop Jermain Loguen and the Reverend Dr. Samuel J. May. Sculpted by Sharon BuMann, it eloquently depicts and commemorates an incident that began on October 1, 1851, when William Henry, known as Jerry, was arrested by federal agents. Daniel Webster's prophetic words warning Syracusans that "the law will be executed … in the midst of the next anti-slavery convention, if the occasion shall arise" may have been in some people's minds when they heard the news. There was much activity in Syracuse on that day. The county fair was in progress, and the Liberty party was holding a convention at the Congregational church. Jerry, who after his escape from Missouri had come to Syracuse on the Underground, worked here as a carpenter and later as a cooper. On the day of his arrest for a trumped-up charge of theft, he was employed in a cooperage on North Salina Street in the First Ward. Handcuffed, he was taken to the office of U.S. Commissioner Sabine in the Townsend Block (demolished, now the site is partly occupied by the Federal Building and the Atrium), where he was informed that he had been arrested as a fugitive slave. The news spread quickly. Church bells rang the alarm. The Liberty party's convention adjourned. A large crowd gathered at the Townsend Block to hear the preliminary examination of the prisoner. Jerry managed to escape but was seized again and, after a desperate struggle, was carried to the police station at the Raynor Block, later known as the Jerry Rescue Building (demolished, now a site adjacent to the Amos Block). Here he was chained and manacled.

6. Jerry Rescue Monument

From the steps of the building, Samuel Ward delivered a rousing speech to the crowd that had gathered at Clinton Square. It was the last address he gave in the United States. (Accused of treason for his part in arousing the crowd, he fled to Canada, where he continued his antislavery work.) Incited by his eloquence, some threw stones at the commissioner's windows and did not interfere when abolitionists, armed with clubs, axes, crowbars, and a heavy beam, forced their way into the building where Jerry was held. The prison guards quickly fled. Jerry was taken out to a waiting carriage, driven along West Water Street, past the Syracuse House and along Washington Street to Brintnall's Hotel at the corner of South Warren and East Fayette streets, where he got into a light buggy and was driven to the residence of Caleb Davis, located at the corner of McBride and East Genesee streets. (The site of the Davis house, long since demolished, is now part of the site of Peck Hall of University College.) Although Davis was said to have been an proslavery Democrat, he sheltered Jerry for humanitarian reasons for four days. On October 5, Jerry was driven along the Cicero Plank Road to Oswego, where he boarded a schooner to Canada. Jerry lived the rest of his life in Kingston, Ontario, where he died from tuberculosis in 1853.

Clinton Square with Jerry Rescue Building (l), ca. 1876, looking west. Courtesy the Koolakian family

The Underground Railroad, filled with mystery, hope, and terror—many a slave would take poison before submitting to recapture—took possession of the popular imagination in later years. There have been many claims that this or that building was a stop on the Underground Railroad, but few of these can be supported, because the operation had to be veiled in secrecy. One of the more persistent claims was associated with romantic Yates Castle, also known as Renwick Castle or Longstreet's Folly (now the site of Weiskotten Hall of Upstate Medical Center), whose Gothic Revival towers and battlements inevitably invoked mystery and created stories that eventually became local legend. According to one of these, the castle was a stop on the Underground Railroad. The existence of a "slave refuge" and of secret underground passageways in the castle was reported in the local paper. And after Yates Castle became the property of Syracuse University in 1905, generations of students rediscovered "secret passageways" and the "hideaway." The romantic stories were much treasured. Finally, Ella Longstreet, daughter of Cornelius Tyler Longstreet, the original owner of the castle, dispelled the myth. Her parents, she said, were not abolitionists. There had not been an underground passageway, but there had been a large attic room where she and her friends often played. In jest it was referred to by family members as the "Fugitive Slave Room."

And then there was the Syracuse resident who called a local historical association a few years ago with the urgent request that someone immediately visit her home to witness the evidence that her house had been a stop on the Underground Railroad. When asked for the nature of the evidence, she breathlessly replied, "The tracks are still in the basement!"

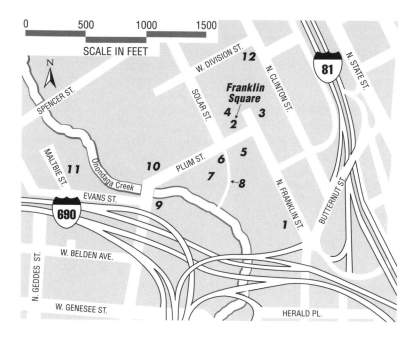

NORTHWEST SIDE

Franklin Square and Vicinity

*Estimated walking time: 1 hour, 30 minutes (**Nos. 1–10**)*

Harvey Baldwin liked to make predictions, and one of them was that "machines would hum." This he said in his famous "Hanging Garden" speech before becoming Syracuse's first mayor in 1848. Half a century later his prophecy came true: machines busily hummed in factory buildings concentrated mainly on the northwest side of the city in an area once occupied by solar salt vats. Baldwin owned many acres of marshland between Onondaga Creek and Geddes Street. In 1884, Thomas Gale purchased land from the Baldwin estate to set up his solar operation, which functioned until 1926.

Twelve million tons of salt were produced in the yards around Onondaga Lake between 1797 and 1904. Two techniques for harvesting salt were used. One was boiling brine in large kettles until salt crystals formed; the other involved evaporation by the sun. The latter was the more economical technique and survived the former by almost forty years. Brine was carried

5–6. Hurbson Office Furnishings Warehouse and the Hub of the Syracuse Salt Pumphouse

in wooden pipes to shallow vats that would be protected from rain by covers on wheels. When rain threatened, a bell located in the central part of the salt field would summon saltworkers—men, women, and children who lived in adjoining single- or multifamily houses owned by the salt manufacturers—to shove the covers. Thus, Syracuse, one of the cloudiest cities in the United States, became the site of the state's first solar-powered industry. Each salt district had a stone pump house, which was always built into a hill because of the fall of water. From the pump house the brine was pumped into the reservoir. The pump house for the Syracuse District was on Spencer Street directly across from the City of Syracuse Department of Parks and Recreation. Only its foundations exist. The only other survivors of an industry that put Syracuse on the map are the foundations and an iron pipe of the Geddes District Pump House at 1800 Erie Boulevard West (CSPS), the head of the Gale salt well on Onondaga Lake Parkway, and the salt block chimney that rises from the Salt Museum in Liverpool.

Springs supplied more than salt: during the second half of the nineteenth century, the Chlorine Swimming Baths and the White Oak Sulphur Springs were hailed as having curative powers and advertised as being the "greatest luxury that Syracuse possesses." They promised relief from rheumatic and blood diseases, as well as entertainment, dances, and cotillion parties by the swimming pond. The location (behind the pump house for the Syracuse District and surrounded by saltworks), however, precluded competition with Saratoga Springs. In 1899, the city bought the White Oak Sulphur Springs property and constructed a public bathhouse (1930; Melvin L. King) The land and its buildings are now used by the City of Syracuse Department of Parks and Recreation. One of the buildings is a maintenance barn built of local limestone in 1934.

During the latter part of the nineteenth century, the declining salt industry was replaced by a more diversified industrial and commercial base. As a rule, nineteenth-century factory buildings were of masonry construction, often including a water tower. Regularly spaced large windows on all floors provided adequate interior lighting. Later in the century, iron was introduced and finally steel-frame construction, providing for larger openings and a safer work place. Before the use of steam power, factory buildings were located near water to provide power and ready transportation. As local industries moved to suburban areas, buildings became vacant, deteriorated, and were torn down. Some of the extant factory buildings are being recycled, especially in the Franklin Square area, which has a number of fine examples of late nineteenth- and early twentieth-century industrial buildings. It was a good site for factories because it was served by the West Shore Railroad. In the late 1980s, streets and sidewalks in this area were repaved and trees planted. In the springtime, the rectangular red brick buildings form a backdrop to pink tree blossoms and yellow daffodils.

1. Mission Landing, ca. 1910

427 North Franklin Street

Renovation: 1990, Holmes/King & Associates Architects, Syracuse

The building was originally used by the Monarch Typewriter Company. In 1915, it was purchased by New Process Gear Corporation and became Plant No. 3. The former Rescue Mission—the Mission came to Syracuse in 1887—used it as a warehouse after it was vacated by New Process Gear. The building is now adaptively reused as a residential complex of forty-three condominiums.

The New Process Gear Division of Chrysler Corporation started as New Process Raw Hide Company in 1888 in Baldwinsville, manufacturing rawhide boats and canoes. The founders held a "new process" patent for producing rawhide of special durability. The name was changed to New Process Gear Corporation in 1912, when the company began making rawhide gears that were durable, practically noiseless in operation, and mainly used for streetcars and stationary motors. The automobile put an end to rawhide gears, and the company began manufacturing steel, brass, and cast-iron gears. In 1957, New Process Gear became a division of Chrysler Corporation and four years later closed its plants in Franklin Square and moved to the town of Dewitt.

2. Franklin Square, 1988

Solar and Plum streets

Landscape architects: Reimann Buechner Partnership, Syracuse

Sculpture: Dexter Benedict, Penn Yan, N.Y.

The park was developed by the Pyramid Companies as payment in lieu of taxes to the city. A larger-than-life bronze statue of Benjamin Franklin stands on a granite base and overlooks the landscaped green space, complete with an ornate fountain and a pavilion of stone columns and wooden beams.

3. One Franklin Square, 1990

Architects: 1988–89, Dal Pos Associates, Syracuse, and
Holmes/King & Associates Architects, Syracuse

The seven-story Post-Modern building that harmonizes in materials and design with the older surrounding buildings was built as housing for senior citizens and contains 136 units of one- and two-bedroom apartments.

4. Former Borden Foods Company Research Center, ca. 1900

600 North Franklin Street

The plant served as a major center for nationwide Borden research operations. The building was originally built for the Merrell-Soule Company, which became nationally known for the manufacture of the None-Such mincemeat they started producing in 1885. Frank Soule developed a process for drying milk and purchased a patent in Europe for the manufacture of powdered milk. This product, named KLIM, became the principal item manufactured by Merrell-Soule when the company was purchased by Borden Foods Company in 1923.

5. Hurbson Office Furnishings Warehouse, 1904
455 North Franklin Street
Redesign and addition: 1908, Merrick and Randall, Syracuse
Renovation: 1990–, Syracuse Restoration, Inc.

The building was once Plant No. 1 of New Process Gear. Merrick and Randall built the new structure and made additions to the earlier building, part of which was destroyed by fire. The building is and will be used as a warehouse. The present renovation work entails cleaning brickwork, installing new windows, and landscaping.

Asa L. Merrick (1848–1922) and James A. Randall (1861–1940) both learned their trade by practicing it. They were partners between 1893 and 1922, and won commissions for a number of churches and school buildings in the area.

6. The Hub of the Syracuse Salt Pumphouse
Plum Street

The cast-iron hub on display relates to the area's salt history. The artifact formed the core of a three-story wooden waterwheel used in the Geddes pump house and is on loan from the Salt Museum.

7. Plum Court, 1906 (former O. M. Edwards Company Building)
526 Plum Street
Architect: Gordon A. Wright, Syracuse
Renovation: 1989–, MacKnight Architects/Planners, Syracuse

This handsome five-story brick building was hailed as a "model manufacturing plant." A panoramic mural at the World's Fair in 1939 included a photograph of the building. Founded by Oliver Murray Edwards, an inventor of various railway devices and padlocks, among other things, the company manufactured steel furniture, window devices, and extension platform doors, the latter invented by Edwards. The building is being recycled for use as office space and loft-style condominiums.

8. Onondaga Creek Walk
Starting point: Plum Street

The walk is intended to link the "Oil City" waterfront development (situated on the southeastern shore of Onondaga Lake and home to oil storage tanks) with Armory Square. It will run to Onondaga Lake. The often-maligned Onondaga Creek is the only survivor of several brooks that once ran through Syracuse. Now considered an asset to the cityscape, it was seen very differently during much of the nineteenth century. The creek was a source of sickness to those who lived along its banks and polluted its waters. Boys liked to swim in it and were arrested for "indecent proceedings."

The story is told that the creek almost participated in the War of 1812. When war was declared with Great Britain, a U.S. Navy lieutenant was ordered to take the brig of war *Oneida* from Oswego to Onondaga Hollow, load it with a cargo of cannonballs, and deliver the ammunition to Fort Oswego. But the ship was unable to enter the mouth of Onondaga Creek, and the ammunition had to be sent by land to the Oneida awaiting its cargo in Onondaga Lake. A mistake had been made on the map, which had shown the creek to be navigable. The incident is the subject of one of the murals in OnBank on Hanover Square. Not only had the creek missed its chance to become a war hero, it was indicted some fifty years later by a grand jury as a public nuisance. There had been much sickness, and the creek's stagnant waters were blamed for it. Most of the old creek bed north of Spencer Street was filled in under the landfill program of the Department of Public Works. In mid-twentieth century, the old course of the creek, principally in Onondaga Valley, was abandoned when the federal government built a straighter creek bed as a flood-control measure.

8. Onondaga Creek with Mission Landing (directly in back)

9. Bridgewater Place, 1912

500 Plum Street
Renovation and additions: 1988–91, Dal Pos Architect, P.C.,
Syracuse

The structure was originally built as Plant No. 2 of New Process Gear and was the largest of the three plants. It was the first building in Franklin Square to be renovated and adaptively reused as office space. Once considered an eyesore, the impressive structure now greets the traveler coming into the city on Interstates 690 and 81. It is difficult to determine the boundaries between the original structure and the new additions; both enhance each other. The tower addition is a focal point and completes the corner. Subtle details and colors enliven the interior, and the lobby is worth a visit. Like a piece of sculpture, the colorful spiral staircase in back of the lobby space is an eye-catcher. The architect received the First Design Award for Renovation or Adaptive Reuse from the Central New York Chapter of the American Institute of Architects.

9. Bridgewater Place

10. Unity Life Building, 1991

507 Plum Court
Architect: Dal Pos Architect, P.C., Syracuse
Sculpture: William Severson

This office building conforms in size and materials to the existing older structures. A hanging sculpture of polished aluminum embellishes the atrium space. Dal Pos Architect, P.C. also designed the Royal Insurance Building to the north of the Unity Life Building.

11. Allen Building, ca. 1920 (former Allen Tool Building)
208 Maltbie Street
Renovation: 1991, Pioneer Development Company, Syracuse
Sculpture: William Severson

The building is now occupied by offices of Environmental Design and Research (EDR), and the entrance faces the creek, the creek walk, and the old railroad bridge.That (rear) facade is ornamented with a brick carving depicting plants that grow on the banks of Onondaga Creek. EDR is one of a few firms in Syracuse that promote public art. Across the creek at 400 Leavenworth Avenue is the Burns Brothers Building, which is being renovated (1988–, Holmes/King & Associates Architects).

12. Spaghetti Warehouse
689 North Clinton Street

An Italian restaurant occupies the first floor of this former factory building that at one time housed Julius Resnick Inc., a company that manufactured handbags for women. A group based in Dallas, Texas is responsible for the renovation. The floor above the restaurant is being renovated by Don Swanson as a rehearsal space and studios for dancers.

Other buildings of interest in the area but not on the tour are

City of Syracuse Department of Parks and Recreation Building, 1930
412 Spencer Street
Architect: Melvin L. King

Originally the public bathhouse for the Chlorine Swimming Baths and White Oak Sulphur Springs, the building is now used by the Department of Parks and Recreation. One of the outbuildings is a limestone barn (1934), which replicates earlier horse barns used for the salt industry. Directly across the street are the foundations of the Second Ward pump house.

Carousel Center, 1990
Hiawatha Boulevard
Architect: Dal Pos Associates, Syracuse

The Franklin Square projects are connected to the Oil City development planned by Robert Congel of the Pyramid Companies. Since the 1950s, sixty-seven oil tanks have occupied about 800 acres of former salt marshes on the shore of Onondaga Lake, hence its name. The showcase of the project is the Carousel Center. The poured concrete and glass building floats on the debris-filled swamp atop a vast raft. This new cathedral to commerce covers six and one-half acres. Because of the effective use of color and artificial and natural illumination, its interior landscaping, and the spatial organization, words such as "Piranesian," "fantastic," and "opulent" have been used to describe it. Four levels containing parking, retail space, movie theaters, and restaurants are connected vertically by escalators and elevators, and are grouped around a central atrium that rises through seven stories to an observation deck. Employees, customers, and visitors tread on floors of Italian marble. But the main attraction is no doubt the melodious carousel at the north end that gives the supermall its name. It was created by sculptor Leo Zoller and built in 1909 by the Philadelphia Toboggan Company. It was once used at an early twentieth century Onondaga Lake resort. The Pyramid Companies bought it at an auction, and Bill Finkelstein of R & F Designs, Inc. restored its forty-two horses, the carriages, the artwork, and the mechanics, and made it go round again.

Former Lipe Machine Shop, ca. 1880
208 South Geddes Street

The building was once known as "Syracuse's Cradle of Industry," where inventors and entrepreneurs worked and exchanged ideas. In 1880, Charles Lipe set up his machine shop in the building. From his invention of the two-speed bicycle gear that was to become the prototype for early automobile transmissions, the Brown-Lipe Gear Company was formed. It later became Brown-Lipe-Chapin and eventually a division of General Motors.

It is reported that Henry Ford came to the old Lipe Machine Shop to oversee the construction of parts of his first car. Here Herbert H. Franklin met John Wilkinson, designer of an air-cooled automobile engine and grandson of the man who named Syracuse. Their encounter led to the founding of the Franklin Motor Company, which became the largest employer in the area. Until 1934, when it fell victim to the Depression, the company was the only one in the country to make air-cooled passenger cars.

Former Brown-Lipe-Chapin Building, 1908
718 West Marcellus Street
Architect: Albert Kahn, Detroit

The office of Albert Kahn (1869–1942) specialized in factories, war plants, and naval bases. Kahn applied techniques of mass production to architecture and was a pioneer in the use of reinforced concrete and steel. The essential features of modern reinforced concrete framing are present in the Syracuse factory, although the particular mode of construction used here has been superseded by more efficient reinforcing systems.

First Presbyterian Church Parish House, ca. 1865
(former James J. Belden House)
620 West Genesee Street

This Italian villa, characterized by a central tower flanked by two gabled wings, reminds us of West Genesee Street's past elegance as a residential street. In 1904, the structure was moved to the rear of the lot to make room for the church building. Some interior changes were made.

First Presbyterian Church, 1905
620 West Genesee Street
Architects: Tracy & Swartaut, New York

Dedicated in 1906, the church was designed in the late Gothic Revival style with pointed-arch openings. In the 1960s, Henry Keck Stained Glass Studio designed and installed two stained-glass windows. They were unfortunately covered by the installation of a new organ in 1991.

St. Paul's Armenian Apostolic Church, 1888
(former Park Avenue Methodist Church)
310 North Geddes Street
Architects: Kirby & Merrick, Syracuse

When it was built, the size, scale, and proportions of this picturesquely massed church fit well into the one-time suburban character of the area. The Romanesque Revival church of red brick with stone trim remains basically unaltered.

James H. Kirby (1844–93) apprenticed with a Cleveland architect. When he came to Syracuse in 1879, he worked in the office of Horatio Nelson White and set up his own office six months later. He was subsequently associated with various Syracuse architects and left Syracuse in 1891 to practice in New York. He specialized in residential architecture and published several portfolios between 1874 and 1887.

St. John the Baptist Ukrainian Catholic Church, 1913
102 South Wilbur Avenue

Its location on the hill and its onion-shaped spires mark the Romanesque Revival church against the skyline. As in Byzantine churches, frescos ornament interior walls and ceiling. An iconostasis—an elaborately decorated paneled screen—conceals the sanctuary and altar from the main space of the church. In 1900, the church was organized by Ukrainian immigrants as St. John the Baptist. It was the first Eastern Catholic church in Syracuse and was given its present name in 1944.

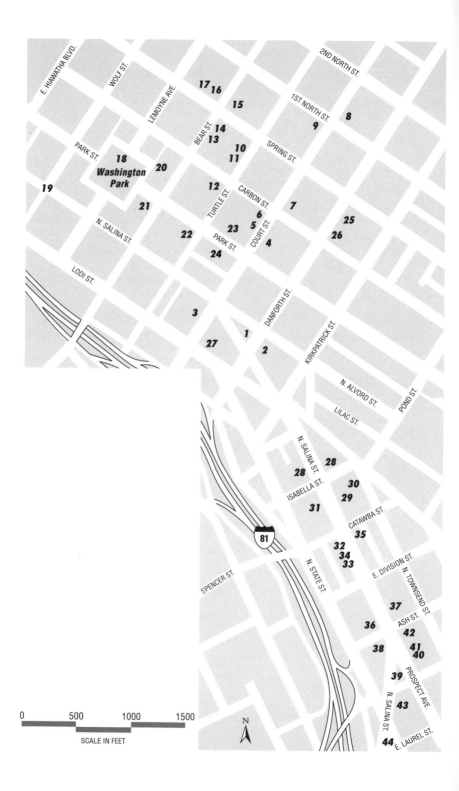

NORTH SIDE

The Old Village of Salina

The information is taken in part from "Boilers, Barons & Bureaucrats: A Tour of an Historic Syracuse Neighborhood," a walking tour pamphlet prepared by Dennis J. Connors (1986).

*Estimated walking time: 1 hour 45 minutes; driving time: 30 minutes (**Nos. 1–27**). The sites are not contiguous; therefore, the tour is most easily taken as a driving tour.*

Because of salt, Salina is older than Syracuse. As early as 1790, squatters were living on the state-owned land surrounding the lake. They set up clusters of iron boiling kettles to evaporate brine from the salt springs and produce salt crystals. It was a shantytown with temporary dwellings of dried mud or of bark and slabs. There was an abundance of fish and game, but swampland surrounding the settlement, mosquitoes, and "the fever" made for miserable living conditions. The commercial developments motivated the state to lay out and lease manufacturing lots, thus organizing production and land use. The communities of Liverpool and Geddes owe their existence to salt manufacturing, but the major center of production, commercial trade, and home building focused at the southeast end of Onondaga Lake, which soon was called Salt Point. The demand for salt in the rapidly expanding nation encouraged the growth of the industry, and the number of people involved grew proportionally. Between 1798 and 1799, a village was laid out on the high ground immediately south of today's Hiawatha Boulevard. Overlooking the salt-boiling operation close to the lake, the new community was called Salina.

The completion of the Erie Canal in 1825 and the addition three years later of the Oswego Canal, which ran through Salina, were tremendous boosts to the local salt industry. Salt blocks, groups of kettles set into rectangular stone foundations and covered with a wooden structure, began to crowd each other along the Oswego Canal. Salt was used for barter. The story is told of one Salt Pointer who bargained with the canal boat captain for a passage for himself and a load of salt to Cleveland in return for one-half the load of salt. After two months there, he bartered his salt for cattle, which he drove back to Salina and sold for more salt. He was, indeed, a fellow "worth his salt."

Syracuse a few miles to the south was no more than an unnamed crossroads when Salina was laid out , but the opening of the Erie Canal through its heart guaranteed its rapid growth as a commercial center. Although both villages were becoming interdependent economically, there was intense political competition between the two settlements for almost thirty years. In 1848, the two villages merged to become the city of Syracuse, with Division Street marking the erstwhile boundary. The village of Salina became the First Ward and continued its critical link to the salt industry for another fifty years. Although several of the houses listed on the tour are architecturally undistinguished, they are of historical interest as survivors of the old village of Salina.

1. Grosso Park
Corner of North Salina and Court streets

From this intersection you can orient yourself to the Syracuse of the nineteenth century. North Salina was the main street linking the commercial heart of Syracuse, one mile south of here at Clinton Square, with its First Ward, the former Salina. In 1859, the city built its first horse-drawn trolley line up Salina Street from Clinton Square to Wolf Street, four blocks to the north of this point. Three blocks to the west of Grosso Park, today's Court Street meets Interstate 81. Throughout most of the 1800s, that highway section was occupied by the Oswego Canal, and numerous salt-boiling blocks lined its eastern edge. Beyond the canal, in the area now covered with oil storage tanks and often referred to as Oil City, were thousands of solar salt-evaporating sheds. The streets immediately northeast of here were laid out in 1799 to accommodate the homes, churches, schools, and stores of the many hundreds of people whose lives were linked to the salt industry. What is quite obvious as one walks through this neighborhood is its stability and continuity across generations.

2. Catherine Murray House

2. Catherine Murray House, ca. 1850

406 Danforth Street

Overlooking Grosso Park stands an imposing Italianate residence, the home of Catherine Doyle Murray for over forty years. A rooftop cupola, wide eaves with brackets, ornate window hoods, and a distinctive porch make this house a good example of the style. The popularity of the Italianate Style coincided with the peak years of the salt industry, and many salt manufacturers lived in Italianate houses. Catherine Doyle Murray and her husband moved into the house as newlyweds, but he died within two years. She successfully continued to manage the salt manufacturing interests that she had inherited from her father and her husband, and died wealthy in 1908. Her son continued the family solar salt business along Old Liverpool Road until 1924, two years before local salt manufacturing ceased.

3. Nehemiah Earll House, ca. 1830s

211 Court Street

This inconspicuous brick house is one of the oldest in the neighborhood and has undergone many changes over the years. From 1842 to 1861, it was the home of Nehemiah Hezekiah Earll, who in the 1830s was appointed New York State's salt superintendent to oversee all salt production on the state lands surrounding the lake.

4. St. John the Baptist Church, 1867

406 Court Street
Architect: Horatio Nelson White,
Syracuse
CSPS

This structure serves the oldest Roman Catholic parish in Onondaga County. In 1826, Salina Catholics, mostly Irish immigrants, asked permission from the bishop in New York to establish a church. The first was a frame building on North Salina Street serving a parish that covered all of Onondaga County. By the mid-1860s, during the peak years of the salt industry, the need for a larger church became apparent. Horatio Nelson White, a prominent local architect, designed the church in the Romanesque Revival style, popular for mid-nineteenth-century churches and characterized by round-arched openings and brick detailing.

4. St. John the Baptist Church

The church has a traditional plan: a semicircular apse, transept, and nave with side aisles. A central tower with doorway and narthex is placed on the west front. The stained-glass windows, some of which were memorials to salt manufacturers, were fabricated by Morgan Brothers of New York and have been restored recently. Neither the basic interior form nor the exterior of the church have been significantly changed since its dedication in June 1871.

5. John Beer House, 1868
409 Court Street

City tax records indicate that John Beer had a small frame house on this site as early as 1852. In 1868, he replaced it with this upright-and-wing of brick, which indicates a change in his financial and social status: in the preceding nine years, Beer had changed jobs three times, moving from "salt weigher" to "salt inspector" to "flour dealer." Weighers and inspectors held important positions. They were hired by the state to ensure the quality of Onondaga salt in the face of stiff competition from other states and from abroad.

6. Rice-Abbott House, ca. 1850
413 Court Street

The gabled board-and-batten cottage bears a strong similarity to a design attributed to architect Gervaise Wheeler and published in Andrew Jackson Downing's *Architecture of Country Houses* (originally published in 1850). The Eastlake-ornamented porch may have been added during the second part of the nineteenth century. It appears that Caroline Rice was the original owner of the house. Henry Abbott, who worked for the Haeberle Brewery, one of many breweries on the North Side, purchased the house in 1884.

6. Rice-Abbott House

7. Ira Williams House, 1856
502 Court Street

Although severely altered by inappropriate additions, its overall form is that of a massive Italianate house almost square in plan. The ornate window surrounds are characteristic features of that style. In addition to owning a salt block, Ira Williams was also involved with the dry- goods and grocery business in Salina and served as one of the village trustees in the early 1840s. By 1850, ownership of more than 250 salt-boiling blocks surrounding Onondaga Lake was in the hands of nearly 200 individuals. Salt manufacturers like Williams often operated a grocery store as part of their business because farmers frequently traded their produce for salt. Note the curbside hitching post for horses on the Carbon Street side. Such artifacts are clues to the age of a neighborhood. If you have a sharp eye you will find more along the way.

8. Amos L. Mason House, 1864
700 Court Street

The stuccoed Italianate house with cupola and side wing was the home of Amos L. Mason and his family. Mason was involved with salt manufacturing and began his own successful construction business at the age of twenty-two. In addition to building the Hall of Languages at Syracuse University and St. John the Baptist Church (**No. 4**), as well as many other commercial structures in Syracuse, he constructed about 1,000 dwellings, 116 salt blocks, and several salt-refining mills.

9. Michael Killian House, ca. 1848
621 Court Street

Originally a modest vernacular Greek Revival house, its age is disguised by recent modifications. Some early cut stonework is still visible in the northeast foundation wall. In most cases, houses once occupied by salt barons and bureaucrats have survived, unlike those of salt boilers. This is an exception. Killian's obituary of 1914 states that he had this house built in 1848, two years after his marriage to an Irish-born woman. Killian's early life paralleled that of many salt boilers. At eighteen he immigrated from Ireland during the potato famine of the 1840s. He settled in Syracuse and became a salt boiler. By 1875, salt boilers averaged $3.50 a day, a decent wage and more than either blacksmiths or carpenters made. In 1884, Michael Killian and his son had saved enough money to go into salt manufacturing but stayed in business for only five years because the industry was by then in decline.

10. Hoyt Freeman House, 1874
513 Turtle Street

11. Augustus Sanger House, 1870s
509 Turtle Street

Once the homes of salt manufacturers and bureaucrats, these modest Italianate houses were severely altered over the years. Hoyt Freeman entered the salt business during its prime, first as bookkeeper, then as salesman, and eventually as manufacturer. In 1903, he was appointed state salt superintendent by the governor, an appointment that was usually a function of patronage. He became the last superintendent because the state sold all its interests in the declining salt industry to private owners in 1908. Less than twenty years later, competition from cheaper salt sources in Western states terminated the Syracuse salt industry.

By 1875, Augustus Sanger was the deputy salt superintendent for the Salina district. His duties included supervising maintenance for the pump house, brine wells, and log pipes in the area immediately northwest of this neighborhood. He died in 1896, and like many of the salt manufacturers and superintendents, he is buried in Syracuse's Oakwood Cemetery.

12. Albert Freeman House, 1856
419 Turtle Street

Like most of Salina's first-generation salt manufacturers, Freeman was born in New England and came to Salina before the Civil War. He was soon involved in flour milling and salt manufacturing. The firm that he and his son Hoyt owned at one time operated six canal boats, shipping salt on the Erie Canal to Buffalo and Midwestern grain on return trips to Syracuse. The rectangular lines of stone window lintels and doorway of this brick house belong to the Greek Revival style, while the roofline with overhanging eaves supported by brackets, the cupola (now altered to look like a roof dormer), and the porch are Italianate. The house was stuccoed in the twentieth century. Note the carriage house at the rear on Carbon Street.

13. Former First Ward Methodist Episcopal Church, 1865
510 Bear Street

After an intermittent history dating back to 1821, the Methodists of Salina secured a pastor in 1840, the Reverend Ebenezer Arnold, who helped to complete organizing the congregation. Steady growth resulted in the need to build a church, and construction started in 1864. Finished in the following year at a cost of $11,000, the church was designed in the popular round-arched Romanesque Revival style and has a centrally placed tower. Today the church is used as a community center. The former parsonage is next door at 512 Bear Street.

14. Dr. Henry E. Pierce House, 1854
514 Bear Street
Porch addition: 1947

This brick structure is notable as Syracuse's only surviving octagon house. Originally the house had only an entrance porch; the enclosed porch is a later addition. In 1853, Orson Squire Fowler, who was not an architect by training, published a book entitled *A Home for All; or, the Gravel Wall and Octagon Mode of Building* in which he suggested the octagon house to be the "healthiest" type of residence and defended the gravel wall as "nature's own building material ... all that is wanted is stone and lime." Fowler was quite innovative for his time, and his plans include light and airy interiors with a maximum of windows and with built-in closets, central heating, running water, speaking tubes, elevators, and indoor water closets. Fowler's own octagonal house on the Hudson River has been destroyed, but hundreds of octagonal houses, still standing, attest to the popularity of his book.

14. Dr. Henry E. Pierce House

15. John Eastwood House, 1862
1316 Spring Street

Eastwood's house is a good example of the Italianate style, complete with cupola, bracketed eaves, bay window, a double-leafed entrance protected by a porch, and decorative hood molds. Eastwood built the house during the Civil War in the year that local salt production peaked at over over 9 million bushels, produced by 3,000 workers. The war helped promote the local salt industry and temporarily protected Syracuse salt makers from Southern competition. The shipment of salt to the Union army was so important that men working in the salt industry were exempt from military service. For some years, Eastman functioned as receiver of salt duties for New York, collecting the tax the legislature levied on each bushel of salt. He also owned a salt block and for some time worked as overseer of barrels, an important job since hundreds of thousands of barrels were used annually for the shipment of salt. An 1865 report lists 175 men and 26 boys employed in the nearly twenty cooperages located in the First Ward.

16. Phillips-Farrell House, ca. 1845
601 Bear Street

Covered by inappropriate siding, this vernacular Greek Revival house is notable for its finely detailed Greek Revival doorway with rectangular sidelights and flanking pilasters complete with classical anthemion leaf designs. The earliest resident identified with the home is Nelson Phillips (1850). A Salina blacksmith, Phillips may have been involved with the fabrication of special tools for the salt industry, as were many of his fellow blacksmiths. In 1860, the house was sold to Richard Farrell, a salt manufacturer and grocer.

17. William G. Clark House, ca. 1845
1408 Spring Street

The house is one of three existing cobblestone houses in Syracuse and is an architecturally important survivor of Salina's early village days. It was the

17. William G. Clark House

home of the William G. Clark family before the Civil War. A salt manufacturer, Clark was a Connecticut native. His three sons also entered the salt
business, and son Henry lived here with his family after his parents' death in
1875. (The house at 1010 Carbon Street was once occupied by another son,
Adolphus.) Cobblestone houses have water-smoothed cobbles from the
shore of Lake Ontario or glacier-rounded fieldstones as an exterior surface.
Here quoins, window sills, and lintels are of sandstone. The eave brackets
have been covered, and the original porch has been removed, exposing the
rubble core of the wall.

18. Washington Square, 1799
Kirkpatric Monument, 1908
Design: Harvey Wiley Corbett
Sculpture: Gail Sherman Corbett

Originally known as Centre Square, the park and its surrounding area were
laid out in 1799. It functioned as the village green, and it may be the oldest
park in the city. A portion of it was originally used as a cemetery, and in
1805 the first schoolhouse in Salina was built in its southwest corner. In
1822, the local Presbyterians erected their first church in the northwest
corner and paid for most of it with salt donations. Before the church was
built, a Presbyterian missionary addressed "the Sinners of Salt Point" in an
old barn on the site of the church.

18. Kirkpatrick Monument, detail

The monument was originally designed as LeMoyne Fountain. A bronze drum sits on a granite base and depicts the discovery of the salt springs around Onondaga Lake by Europeans in 1654. The figures represented in relief are Father Simon LeMoyne, companion Jean Baptiste, the Iroquois leader Garakontie, and an Onondaga woman and man. An oak tree represents Christian faith, a pine tree protection and tribal unity. The fountain, now closed, was originally hollowed out and divided into quadrants to water people and horses. The monument was one of three given to the city by William Kirkpatrick, son of Dr. William Kirkpatrick, who for more than twenty years was closely connected with the salt industry. The artist grew up in Salina.

Look to the north toward Onondaga Lake and imagine the late nineteenth-century scene with thousands of salt-evaporating sheds lining its shores.

19. Wolf Street and Intersection of Wolf and North Salina streets

One block north of Washington Square lies Wolf Street. Its intersection with Salina Street marks the old commercial heart of Salina village. Some of the mid-nineteenth-century buildings, especially those on the south side of the street that once housed grocery stores, dry-goods establishments, taverns, and cooper shops, still stand. On top of the Penfield Manufacturing Company building (1710 North Salina Street) is a penthouse built in the 1880s by H. A. Moyer Carriage Construction Company, which at that time occupied the building. The penthouse (visible from Washington Square looking north) carried a carriage on its roof and was built as an advertisement. The carriage is gone, and the structure houses machinery and sprinkler systems. At one time, many salt boilers lived along the easterly stretches of Wolf Street and Hiawatha Boulevard, and in the area between the two streets.

20. John Lynch House, ca. 1860
118 Washington Square
Renovation: 1989–, Gary Parker, Syracuse

The Italianate house, consisting of a main block with cupola and two side wings, was the home of the family of John O. S. Lynch, who was one of several family members involved in salt manufacturing. Its size and detailing suggest that this was once a grand home. It is of frame construction, is covered with flush boarding, and has quoins to imitate masonry construction. Note the decorative medallions running along the frieze board between the paired roof brackets and the open-topped hood molding above second-story windows.

21. Avery-Burton House, 1854
317 Bear Street

Like many other houses in Salina, this brick house combines Greek Revival with Italianate features. At the time Benajah A. Avery built his brick house, he owned a fifty-kettle salt block near the Oswego Canal. He helped organize the Central City Railroad, which in 1860 started to run between Clinton Square and Wolf Street as the city's first horse-drawn trolley line. In 1865, Avery sold his home to Henry Burton, a second-generation salt manufacturer.

22. Westminster Presbyterian Church, 1855
1601 Park Street
Architect: G. P. Randall, Syracuse
Alteration of tower: 1946

The congregation was formed in 1810, making it one of the oldest in the city. Its growing numbers necessitated a larger church than the one on Washington Square, and a new brick structure in the Romanesque Revival style was constructed in midcentury. Only a few changes have been made since the structure was completed: the brick facades were stuccoed, and the tower was modified and lowered in 1946. The interior is in a remarkable state of preservation. Important original features are the walnut pews, plaster decorations, and the city's oldest organ. Its stained-glass memorial windows affirm that many prominent area residents were members of the church. The present congregation has a deep appreciation of the history of the church and its links to the salt industry.

23. Clark-Kearney House, ca. 1830
1506 Park Street
Remodeling and addition: 1875

The Georgian brick house has a symmetrical main facade flanked by chimneys, a finely detailed roofline, and semicircular attic windows in the gables. When the house was remodeled in 1875, the double entrance doors and the rear section were added. Built for salt manufacturer, banker, and merchant William Clark, the size of the house demonstrates the prosperity of Salina after completion of the Erie and Oswego canals. The Clark family lived in this house until 1871, when William Kearney purchased it. Sale notices advertised many fine fruit trees on the lot, which then occupied one-fourth of the entire block. Kearney, an Irish immigrant, had become a successful brewery owner, and his former brewery buildings still stand at the northwest corner of Wolf and Salina streets. Breweries played an important role in the city's economy after the Civil War.

24. Parke Avery House, 1850
1509 Park Street
CSPS

The house shows the classic forms of the Greek Revival style in its porch and entrance; roof bracketing and a bay window are Italianate features. Three generations of the Avery family lived here for over one hundred years. Parke, one of several Connecticut Averys who came to Salina in the 1830s, entered salt manufacturing like his cousins Benajah and Latham. He owned two coal-fired blocks, each containing over fifty boiling kettles, and a grocery on Wolf Street; he ran a cooperage near the Oswego Canal as well. In 1874, Avery's six coopers produced approximately 15,000 barrels. After the death of Parke and his wife in 1898, other Averys or their in-laws lived here until 1980. Since 1982, the house has been occupied by the Preservation Association of Central New York, which maintains part of it as a house museum that is open to the public.

24. Parke Avery House

25. George Zett House, 1899
702 Danforth Street
Architect: Archimedes Russell, Syracuse

Brewery owner George Zett commissioned Archimedes Russell to build two houses, this one for himself and his family and the other next door for his daughter and son-in-law Charles A. Frank. The interior of the Zett house is finished in white oak, and plate-glass and stained-glass windows imported from Munich were used throughout. There was a ballroom on the third level and a bowling alley in the basement.

26. Charles A. Frank House, 1899
700 Danforth Street
Architect: Archimedes Russell, Syracuse

A gambrel roof (a roof with a double pitch) with hipped dormers, a symmetrically articulated main facade with a projecting central section and a Palladian window, quoins, and a Federal style-inspired entrance porch make this house a good example of the Colonial Revival style. Stained-glass windows were imported from Germany, and the interior is embellished with finely carved woodwork.

26. Charles A. Frank House

27. Former Zett Brewery, 1887
Corner of Lodi and North State streets

A German brewer, Xavier Zett, uncle of George, established a brewery and malthouse here, but Prohibition forced them to produce soft drinks. Fire destroyed the main building in 1943. The annex (1887; Louis Lohman) is extant and is adaptively reused. Between 1860 and 1930, Syracuse was the brewing capital of upstate New York. Its breweries could be found in the center of the city near canal and railroad and on the North Side. The Greenway Brewery, the largest in the United States outside of New York City, stood on the north side of the Erie Canal where the Niagara Mohawk Building now stands. Some breweries sponsored saloons, with the proviso that they sell their product, in much the same way that gas stations are operated today. A restaurant and bar at 312 Park Street, now known as Riley's, started as a saloon run for the Haeberle Brewing Company. After Prohibition, saloons were individually owned, and Riley's is believed to be the only one surviving in Onondaga County in continuous use since its beginning in 1897. A few of the old North Side brewery buildings and homes of former brewery owners have been adaptively reused.

North Salina Street Commercial District

NRHD

A short drive or ten-minute walk will get you from **No. 27** to **No. 28.**

Estimated walking time: 40 minutes **(Nos. 28–44)**

This is the largest historic district in the city and consists of ninety-eight properties, mostly commercial. North Salina Street, at one time called Cooper Street, was the original route of transportation and trade between the villages of Syracuse and Salina. It initially developed as a commercial area to service the salt industry. By midcentury, the North Side was being built up by German immigrants who made barrels and vats for salt production and North Salina Street developed as the center of their community. After the salt industry declined in the 1860s and following the Civil War, German artisans transferred their carpentry skills to the manufacture of domestic goods. The area developed as a commercial and small manufacturing center, encouraged by paved streets and sidewalks and a street railway. German immigrants built the majority of the existing brick row buildings during this period. The shop would be on the first floor, with the owner's

North Salina Street, 1927, looking north. Courtesy Onondaga Historical Association, Syracuse

apartment or rental property above. Italian immigrants came to Syracuse in the 1880s; many of them helped build the West Shore Railroad and settled in the predominantly German area, transforming it into an Italian neighborhood by the early decades of the twentieth century.

28. 900 Block, North Salina Street

NRHD (both sides)

The northern part of the street has the older buildings, which are smaller and simpler in design than those erected later at the south end of the street closer to the city's business center. All buildings on the 900 block are two stories high and are of brick, with fine brickwork along the cornice lines and on window surrounds. Most of them were built in the mid-1860s. One of the exceptions is the building at 911 North Salina, constructed in 1919 as the North Side Garage and representing the early popularity of the automobile in this city.

The 800 block of North Salina Street (both sides) has some of the most distinctive buildings in the district.

29. Assumption Church, 1865–67; Parish Center, 1880; Convent, ca. 1900; Rectory, ca. 1934

804, 808–812 North Salina Street

Architect for Assumption Church and parish center: Horatio Nelson White, Syracuse

Remodeling of interior: 1934

Restoration of parish center and convent: ca. 1934

NRHD CSPS (Assumption Church)

The church was the focal point of the German community and was formerly known as St. Mary's German Catholic Church. In 1845, German-speaking Catholics in Syracuse built a small frame church on the site of the present church. The growth of the congregation demanded a new building, and in 1865 the cornerstone for the new structure was laid. Horatio Nelson White designed the church building and its convent in the Romanesque Revival style. Two symmetrically placed domed towers, added in 1872, can be seen from afar. Frescoed walls in the interior and a 4,000-pipe organ speak of the financial success of the original parishioners. In 1880, the adjoining parish center (804 North Salina) was designed by White. The interior of the church was remodeled after a fire in 1934. That fire also severely damaged the parish center and convent. Both buildings were restored and reconstructed. The rectory house at 812 North Salina Street was constructed at that time.

29. Assumption Church

30. Academy Court Apartments, 1890 (former Church of the Assumption School Building and Sisters' Dwelling)
1119 North Townsend Street
Architect: Archimedes Russell

Located behind Assumption Church and at one time part of its building complex, this brick structure is now adaptively reused. It is not part of the Historic District.

31. 839–841 North Salina Street, ca. 1890
NRHD

The three-story, bow-fronted building has an elaborately detailed sheet-metal facade. One of the most successful North Side merchants, Francis Baumer, built the structure for his candle business that he previously operated in a building at 831–833 North Salina Street. Francis Baumer was one of the founders of Will & Baumer Inc., a candle company that still exists in Liverpool. The manufacture of candles, which was started as a cottage industry by German immigrants in the nineteenth century, continues as an important industry in Syracuse. The building also functioned as a theater at one time, later as a saddlery; it is now used as an office building.

Several of the commercial buildings on this block have ornate window surrounds of cast iron. An acanthus leaf-ornamented keystone seems to have been a favorite among many property owners. During the second half of the nineteenth century, with the Industrial Revolution in full swing and with good transportation routes, these features could be ordered ready-made from trade catalogues.

32. Walier Block, ca. 1890
755 North Salina Street
NRHD

A large commercial structure, the Walier Block was built by Joseph Walier to house his flourishing confectionery business. Its size exhibits a growing prosperity in this area.

33. Former Christian Freeoff Building, 1889
745–747 North Salina Street
Architect: Charles E. Colton, Syracuse
NRHD

An elaborate Romanesque Revival main facade of brick and stone distinguishes this structure originally owned by Christian Freeoff. He had his office as a "conveyancer" (notary public) here, as well as his home.

34–35. 753 and 758 North Salina Street
NRHD

These structures were both built before 1850 and are the oldest surviving buildings in the area. 753 North Salina Street **(34)** has been altered and covered with synthetic siding, but the original clapboard-covered frame structure is still visible in the rear, as are reeded pilasters and a denticulated cornice framing the entrance. Jacob Brand lived and operated his bakery in this building for over forty years. The structure at 758 North Salina (35) has received a modern storefront, but the original temple-front facade is still visible above it and can best be seen from across the street or from Catawba Street.

38. 571–573 North Salina Street

36–37. 601 (1892) and 600–608 North Salina Street

Renovation of 601: 1991–, Holmes/King & Associates Architects, Syracuse

NRHD

When the Clinton Square area became the city center, demand for property at the southern end of the district increased, and several large buildings were constructed in the 600 and 500 blocks of North Salina Street. In 1892, Jacob Haas built his large Queen Anne building at 601 North Salina Street (36) with a saloon on the first floor and apartments upstairs. The business block at 600–608 North Salina (37) exemplifies the post–Civil War taste for architectural ornament and its ready availability.

38. 571–573 North Salina Street, 1885

Renovation: 1988–, Holmes/King & Associates Architects, Syracuse

NRHD

This commercial brick structure occupies an important corner position. Queen Anne elements such as textures and gables filled with semicircular flower symbols combine to make the main facade visually interesting. According to Bruce King's research, the building at one time accommodated a pool hall downstairs and doctors' offices above. It still functions as a multi-use building, with the architects' offices on the second story.

39. Albany Block, 1896
530–536 North Salina Street
Builder: Louis Lohman, Syracuse
NRHD

Considerably larger than others along the street, this bow-fronted commercial block, housing shops, apartments, and offices, introduces a new scale to the street.

40–42. 512, 514, and 518 Prospect Avenue
NRHD

The 500 block of Prospect Avenue was developed by German middle-class families who built their detached homes here during the 1880 and 1890s. Representative of these are two, almost identical, bay-fronted brick dwellings at 512 and 514 Prospect Avenue, both built in 1886. The house at 512 Prospect (**40**) was originally occupied by William H. Haeberle, treasurer of Haeberle Brewing Company, one of Syracuse's largest at that time. Its neighbor at 514 Prospect (**41**) was owned by physician Dr. Leonard A. Saxer, who had his home and his practice in the house. Both men were business partners of Charles Hoffman, whose success in the business world was exhibited in his home at 518 Prospect (**42**). Sometimes referred to as the "Hoffman Castle," the picturesquely massed brick structure was built in 1889 and designed in the Romanesque Revival style, unusual for residential work. Large arches, unusual and very ornate dormers, a turret, a rounded bay, and stained glass are stylistic features that distinguish the house. The Romanesque or round-arched mode was so popular in Germany that it was considered by some to be a "national German style." The original owner may have had this in mind when he asked his architect (unknown) to design his home.

43. 400 Block, North Salina Street

The buildings here are not part of the Historic District. Some of the two-story commercial brick buildings (433–435 North Salina Street) with straight stone sills and lintels and fine brickwork along the cornice line are reminiscent of the Phoenix and Franklin buildings on Hanover Square. Of note is the Learbury Center (ca. 1903) at 401 North Salina Street. It housed Learbury's Clothing factory from 1922 to 1988. Zausmer-Frisch Associates, Inc. of Syracuse renovated the building (1988–89), which is now used as retail and office space.

44. Sniper Monument, 1905
Sculpture: Frederick Moynihan

The monument was erected in memory of the Civil War General Gustavus Sniper.

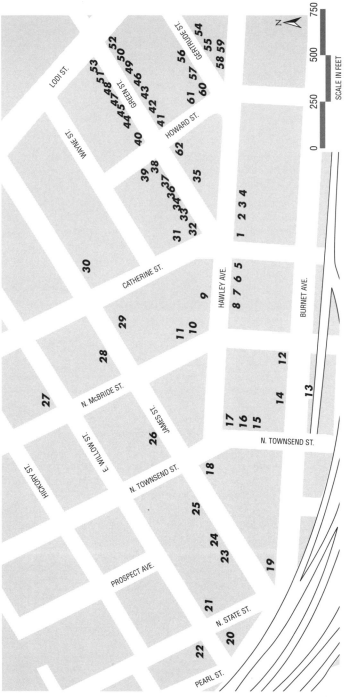

NORTHEAST SIDE

Lodi-Burnet-James Street Triangle and Vicinity

The Hawley-Green Street area is a National Register Historic District (NRHD) and includes fifty-four properties. Because of space constraints, not all have been included here.

*Estimated walking time: 2 hours, 15 minutes (**Nos. 1–62**)*

Lodi Street, Burnet Avenue, and James Street enclose a coherent neighborhood that was settled in the 1840s. As early as 1826, Lodi Street, a wide road that ran on high ground from the Erie Canal to Salina, was opened by Captain Oliver Teall and his associates. It followed an Indian trail, known as the "upper trail," and avoided the swamp that is now the site of Syracuse. Burnet Avenue and James Street (originally Foot Street) were named after men of the Syracuse Company, as were other streets in the area, such as Howard Street, Hawley Avenue, and Townsend Street. Here lived artisans and workers, bankers and lawyers, shopkeepers and manufacturers. The triangle combined residential with commercial development. Typically, people who came here during the early decades of the nineteenth century built modest frame or brick houses, sometimes with Greek Revival details. The particularly popular Italianate house and the Second Empire and Queen Anne houses built here in the 1870s and 1880s, during the next wave of development, reflect the greater affluence of the residents. When the trolley arrived in the area later in the nineteenth century, development reached its peak and land values rose. The trolley lines ran down Hawley to Green, up Green to Lodi, from where they went north.

Speculators built apartment houses. Older houses, set far back from the road, were replaced by larger structures. Quite often a small older house received an addition to the front. Although some of the smaller houses of early nineteenth-century vintage remained as single- family residences and were well maintained, economic changes in the twentieth century made it increasingly difficult for one family to keep a large house, and many of them became apartment buildings or were left vacant. Plagued by burned-out and abandoned buildings, largely a collection of rooming houses and battered apartments, the neighborhood deteriorated. In recent decades, this trend was turned around by civic agencies and private investors who helped to make the area viable again.

The renaissance began in the early 1970s when the Landmarks Association of Central New York (now the Preservation Association of Central New York) became interested in a row of Italianate brick houses on the south side of Hawley Avenue (300–306). They are known as the "Beadle Houses" after their builder, George Beadle. Originally built as single-family residences and as rental properties, they are now adaptively reused. Other buildings were restored and adaptively reused, and the Hawley-Green Street area was listed on the National Register of Historic Places.

1. 300 Hawley Avenue, 1878
Renovation: 1982, JCM Architectural Associates, Syracuse
NRHD

The Italianate brick house served as Beadle's home for ten years and then became the home of John Greenway, Jr., treasurer of the Greenway Brewery. At present, it contains architectural offices. Italianate style houses (of which 300–306 Hawley are good examples) were so popular in this country in the 1860s and 1870s that the style was sometimes referred to as the "American style." Writer and landscape gardener Andrew Jackson Downing, who worked with architect Alexander Jackson Davis, promoted the Italianate style in his books.

The ornate hood moldings above windows, the almost-flat roofs with wide eaves supported by brackets, and ornate entrance porches on 300–306 Hawley are characteristic elements of the Italianate house. The Eastlake-inspired entrance porches and the hood molds are identical on 304 and 306 Hawley which suggests that these features were ordered from catalogues. The porch on 300 Hawley comes from an 1870s pattern book by A. J. Bicknell & Co. In 1975 the Landmarks Association of Central New York, Inc. bought the house.

2. 304 Hawley Avenue, 1874
304 Hawley Avenue
Renovation: 1984, JCM Architectural Associates, Syracuse
NRHD

The house was at one time home of Henry Rowling, clothier and later president of Onondaga County Savings Bank.

3. 306 Hawley Avenue, 1874
Renovation: 1978, JCM Architectural Associates, Syracuse
NRHD CSPS

This was also a Beadle residence originally, and for many years functioned as the residence of a physician. In 1975, the Landmarks Association of Central New York, Inc., shared office space with other businesses in this building, before the organization moved to the Parke Avery House on the North Side.

3. 306 Hawley Avenue, detail

4. 308 Hawley Avenue, 1888
Renovation: 1981, JCM Architectural Associates, Syracuse
NRHD

It is believed that Beadle also built this brick house. Notice the Eastlake-inspired ornamentation on the porch, the Palladian window in the clapboarded gable, and the block ornament under the cornice. The building now functions as an apartment house. When in the early 1980s the Junior League used it as a show house, the carriage house in back was torn down and a replica was constructed.

4. 308 Hawley
Avenue

5. MQ Camera Center, ca. 1970
226 Hawley Avenue
Renovation: 1986, MQ Camera Center; preservation consultants, Crawford & Stearns, Syracuse

Originally an ugly cement-block duckling, the small commercial structure has been transformed into a contextual building that meets the street well. It is not included in the National Register Historic District.

6. 222–224 Hawley Avenue, 1872
Renovation: 1984, JCM Architectural Associates, Syracuse
NRHD

This duplex was probably built for rental purposes for the Reverend F. A. Spencer, an active member in the local temperance society. Since the building exhibits no other Second Empire style features, its mansard roof with dormers may have been added as an afterthought.

7. 218 Hawley Avenue: Back House, ca. 1840; Front Addition, ca. 1880

Renovation: 1984, Siegrid Tuttle, Syracuse; preservation consultants, JCM Architectural Associates, Syracuse

NRHD

The original one-room house became the kitchen when the larger front addition was built forty years later. The back section now accommodates an apartment, while the front has been recycled into a townhouse.

8. 210 Hawley Avenue, 1898

NRHD

Classically inspired ornamentation embellishes the frieze of the second story. Special attention was also paid to the second story-window, which is framed by Ionic pilasters. This Georgian Revival frame house was built by local lumber merchant John H. MacDowell.

9. Greenway Place, 1882

201–223 Hawley Avenue
Renovation: 1983, JCM Architectural Associates, Syracuse

NRHD

This was built by John Greenway, a prominent Syracuse brewer, on the site of the Greenway Brewery that had been destroyed by fire. The brick structure consisted of fourteen units that were sold individually, a townhouse concept then unusual for Syracuse. The original Second Empire style building received Tudor style facades of stucco and half timbering and Tudor-arch entrances in the early years of the twentieth century. The building was restored and now consists of approximately sixty rental units that are built around and open up into a landscaped courtyard. A Gothic cottage located there features a steep gable with vergeboards and functions as the caretaker's house.

9. Greenway Place

10–11. 304 and 306 North McBride Street, ca. 1881

Architect: attributed to Archimedes Russell, Syracuse

Renovation: 1981–82, Siegrid Tuttle, Syracuse; preservation consultants, JCM Architectural Associates, Syracuse; renovation of the exterior: 1981, Allen Silberman of Crown Restoration, New York

NRHD

11. 306 North McBride Street, detail

These two houses exhibit the taste of their time for artistic expression and individuality and of our time for color. They became "Painted Ladies" in the early 1980s, thus following a colorist movement that developed spontaneously but haltingly in the 1960s in San Francisco. "This is my gift to the community," says the owner, Siegrid Tuttle. The earliest Painted Ladies in the district, they were traffic stoppers. 304 North McBride Street (**No. 10**) is a clapboard-covered frame house, featuring an exuberant display of ornament, including Stick style elements and a sunburst in the roof gable. By the late 1800s, these decorative elements were machine-made and could be ordered by catalogue.

10. 304 North McBride Street

The house was built for real estate agent Edward Townsend. 306 North McBride (**No. 11**), constructed for Alfred E. Lewis, an executive at the Syracuse Savings Bank, is of brick and keeps up with its neighbor in display of ornamental detail. It has a fine beveled-glass entrance and an interior with scrolled ceilings and black walnut fireplaces. Both houses, recycled as rental units, are fronted by Eastlake-inspired porches with gazebo. A former carriage house in the back, 306 1/2 North McBride, has also been renovated by JCM Architectural Associates and accommodates two rental units.

12. 219 Burnet Avenue, 1892

Renovation and partial restoration: 1974–, Zausmer-Frisch Associates, Inc., Syracuse

One of the finest buildings in the area is this Second Empire style brick house with a high stone basement and stone trim that was constructed for Edward A. Dollard, vice-president of the National Brewing Company. Notice the cast-iron cresting that tops the mansard roof. Like so many of its neighbors, the house fell on hard times. "We moved into a three-family slum seventeen years ago," said Garson Zausmer, "and we have been renovating and restoring since." Downstairs rooms have high pressed-tin ceilings, mahogany woodwork, and original fireplaces, which were used in combination with cast-iron stoves. With a beautifully restored exterior, the house is again an asset to the neighborhood.

12. 219 Burnet Avenue

13. Midtown Auto Body Service Corporation, 1950s
212 Burnet Avenue
Murals: 1976, Jeff Davies

The small commercial building was originally constructed as a carriage house for the Century Club on James Street. Changes were made to the building in the 1950s when it became the Auto Body Shop. The facade has been enlivened by glass blocks and more recently by murals painted by local artist Jeff Davies. The building faces an Italianate brick house (211 Burnet) with fine Eastlake-inspired window surrounds.

13. Midtown Auto Body Service Corporation

14. 207 Burnet Avenue, ca. 1900
Renovation: 1982, NEHDA, Inc., Syracuse

The two-family frame house, once gutted by fire and abandoned, is now a mixed-use building. It was rehabilitated by the Northeast Hawley Development Association, Inc. (NEHDA, Inc.), a grassroots not-for-profit community improvement organization that was founded in 1974 by the residents of this neighborhood, the near Northeast Side of the city of Syracuse.

A clipping from the *Syracuse Standard* of 1855 informs readers that the Townsend Street sewer was completed. Taxation may be next! And it is about time, the reporter continued, that the city fathers do something to prevent Prospect Hill from being rushed into gardens, cisterns, and basements of the dwellings in that part of the city every time there is a slight shower.

15. 206 North Townsend Street, ca. 1840
Renovation: 1954–55, Dorothy and Robert Riester

The small vernacular Greek Revival house of brick with sandstone lintels, once a residence, now accommodates office space. It is said that Moses DeWitt Burnet, agent for the Syracuse Company, built the house. The front portion, featuring a Greek Revival door with sidelights and transom, probably dates to 1840. The original kitchen section in the rear is slightly lower than the living areas. In the 1860s, a lawyer added the side wing, where he maintained his office. It has Italianate features such as arched windows with denticulation and keystones. A wooden porch, not original to the structure, was removed. Said Dorothy Riester, "we were the first in the city to move into an old house and restore it, and it was difficult!"

15. 206 North Townsend Street

16. 208–210 North Townsend Street, ca. 1912
Mural: 1985, Monica Seaberry

In 1947, this former trolley barn became the Carpenters' Union Hall, home to the United Brotherhood of Carpenters and Joiners of America. It now houses offices. Modest Neoclassical Revival ornamentation, such as dentils along the cornice line, pilasters dividing window bays, and a mural, enliven the brick facade.

17. The Syracuse Home, 1869–70
Corner of North Townsend Street and Hawley Avenue
Architect: Horatio Nelson White, Syracuse
Addition: 1956, King & King Architects, Syracuse
Renovation: ca.1980

Also called "The Home," it was built for the Ladies' Relief of the Poor and Needy and Home Association. Established in 1851 by Protestant women, the organization was housed in several locations in the city until Moses DeWitt Burnet donated the site in 1868 and this building was constructed. It was a place of refuge for old or infirm women, for children too old or not old enough to go to an orphanage, and for young women temporarily out of work. The Second Empire style building of three stories on a high stone basement is embellished with fine brickwork. The mansard roof above the central tower has been removed. Apparently White's own house on James Street, begun in 1870 (now demolished), was similar in character. The Home has been used as a low-income apartment house since the 1970s, when the association moved to another location.

17. The Syracuse Home

18. Century Club, 1842
480 James Street
Renovation: 1890; addition to rear: 1911

Architectural historian Talbot Hamlin maintains that "nowhere more than in upstate New York is Greek Revival work more vital and more varied." The former home of Moses DeWitt Burnet was the first of the large houses that were later built on James Street, and it was designed in then-fashionable Greek Revival style. Its owner was delighted about the fact that he was able to watch canal traffic from a loggia (now removed). In 1881, the house became the home of the Century Club, a social club chartered in 1876 for Syracuse business and professional men. Before then, a cupola and a balustrade along the roofline had been removed, and when the Century Club purchased the building, further alterations were made to the interior with its impressive fireplaces and oak and maple woodwork. The basement space, formerly used by staff, was given over to members who also used the two floors above. The original entrance on the second level, with twenty-one steps leading up to it, was changed to a basement-level entrance with a Neoclassical Revival porch. A wood-frame addition was built in 1911.

Century Club (l) and May Memorial Church, 1899. Courtesy Onondaga Historical Association, Syracuse

19. Snowdon Apartments, 1902–4
Corner of James Street and Burnet Avenue
Architect: Archimedes Russell, Syracuse
Renovation: ca. 1978, Phelps Corporation, Binghamton

Walter Snowdon Smith built this apartment house on a triangular corner site. The six-story brick structure rests on a high limestone basement and consists of two main wings that frame a wedge-shaped courtyard. Elements such as bow fronts, vertical rows of balconies with decorative wrought-iron work, and a semielliptical entrance porch supported by fluted composite columns make this a good example of the Georgian Revival style. Between the time of its opening and the 1920s, it was considered to be a luxury apartment house in the city with only two or three units per floor. Occupied by transient hotel residents during the 1960s and 1970s, it fell victim to inner-city decline and was reputed to be Syracuse's highest crime address. A fire destroyed much of the south wing; renovated, the building is again used as an apartment house.

20. St. John the Evangelist Roman Catholic Church, 1853–55
215 North State Street
Alterations: 1875; 1887

In 1886, this Gothic Revival church became the first Cathedral of the Roman Catholic Diocese of Syracuse and served in that capacity until 1904, when St. Mary's (now the Cathedral of the Immaculate Conception) was completed. At the time it was built, St. John the Evangelist Church was located at the junction of the Erie and Oswego canals. The handsome building with central tower, buttressing, and pointed-arch openings served its predominantly Irish neighborhood for generations. The exterior remains basically unchanged, but a steeple was added in 1875 and the sanctuary was enlarged in 1887. The building is endangered because the number of parishioners has declined in recent years. The adjacent school building was demolished after the school was closed in the late 1960s.

21. Rectory of St. John the Evangelist, 1874
214 North State Street and Willow Street
Architect: Archimedes Russell, Syracuse

The three-story High Victorian Italianate building, more ornate than its Italianate contemporaries, is square in plan and has a two-story wing. It is used as a rectory and church office. The exterior is resplendent with a cupola on an almost-flat roof with projecting eaves and paired brackets. Ornate window surrounds, two bays, and an entrance with a second-story porch lend the main facade a baroque plasticity characteristic of the style. It is likely that the enclosed porch above the entrance was originally open.

22. Nettleton Commons, ca. 1882
313 Willow Street
Renovation and addition: 1899; 1922, T. Walter Gaggin, Syracuse; renovation: 1988, Holmes/King & Associates Architects, Syracuse

Directly to the north of St. John the Evangelist is a building that once housed the A. E. Nettleton Company, which occupied the structure until 1983. Considered to be "the Rolls Royce of footwear companies," A. E. Nettleton was established in this city in 1879. The company manufactured men's shoes and invented the loafer in 1937. The present building was constructed around an earlier structure and, according to architect Bruce King, "represented a happy medium between the old time individuality of the craftsman and the modern large scale manufacturing space." The building now accommodates office and retail space on the first floor, and apartments above. Originally, the structure could be entered from Pearl Street by a carriageway on the first floor, but it was closed when the carriageway entrance from North State Street on the second level was opened. During rehabilitation, both carriageways were reopened, and an unused boiler room was excavated and became a two-story atrium space, linking pedestrian circulation from both street levels to the parking area and the elevator lobby. Various artifacts, such as a boiler door (now on the Pearl Street entrance), were incorporated into the renovation. Holmes/King received awards for design excellence and for historic preservation for this project from the Central New York Chapter of the American Institute of Architects.

23. 427 James Street, ca. 1842

23. 427 James Street

This is a fine temple-front build-ing, a survivor of earlier days when houses like this lined the city streets. Despite changes that were made, its scale and its portico with Doric columns that carry a pedi-ment embellished with Federal style ornament make this frame house a good example of the Greek Revival house. Moses DeWitt Bur-net sold the lot to local banker John D. Norton, who may have built the house.

24. Church of the Savior, 1912
437 James Street
Rebuilding of original church: Ralph Adams Cram, New York
CSPS

This small Gothic Revival brownstone and brick building replaced St. James Episcopal Church, later renamed Church of the Savior, which burned in 1912. Only the original walls and piers remained of the previous building, which had been designed by local architect Asa L. Merrick. Cram lowered the floor and inserted a beam ceiling with heavy timber trusses. A soaring nave is bordered by obtuse brick arches and brick lancet tracery with clerestory windows and window blanks. In this simple interior of white plaster walls and carved oak woodwork, nothing interferes with the focal point, the high altar of Caen stone and marble. Ralph Adams Cram (1863–1942) is best known as the architect of the Cathedral of St. John the Divine in New York.

25. Newell House and Carriage House, 1872
457 James Street
Renovation and partial restoration: 1985, King Landmark Properties, Inc., Syracuse

Built for carriage maker Joseph Newell, the building originally consisted of two townhouses visually unified by a symmetrical facade. The one to the east was torn down in 1962. With mansard roof and bold cornice, with ornate windows and dormers, and with elaborate woodwork, high ceilings, and marble mantels in the interior, the house is a fine example of the Second Empire style. Notice also the addition of Second Empire style elements to the carriage house in back. One of the few survivors among the stately homes that once graced James Street, the house is now adaptively reused.

26. First English Lutheran Church, 1910–11
507 James Street
Architects: Russell and King, Syracuse

The architects designed this church in the Mission style, which was California's answer to the Georgian Revival in the Eastern states. The structure is of gray sandstone, roofed with red tile, and embellished with fine stained-glass windows. A large bell tower, centrally placed and flanked by two smaller towers, articulates the narthex. The decorative work in the bell tower as well as brackets underneath the cornices are of wood. In the 1960s, a building containing schoolrooms and offices was constructed and added to the rear of the rectangular sanctuary. Descendents of German immigrants, weary of having to listen to church services in German, organized the English Lutheran Church in 1879.

26. First English Lutheran Church

27. 500 North McBride Street, 1894

Restoration and renovation: 1985–87, Dr. J. Rene Wilett; preservation consultants, Holmes/King & Associates Architects, Syracuse

CSPS

Located on a hill with a view over the city, this is one of the finest Queen Anne houses in the area. It has been suggested that the design came from a pattern book by George F. Barber, who was the first to supply entire prefabricated houses and one of many who emphasized artistic achievement, creative expression, and individuality. The plans could be ordered for a nominal fee. The picturesquely massed frame house sits on a stone foundation and is faced with horizontal clapboards and fish-scale shingles, creating a rich textural variety characteristic of the style. Ornament and detail are emphasized by a well-executed paint job. Porches featuring Eastlake ornamentation, large plate-glass windows enhanced with stained glass, a three-story hexagonal corner tower, and a ground-floor porch with a central gazebo add to its picturesqueness. The elegant interior of the house has an ornate oak staircase, wooden paneling, ornate plaster ceilings, and parquet floors. In the 1920s, local attorney Edward Schoeneck, former mayor of the

27. 500 North McBride Street

city and lieutenant governor of the state, bought the house from the original owner, John Truesdell. The house is now adaptively reused by Reach-Out, a local drug abuse agency. Visits to the house may be arranged through the Preservation Association of Central New York.

At the turn of the century three apartment houses on James Street, once the most elegant residential street in the city, were built for the affluent middle class. To attract the "right kind" of tenants, exteriors would be designed in the fashionable style of the day, featuring elegant lobbies and public rooms. James Street seemed the "right" location, because it was associated with the homes of the wealthy. However, these changes in urban life came under attack: "The promiscuous exclusivity of the apartment hotel is the most dangerous enemy American domesticity has had to encounter" wrote an observer in *Architectural Record*, and another in *Ladies Home Journal* warned that American women would come under Bolshevik influence because of apartment living. It was generally urged and accepted that the American woman's place was in the detached home.

28. Leavenworth Apartments, 1912
615 James Street
Architect: Charles E. Colton, Syracuse

The structure occupies part of the former site of the Leavenworth house and its extensive gardens. When constructed, the building was advertised as being "fireproof ... a model in architectural beauty ... containing 48 suites and bachelor apartments, with a public dining room in the basement." The curved Flemish gables of the two apartment towers and their central connecting link refer to Colonial forms. A twentieth-century entrance porch is inconsistent with the Colonial Revival details of the facade.

29. The Kasson, 1898
622 James Street
Architects: Merrick and Randall, Syracuse

The seven-story apartment house was designed in the Second Renaissance Revival style. The building is faced with light-colored brick and terra cotta featuring Neoclassical ornamentation. Notice the cartouches along the cornice line and the arrangement of the balconies with wrought-iron railings. The first-level balcony is supported by paired Doric columns, the second by Ionic, and the third by columns with Corinthian capitals.

30. Schopfer Court, 1917
708 James Street
Architect: Albert L. Brockway

The Neoclassical arrangement of apartment blocks was designed in combination with formal gardens. The building originally featured rooftop gardens, giving expression to a concern prevalent at the time for fresh air and healthy living.

31. 306 Catherine Street, ca. 1890

Renovation: 1983, NEHDA, Inc., Syracuse

A one-family residence, this frame house had been abandoned by its owners and was rehabilitated by NEHDA. The house, featuring a bay and an East-lake-inspired front porch, is a small version of then-popular architectural themes for larger houses. Built on a small lot, it served a family with a modest income as a home in a suburban neighborhood.

Because of its many trees, Green Street was once known as "the Grove." It boasted the first tennis court in the city. Middle-class Syracusans lived here, and the size and style of their homes attest to the owners' social position and affluence.

32. Gouldner's Pharmacy, 1885

101–105 Green Street

NRHD

A drugstore has been on this site since 1865. The present pharmacy is housed in a two and one-half-story gabled frame structure that was built by surgeon and pharmacist Judson J. Taylor, who most likely lived above the shop.

33. Brick House, 1897

121 Green Street

NRHD

This Georgian Revival house built for physician Dr. Lewis F. Weaver is now called Brick House; the Brick House Association owns and uses it as a drug rehabilitation center.

34. 125 Green Street, 1876

NRHD

Rasselas Bonta, a banker and later president of the Onondaga County Savings Bank, built this Italianate house. Notice the leaded glass in the windows. Adaptively reused, the house now functions as a rehabilitation center.

35. 124 Green Street, 1855

Restoration: 1985, Jamieson R. Steele; preservation consultants, Crawford & Stearns, Syracuse

NRHD

The one and one-half-story Gothic Revival cottage is distinguished by a steep gable and label hood molds around windows. The vergeboards original to the house were removed, and the porch and two sections were later added to the rear. The cottage now functions as a two-family home.

36. 127 Green Street, ca. 1890

Restoration: 1986–, Jamieson R. Steele, Syracuse

NRHD

Facing the street brightly colored, this Painted Lady does not look like a haunted house. But it is, says owner Jamieson R. Steele, who has lovingly restored the erstwhile one-family home. While he occupies the front part of the house, the former maids' quarters in the back have been converted into a studio apartment. Notice the Eastlake ornamentation, the fine stained glass, and the characteristic Queen Anne textures on the facade, including a frieze of pie motifs above the second-story windows. The interior woodwork has been restored to its original beauty: cherry was used for the ceiling in the parlor and also for the staircase. The house comes complete with a set of pocket doors, a terra cotta fireplace, and a ghost.

36. 127 Green Street

37. 129 Green Street, ca. 1890

Renovation: 1983–84, Crawford & Stearns, Syracuse

NRHD

Various fires had damaged the house. During renovation work, the interior was changed; only the living room and most of the foyer are original. Creative recycling was employed by using the interior woodwork from the neighboring house in the renovation of this one, now divided into five rental units. The exterior, except for the new porch, has been restored to its original appearance.

38. 133–135 Green Street, 1879

Restoration (exterior) and renovation (interior): 1982-83, JCM Architectural Associates, Syracuse

NRHD

Built as income-producing property for two families, the apartment house now contains five rental units. Eastlake ornamentation on the porches and Stick style elements in the gable enliven the facade.

39. 401–407 Howard Street, 1879

Renovation: (403), 1991–, Jamieson R. Steele, Syracuse; (405), ca. 1984, Joan Farrenkopf, Syracuse; (407), 1981, NEHDA, Inc.; and 1985, Joan Farrenkopf, Syracuse. Joan Farrenkopf also renovated 409 Howard Street in 1984.

NRHD

The row-house complex of wood-frame construction was built in response to the trolley service along Howard Street.

40. 201–203 Green Street, 1888

Renovation and partial restoration of 201: 1982, Joan Farrenkopf; preservation consultants, Crawford & Stearns, Syracuse

NRHD

Despite appearances, these are not two separate houses but a duplex with a tower connecting the two parts. The viewer is presented with a collage of architectural detail: stone, brick, and shingling provide textural variety on the exterior. Romanesque Revival elements such as large round-arched openings frame porches, Eastlake-inspired designs ornament an entrance porch, and stained glass beautifies windows. Its carriage house is on Howard Street. In 1895, the rivals in the mayoral race, Republican Charles Baldwin and Democrat James McGuire, lived side by side in this two-family structure. The winner was McGuire, aged 27, who served as "boy mayor" until 1901.

The carriage house in back of 201 Green Street is now used as rental property. It was renovated around 1982 by Joan Farrenkopf with preservation consultants Crawford & Stearns of Syracuse.

41. 200–202 Green Street, 1890
NRHD

Built as a two-family house, this picturesquely massed Queen Anne house has some Stick style ornamentation and notable details, such as wood ornamentation in the small triangular pediments of the entrance porch and circular windows in the pediment of the main gable.

42. 208 Green Street, 1911
NRHD

The design of this frame house may have come from a plan book. Some years ago, the city included the house in its homesteading program, and it was rehabilitated by the owners.

43. 210 Green Street, ca. 1860
NRHD

Local businessman Henry Phelps built this handsome Italianate house with cupola for his family. Although it is of frame construction, flush boarding and quoins simulate masonry.

44. Russell-Farrenkopf House, 1869
209 Green Street
Restoration: 1976–, Joan Farrenkopf; preservation consultants,
Sheldon Williams, Syracuse; Crawford & Stearns, Syracuse;
interior: Glenn Hinchey of Salt City Restoration Company, Syracuse
NRHD

This was a pioneering effort in restoration in the district. Like so many houses in the area, this one too had deteriorated, and owner Joan Farrenkopf, a self-proclaimed "preservationist by trial and error," brought it back to its one-time elegance. The house functions again as a one-family home and serves as bed-and-breakfast place for half of the year. The two-story frame structure with side wing topped by mansard roofs and dormers, and with a veranda and tall first-story windows is a good example of the Second Empire style, displaying a wealth of decorative motifs. The front facade is cov-

44. Russell-Farrenkopf House

ered with flush boarding. Richly ornamented pilasters articulate corners and window bays, and also frame a handsome entrance. The porch was restored by Glenn Hinchey, as was most of the interior. Hinchey is responsible for much restoration and renovation work in the Hawley-Green Street district. The ten-room house has grained floors, ornate plaster cornices, and ornamental fireplace mantels. The house was originally heated with cast-iron stoves. It was built by local contractor Henry Russell as his residence. Russell worked for Horatio Nelson White, and it is believed that White designed the house.

45. 211 Green Street, ca. 1850
Addition: 1885
Renovation: 1983, Sheldon Williams, Syracuse
NRHD

The older part (1850s) was designed as a Gothic cottage with a steep gable and vergeboards and is covered with board and batten. When the house received a Queen Anne frame addition in 1885, the Gothic cottage became a side wing. At present, the house is adaptively reused as rental property.

46. 212 Green Street, 1853
NRHD

One of the earlier homes in the area, this was built for carpenter Oliver P. Ives. Between 1886 and 1934, it was the residence of Judge William Ross, who presided over the well-publicized murder trial of one-time heavyweight boxing champion Bob Fitzsimmons.

47. 213 Green Street, 1883
NRHD

Contractor Irwin M. Allen built this splendid Queen Anne house. With its fine detailing—notice especially the sunflower in the main gable, an architectural element available from catalogues—picturesque massing, and porches and entrance framed by large round-arched openings, the house is a fine example of the style.

48. Woodruff House, 1880s
215 Green Street
Renovation and partial restoration: 1982–83, Joan Farrenkopf; preservation consultants, Crawford & Stearns, Syracuse
NRHD

The house had an Italianate roof originally but a gabled roofline at the time the National Register Historic District survey was conducted. This determined the restoration of the gabled roof when the house was renovated after a disastrous fire. Built as a one-family residence, it now houses apartments.

49. Chapman-Clark House, ca. 1850
214 Green Street
Addition: 1870s
Renovation: 1984, Sheldon Williams, Syracuse
NRHD

The house started as a vernacular Greek Revival house set far back from the street. Part of the Italianate addition to the original brick house is still visible. The house is adaptively reused and accommodates rental units.

50. 216–218 Green Street, 1890
Renovation of 218: 1982–83, Joan Farrenkopf; preservation consultants, Crawford & Stearns, Syracuse
NRHD

The Queen Anne house was once the home of "honest Mike," a nickname given to the original owner, Michael E. Driscoll, who served seven terms in Congress and helped to obtain funds for the construction of the former Federal Building on Clinton Square. The frame house has a corner tower, a later Queen Anne development, as well as a roof turret. A small, finely detailed balcony on the second level may have been used as a sleeping porch at one time.

51. Ira Waterbury House, 1856
219 Green Street
Renovation: ca. 1984, King Landmark Properties, Inc., Syracuse; interior (in part): Sam Gleasman and Dave Wishart
NRHD

Now recycled into a two-family home, this is one of the last remaining vernacular Greek Revival houses on the street. It was built by peddler Ira Waterbury. A porch was added later and has also been restored. Like most houses on Green Street, it is set back a good distance from the street.

52. 220 Green Street, 1868
NRHD

The modest Italianate house with an ornate Eastlake-inspired entrance porch was built for ironworker Lewis K. Cole of Draper & Cole, a local firm that manufactured cast-iron fences.

53. George Cook House, 1895
701 Lodi Street
Renovation: 1985, Al De Dominicis of Redwood Construction, Syracuse
NRHD

The George Cook House was built as a two-family house and now accommodates seven apartments. A tower on the Green Street side and textural variety on the exterior lend visual interest to this Queen Anne style structure. The building was damaged by fire and water, and the tower, octagonal in plan but with unequal sides, presented renovation problems that were nevertheless successfully resolved. The interior was rehabilitated with salvaged materials from demolished late nineteenth-century houses.

Gertrude Street was largely inhabited by artisans and workers. Less affluent than the residents of Hawley Avenue and Green Street, they lived in vernacular Greek Revival and modest Italianate houses of comparable scale and proportion that date to mid-nineteenth century. The properties on Gertrude Street are not part of the Hawley-Green Street National Register Historic District.

54–57. 118 Gertrude Street, 1850s (54), a one-family home, and **114–116 Gertrude, 1870s (55)**, an Italianate two-family house, were renovated in 1986–87 by Jamieson R. Steele, Syracuse. **117 Gertrude, 1860s (56)**, a vernacular Greek Revival house with gable-end returns (gable with a gap in the base molding) and a later porch addition, was used as a one-family dwelling and was restored in 1989–91 by Glenn Hinchey. **105 Gertrude, 1852 (57)** received an Italianate front addition in 1876. The two-family house was restored in 1984–86 by Glenn Hinchey.

The following properties are not part of the Hawley-Green Street National Register Historic District.

58. Former Babian's Market, ca. 1850
401 Hawley Avenue
Restoration: ongoing, Sheldon Williams, Syracuse

The two-story brick building anchors the triangular site between Hawley Avenue and Gertrude Street. It is the oldest commercial building in the district and was first known as Healy's Store and then as Babian's Market. The original owner, John F. Bradt, operated the store between 1850 and 1854. The building was used for retail business since that time until 1978 when the present owner bought it. During restoration, a projection dating from the 1920s on the facade facing Hawley Avenue was removed, revealing a French window. The present owner would like to install an iron balcony that he believes was once in front of it. The interior, relatively unaltered, is in the process of being restored and will accommodate two retail stores. An old walk-in oak cooler is still in place. The second floor, once residential, will again be used in that capacity.

59. 405 Hawley Avenue, mid-1880s
Renovation: ongoing, Sheldon Williams, Syracuse

The interior of the picturesquely massed Queen Anne house still has the original trim and hardware. The exterior will be painted in historic Queen Anne colors. Two-bedroom flats on each floor will occupy this former single-family house.

60. 101 Gertrude Street, 1873

Renovation: ca. 1976, NEHDA, Inc., Syracuse

The Italianate frame structure was built as the Henry Schaefer General Store. It now functions as headquarters for the Northeast Hawley Development Association, Inc. (NEHDA, Inc.), a grass roots, not-for-profit community improvement organization, founded in 1974 by the residents of this area.

60. 101 Gertrude Street

61. 304 Howard Street, 1851

Restoration and renovation: 1991–, Glenn Hinchey of Salt City Restoration Company, Syracuse

The restoration and renovation of this frame-house consisting of upright-and-wing involves the re-creation of an 1860s house. It is being used as a two-family dwelling, with a handsome fence framing the property.

62. 134–136 Green Street, 1986

Architect: Peter Arsenault, Syracuse

Built for NEHDA on a former community garden site, this modern frame house is representative of good, affordable housing designed within the context of an older neighborhood.

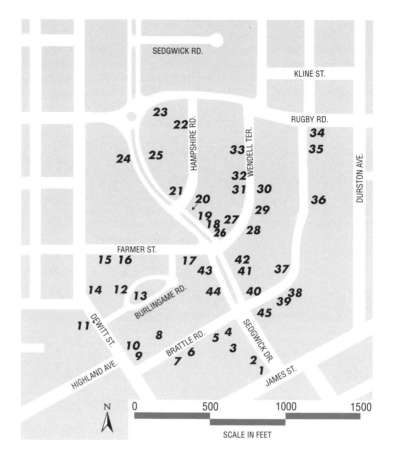

SEDGWICK RD.

KLINE ST.

RUGBY RD.

HAMPSHIRE RD.

WENDELL TER.

DURSTON AVE.

23
22
34
35
24   25   33
32
21   20   31   30   36
19   29
18   27
26   28

FARMER ST.

15 16   17   42   37
43   41
14 12 13   44   40   38
39
45
11
8
10   5 4
9   7 6   3
2 1

DEWITT ST.

BURLINGAME RD.

BRATTLE RD.

SEDGWICK DR.

HIGHLAND AVE.

JAMES ST.

N

0   500   1000   1500

SCALE IN FEET

Sedgwick Tract and Vicinity

The Sedgwick-Highland-James Street area is a City of Syracuse Preservation District (CSPD) and includes, at present, 289 properties. They are located on Brattle, Burlingame, Hampshire, and Rugby roads; DeWitt, Dorothy, Farmer, upper James, and Oak streets; Durston and Highland avenues; Sedgwick Drive; and Wendell Terrace. Because of space constraints, many of these properties are not included.

*Estimated walking time: 1 hour, 30 minutes (**Nos. 1–45**)*

The Sedgwick Tract is Syracuse's first planned suburban community and is named after Charles and Deborah Sedgwick. Politically active and an outspoken antislavery leader, Charles came to Syracuse in 1842 and established the law firm of Sedgwick, Andrews, and Kennedy. Deborah was educated at Brook Farm, an experimental farm in Massachusetts based on principles of cooperative living. She was an early member of May Memorial Unitarian Church and also an abolitionist. In 1858, the Sedgwicks moved from their Gothic cottage (1834; Alexander Jackson Davis; demolished) at the foot of James Street to the top of the hill. Here they bought eighty acres of farmland, built "the Homestead" (which was slightly northeast of the corner of Sedgwick Drive and James Street), cultivated the land, developed the property, and called it Sedgwick Farm. Family members lived in close proximity to each other. Each of the Sedgwick daughters received a parcel of land as a wedding gift, and each, in turn, gave part of her original share to those of her children who stayed in town. After her husband's death in 1883, Deborah Sedgwick turned the farm into a playground for her fifteen

The Homestead, 1870. Courtesy Onondaga Historical Association, Syracuse

201

grandchildren and their neighborhood friends. After her death in 1901, the property was divided among the heirs. They formed the Sedgwick Farm Land Company, which began to develop the area. The tract, hailed as the most desirable location in the city, was opened up in sections. Double houses and stores were not permitted. Large lots on curving tree-lined streets offered the perfect setting for the American Dream, and the Sedgwick Farm Tennis Club (no longer existing) provided sports facilities and entertainment. Within twenty years, the greater part of the land was developed and sold, a process that reflected a national trend. By the 1890s, the well-to-do had left the inner cities; by 1900, the middle class had followed. The 1920 census indicated that for the first time in U.S. history, the majority of Americans lived in cities or its suburbs, with the suburbs growing twice as fast as the central cores. Those who invested in the suburban way of life hoped to find social stability as well as individual freedom. Although some critics denounced this "delusion of the suburbs" with its "selfishness and aimlessness," others saw the suburban trend as the "saving grace of America," praising it as "a haven of normalcy."

First Sedgwick Farm Tennis Club, 1908. Courtesy Onondaga Historical Association, Syracuse

By 1908, eighty-two plots were delineated, and seventeen houses were built south of Farmer Street, set back from tree-lined streets. Most of these are period houses in styles such as Mission, Colonial Revival, Georgian Revival, and Tudor Revival. They are simpler in form than houses built fifty years previously. In plan they are more open, with fewer but larger rooms. Verandas and porches are replaced by terraces and carports. Historic styles are suggested in massing and in details, but the emphasis is on new technologies in relation to kitchens and bathrooms. While some observers saw this historicism as an architectural security blanket that could not yet deal with the unornamented house, others felt that a revival of past American styles would give emotional comfort and display the correct symbols. In contrast, the "progressive" or "natural" house, of which there are a few in the district, was seen as an integral part of nature and was designed with only the structural form and texture of the materials as ornament. An open plan and organic relationship to the site was important; to provide shelter was the primary function. The natural house favoring organic principles was best expressed in the work of Frank Lloyd Wright before 1914 and most clearly in the architectural writing of that time.

1. 101–103 Sedgwick Drive, 1985
Architect: R. J. Engan & Associates, Syracuse

The modern house is designed along Prairie style lines: the eaves of the low-pitched roof extending well beyond the wall, low chimneys, and an exterior of narrow bricks emphasize horizontality. The house has an open interior plan and was designed as a duplex. It fits well into its immediate surroundings and coexists happily with its older neighbors.

2. 105 Sedgwick Drive, 1908
Alterations: 1925–26, Dwight James Baum, New York
CSPD

Originally a simple farmhouse, this was the home of Frank S. Tracy. Between 1925 and 1926, a new owner hired architect Dwight James Baum to classicize the house. The central section of the the facade facing the street sits on a raised stone platform with semicircular steps. It is covered with flush boarding and articulated by attached Ionic columns that rise through two stories. A small round window opens the pediment. The lower side wings are faced with siding. The open-topped pediment above the main entrance is a design feature borrowed from Georgian houses. The west facade of the house features a full portico.

Dwight James Baum (1886–1939), who graduated from the School of Architecture at Syracuse University, received a gold medal in 1923 from the Architectural League of New York for the "simplicity and charm of his residential work." He also served as critic and architectural editor for *Better Homes and Gardens* and in 1932 was awarded the gold medal of Better Homes in America by President Hoover for his design of the best small two-story house in the United States.

During the second half of the nineteenth century, some American architects, whose efforts were widely publicized in books and periodicals, began to restore colonial buildings. Following the centennial, interest in replicating colonial structures grew, and the restoration of Williamsburg in Virginia during the early decades of this century was not a negligible factor in giving "Olde Colonial" a pride of place. The Colonial Revival house not only borrows from the Georgian and from English and Dutch Colonial farmhouses but freely uses noncolonial sources such as Federal and Greek Revival details as well. The appearance of mass-produced windows, entrances, trim, paneling, and reproductions of early American hardware augmented this trend. In most of these houses the center-hall plan of the Colonial house is followed, but the dimensions are considerably larger in the Colonial Revival house than in its predecessor. This was a time when the well-to-do had live-in servants and provisions were made for their housing. Many of these houses have flanking terraces, sunrooms, and porte cocheres, features that are not Colonial but decidedly modern.

2. 105 Sedgwick Drive

3. 107 Sedgwick Drive, ca. 1895
Additions: 1911
CSPD

The house was built for James G. Tracy and family, and it originally faced James Street. According to one of the former owners, "the house was surrounded by apple trees before Sedgwick Drive was put in, changes were made to the house, and it received additions in 1911. The sturdy child-proof furniture was made by Gustav Stickley; some of it was later given to the Syracuse Boys' Club." Its claim to fame: the Civic Morning Musicals series was organized within its walls.

Curving and tree-lined, Brattle Road is a picturesque setting for its comfortable houses.

4. 12 Brattle Road, 1908

Architects: Gibb & Waltz, Ithaca, N.Y.

CSPD

The Georgian Revival house, prominently sited, was built for Lyndon S. Tracy, an executive at the newly established Solvay Process Company, which manufactured soda ash from salt and limestone and later became part of Allied Chemical and Dye Corporation. Mrs. Tracy had grown up in the South and wanted a house with a grand entrance. She got it as a wedding gift. A long stairway leads to a classically inspired entrance porch supported by paired fluted Doric columns. This, as well as prominent roof dormers and a symmetrically articulated main facade, with a broad staircase and Neoclassical ornament in the interior, makes the house a good example of the style.

5. 10 Brattle Road, 1908

Architect: Gustavus Young, Syracuse

CSPD

Unornamented except for textured shingling underneath the eaves and an entrance porch with paired columns carrying a second-story porch, the frame house was built for Justin Seubert, who previously lived at 405 Oak Street. Seubert had immigrated from Germany and established a successful cigar business in this city in 1866.

6. 6 Brattle Road, 1910

Architects: Taylor & Bonta, Syracuse

CSPD

Neoclassical features such as a symmetrically articulated facade, prominent eyelid dormers (small openings that have the form of an eyelid), a Palladian window on the second story, and an entrance porch framed by paired columns that carry a second-story porch distinguish this stuccoed house.

7. 4 Brattle Road, 1908

Architects: Taylor & Bonta, Syracuse

CSPD

The one and one-half-story frame cottage was originally the home of A. R. Grant, president of Alexander Grant's Sons Inc., one of Syracuse's oldest and largest retail hardware stores. The unornamented house exemplified the new trend toward the progressive house. Economy, simplicity, and dignity for everyone were strongly urged by the publicists of the day who protested the "degrading luxury of mansions ... the painful contrast of class." Instead, technological systems were emphasized, along with an

7. 4 Brattle Road

open plan, a centrally located kitchen, uniformity in regard to neighboring houses, and landscaping that allowed the house to blend with well-groomed nature.

8. 5 Brattle Road, 1908
CSPD

The rambling two and one-half-story residence was designed for attorney Alexander P. Jenney. It won a national award given by the National Association of Realtors for "the most representative home built in 1908." The original slate roof was replaced. Eyelid windows allow light to enter the attic. Form and features such as irregular massing and exposed rafters underneath the roof of the entrance porch are often used in Craftsman houses, which ranged from simple cottages or bungalows to large residences, such as this one. What made them Craftsman houses, according to Gustav Stickley, was their emphasis on durability, economy of space and material, an open interior plan, and the "avoidance of any kind of crowding," meaning that as much as possible furniture should be built-in.

9. 1 Brattle Road, 1915
CSPD

This five-bay Georgian Revival house is symmetrically articulated and has corner pilasters and a handsome entrance with an elliptical transom. It is flanked by composite columns carrying a pediment. Here stylistic elements of the Federal and the Georgian house are combined. The north and south facades of the house are clapboard-covered, while the east and west facades have end-wall chimneys and are faced with brick, features often used in Colonial houses of the eighteenth century.

10. 162 DeWitt Street, 1914
Architect: attributed to Ward Wellington Ward, Syracuse
CSPD

The house was built for Alfred H. Lewis. The round-arched doorway with paired columns is one of several types typically used in Tudor Revival houses. Diamond-shaped windows in dormers and upper window panes are also characteristic of the Tudor Revival style, which is loosely based on a variety of late medieval English houses. Most houses of this type have stuccoed, masonry, or masonry-veneered walls and false half timbering. Slate, long-lasting but expensive, was the preferred roofing material.

By the mid-1920s, Tudor Revival had come to symbolize the comforts of the ideal American home and was considered by some to be the most livable and charming house. The style also represented proper antecedents and an English past, whether real or imagined, and was sometimes referred to as Stockbroker Tudor. Using the English Tudor as an inspiration, the Tudor Revival house that you see in this area is, however, decidedly North American. It usually has a slate roof and a large chimney that anchors the irregularly massed structure to the ground. False half timbering and casement windows with small panes are often used, as are exposed wood beams, massive fireplaces, and wood paneling in the interior.

11. 223 DeWitt Street, 1915
Architect: Ward Wellington Ward, Syracuse
CSPD

The hipped-roof house was designed for John G. Ayling. Houses with clipped roof gables, such as the one you see here, point to continental rather than English sources and are sometimes referred to as "Germanic cottages." An unexpected buttress pretends to support one of the corners of the main facade. Exterior elements representative of Ward-designed houses are Mercer tiles, which are embedded in the stucco of the facade facing DeWitt Street, as well as Henry Keck window details.

Ward Wellington Ward (1875–1932) studied architecture at MIT and Chicago. He started to work in Syracuse in 1908, and his practice flourished. He primarily designed residential architecture and two-thirds of his houses, reflecting design principles of the Arts and Crafts movement in the United States, are in Syracuse. Of those, several can be found in the Sedgwick-James Street area.

Henry Chapman Mercer (1856–1930), a lawyer, became an archaeologist and ceramist and founded the Moravian Pottery and Tile Works in Doylestown, Pennsylvania in 1898. His handcrafted storybook tiles were popular with Arts and Crafts architects and were used as pavings and as fireplace facings. Ward used Moravian tiles in more than 200 installations in

11. 223 DeWitt Street

upstate New York residences. After Mercer, who was not an architect by training, had constructed his house Fonthill (1908–10) of poured reinforced concrete, an observer in *Progressive Architecture* noted that "... this building with its unique spatial plan and its frank and bold construction techniques should establish HCM as one of the important forerunners of the modern movement in architecture. ..."

Henry Keck (1873–1956) apprenticed with Louis Comfort Tiffany and studied glass design and glass painting in Munich. His business (Henry Keck Stained Glass Studio) existed in Syracuse from 1913 to 1974 and produced many church windows and Arts and Crafts style windows for Ward houses.

12. 100 Burlingame Road, ca. 1880
CSPD

The Burlingame estate was the only developed residential plot in the Sedgwick Tract before 1908. The multigabled frame house was built for Katherine and Walter Burlingame, daughter and son-in-law of Charles and Deborah Sedgwick.

13. 101 Burlingame Road, 1928
CSPD

This simple frame house set back from the road is nearly hidden by the fine landscaping of which it is an integral part. A round-arched window, with keystone and lancets in the upper sash, calls attention to the gable. At one time, the house became the home of Fanny Goodyear, who came to Syracuse with her sister in 1881. Fanny Goodyear founded the Goodyear-Burlingame School, which she directed until 1925. Her obituary noted that "Miss Goodyear is remembered as one of the first Syracusans who campaigned for women's suffrage."

Only the east side of DeWitt Street formed the western boundary of the original tract.

14. 308 DeWitt Street, 1912
Architect: Ward Wellington Ward
CSPD

A mark of the architect is the brick detailing on the exterior of the house, which was designed for E. B. Salmon. The arcaded two-story staircase window, eyelid dormers, and three paired casement windows crowned by narrow bands of tiles are distinctive features. A decorative brick stringcourse between the second and third stories emphasizes the horizontality of the house. The original slate that covered the variegated roof has been removed, and a porch was closed in.

Lots on Farmer Street are smaller than those on other streets in the tract. By 1908, at the same time as Sedgwick Drive and Brattle Road, Farmer Street was laid out in lots and developed between 1908 and 1917. Most houses here are of Colonial or Georgian Revival style.

15–16. 304 and 308 Farmer Street, 1917
CSPD

Both houses are examples of the free application of classical details often found in Georgian Revival houses. Overall symmetry, with visual emphasis given to the entrance, usually sheltered by a portico, and the use of block ornament along the cornice line and porch roof are derived from the Georgian house. The elliptical fanlight and the sidelights that distinguish the entrance of 304 Farmer Street (**15**) are Federal style features, while the rectangular transom and sidelights on the entrance door of 308 Farmer (**16**) were inspired by Greek Revival houses.

17. 332 Farmer Street, ca. 1925
Alterations to exterior: 1980s
CSPD

The steeply gabled Tudor Revival cottage of brick and shingles with a prominent chimney was built for Austin Barnes, who worked as an engineer at Solvay Process during the company's early years.

Turn left on Sedgwick Drive. The 300 and 400 blocks as well as all points north were not developed by 1924 but were laid out in lots. The last stage of construction work in the tract began in the mid-1920s and coincided with the development of Hampshire Road and Wendell Terrace. The center garden aisle of Sedgwick Drive was also laid out in 1924.

18. 306 Sedgwick Drive, 1925
Architect: Paul Hueber, Syracuse
CSPD

The house was designed for Nelson P. Snow and his family. With its rough stucco finish, red tile roof, and ornamental wrought-iron balustrade and window screen, it is a good example of the Mission style, which was popular in the United States during the early part of the twentieth century and was a West Coast counterpart to the Eastern Colonial Revival styles. Smooth facades, tiled low-pitched roofs, and arched openings are hallmarks. The simplicity of form and lack of ornament foreshadow modern architecture.

Paul Hueber (1892–1943) graduated from the Syracuse University School of Architecture and was awarded the Luther Gifford Prize for excellence in design. In 1916, he founded the architectural firm in Syracuse that continues today as Hueber Hares Glavin. Apart from the Sedgwick area, houses designed by Hueber can be found in the Bradford Hills area and in Eastwood.

19. 310 Sedgwick Drive, 1924
Architect: Paul Hueber, Syracuse
CSPD

The clipped front gable of this Tudor Revival house is its dominant feature. Notice the slate roof laid in herringbone patterns. Physician Dr. Thomas Halstead, the original owner, opened the Syracuse Clinic in 1923. It was one of the first in the city, but opposition to the clinic concept caused it to be closed down three years later.

20. 318 Sedgwick Drive, 1927
Architect: Paul Hueber, Syracuse
Renovation: 1978, R. J. Engan & Associates, Syracuse
CSPD

The Georgian Revival house of brick with sandstone trim was originally built for James F. O'Donnell, one-time superintendent of Prudential Insurance Company.

21. 400 Sedgwick Drive, 1927

Architect: Paul Hueber, Syracuse

CSPD

This is a Tudor Revival house of many gables, steeply pitched; they are on dormers and on a bay with flared roofline that relieves the angularity. The door is surrounded by small tabs of cut stone that project into the brickwork, giving it a quoinlike effect, a design commonly used for Tudor Revival entrances. The house was designed for Stuart B. Taylor.

22. 107, 109, and 113 Hampshire Road, 1927–30

CSPD

Go up Hampshire Road, the last street to be developed in the Sedgwick Tract area. Many of its houses are surrounded by beautifully landscaped gardens. On the west side of the tree-lined street, these three Tudor Revival houses form a coherent group.

23. 715 Rugby Road, 1932

CSPD

This picturesquely massed Tudor Revival house is surrounded by a fine landscaped garden. A prominent chimney, a variegated roofline with pitched gables, stone and brick facing, as well as false half timbering and casement windows with small lights are elements that make this house a good example of its style.

24. 411 Sedgwick Drive, 1957

Architect: Charles Umbrecht, Syracuse

CSPD

The shingled two-story cottage with one-story side wings fits well into its surroundings. Its size and form and the use of 6/6 double-hung windows is reminiscent of a Cape Cod, a vernacular house that has been built since colonial times. It was designed and built by Charles Umbrecht (1888–1969), who worked in this area as an architect and builder. He specialized in residential buildings and looked toward vernacular Colonial architecture and early nineteenth-century designs for inspiration. After he graduated from Syracuse University's School of Architecture, he was hired by Henry Bacon to design the outside columns and the housing of the tablets containing the Gettysburg Address in the Lincoln Memorial in Washington, D.C.

25. 408 Sedgwick Drive, 1924

Architect: Paul Hueber, Syracuse

CSPD

If one ignores the northern vegetation and the absence of livestock in the yard one might feel transplanted to somewhere south of the border by looking at this Mission style house. Built for Arthur Weiler, the house was constructed around a courtyard. A tile roof, a second-story loggia, and fine ironwork are distinguishing features. But, as noted by the architectural firm, "more notable and unseen is the construction of the house. It has reinforced concrete floor systems, supported on steel and masonry columns, and solid exterior walls of poured concrete, which are stuccoed on the outside and lined with cork on the interior."

25. 408 Sedgwick Drive

26. 300 Sedgwick Drive, 1926–27

CSPD

Textured brick, false half timbering, and a slate roof on the exterior of this picturesquely massed Tudor Revival house provide textural variety. Notice the chimney pots on top of the prominent chimney.

By 1924, Wendell Terrace was laid out in lots somewhat larger than those on Farmer Street or Brattle Road north of Sedgwick. The houses, too, tend to be larger.

28. 104 Wendell Terrace, detail

28. 104 Wendell Terrace

27–29. 101, 104, and 106 Wendell Terrace, 1925–30
CSPD

All are Georgian Revival houses. Noteworthy is the entrance at 104 Wendell Terrace (**28**). Emphatically three-dimensional, its open-topped pediment as well as the keystone above the windows are of cast stone, presenting a welcome color contrast to the dark brick.

30. 108 Wendell Terrace, 1929–31
Architect: Albert L. Brockway, Syracuse
CSPD

Local physician Dr. H. B. Doust lived here with his family. In 1908, Doust founded one of the first tuberculosis clinics in New York State outside of Saranac Lake and New York City. He also helped to establish the Onondaga County Sanatorium (1916) and was named health commissioner in 1938. The house of cottage design has a roof covered with slate. The stone used for the first story and the chimney, replete with chimney pots, came from Brockway's farm, Knollwood, in Dewitt, New York.

31. 109 Wendell Terrace, 1925

CSPD

A good example of the Mission style, this house has a tile roof, stuccoed facades, and a pedimented entrance bay that is marked by a curvilinear gable. Local legend has it that the house functioned as a speakeasy during the years of Prohibition.

32. 111 Wendell Terrace, ca. 1925

CSPD

The house was built for Joseph Cashier, owner of a sheet-metal and roofing business. It displays some Tudor Revival elements, such as false half timbering in the gabled roof dormer and decorative vergeboards, multipaned casement windows, and a Tudor-arch entrance with cast-stone surrounds and a crocket (an ornament carved in various leaf shapes). Note the decorative copper gutters and downspouts, and the multicolored slate roof.

33. 115 Wendell Terrace, 1926

Architect: James A. Randall, Syracuse

CSPD

Designed for Dr. Charles Blum and his family, the house is almost square in plan and features some eclectic details, such as lancet windows and an open-topped entrance, inspired by Georgian architecture. A champion tennis player, architect James A. Randall was a founder of the Sedgwick Farm Tennis Club.

Turn right on Rugby Road and make another right on Brattle Road. Here houses are set back at equal distance from the tree-lined road, and most of them are of Colonial, Georgian, and Tudor Revival styles.

34–35. 268 (1928–30) and 264 Brattle Road (1928)

Architect: Paul Hueber, Syracuse

CSPD

Both Tudor Revival houses are distinguished by steep gables and false half timbering. 264 Brattle Road (**35**) features a stacked chimney. It was built for Louis J. Steigerwald, president of the Cathedral Candle Company that was founded by his father Jacob in 1897. The latter worked as an apprentice candle maker for Francis Baumer, whose firm later became Will & Baumer Inc., well-known local candle makers.

36. 240 Brattle Road, ca. 1950

Architect: Charles Umbrecht, Syracuse

CSPD

This shingled two-story cottage with two prominent end chimneys and two narrow side wings is a twentieth-century version of the Cape Cod cottage, a folk house, usually of one to one and one-half stories, that has been in use for about 200 years.

36. 240 Brattle Road

37. 209 Brattle Road, 1910
Architect: William H. Miller, Ithaca, N.Y.
CSPD

At one time, Adelaide White, wife of Hamilton S. White, owned this two-story frame house. The glassed-in front porch was added later. Notice the details in the main gable.

William H. Miller (1841–1922) was a successful architect in Ithaca, New York. His connection with Cornell University President Andrew Dickson White brought him a number of commissions at Cornell University. In Syracuse, he designed the Howard G. White mansion (now demolished) on James Street and the Nettleton House at 705 Walnut Avenue.

38–39. 206 (1922) and 204 Brattle Road (1924)
Architect: Merton E. Granger, Syracuse
CSPD

Both are Tudor Revival houses. 206 Brattle Road (**38**) was built for J. F. Friedl, who owned a paper-box company. The landscaping, of which the house is an integral part, is especially handsome. 204 Brattle Road (**39**), which still has its original slate roof, was the home of Dr. Carl E. Muench, who practiced medicine here for over fifty years and helped establish Crouse-Irving Memorial Hospital.

Merton E. Granger (1882–1974) graduated from the School of Architecture at Syracuse University in 1909 and started his practice in Syracuse in 1917. In 1944, he became the senior partner in the firm of Granger and Gillespie, from which he retired in 1973. In addition to designing residences—Granger at one time worked in Ward's office—the firm specialized in the design of hospitals and health centers.

38. 206 Brattle Road

40. 201 Brattle Road, 1930
Architect: Paul Hueber, Syracuse
CSPD

Simple lines distinguish this two-story Colonial Revival house. The five-bay facade of the main section is flanked by end chimneys and is symmetrically articulated. The centrally placed entrance was inspired by that of Federal style houses. The form of the house replicates colonial building practices, giving the appearance that additions were made and that the house grew slowly over the years, thus reflecting changing needs of the household. The brick house was built for Tyler Gregory, and it was the largest residence that Paul Hueber designed. The first Sedgwick Farm Tennis Club once occupied this site.

41. 202 Sedgwick Drive, 1915
Architect: Ward Wellington Ward, Syracuse
CSPD

Harrell S. Tenny commissioned Ward to design this asymmetrically massed Tudor Revival house of brick and false half timbering with ornamental work above first-story windows. A roof detail in the form of a gable makes this "the house of three gables."

42. 204 Sedgwick Drive, 1926
Architect: Melvin L. King, Syracuse

CSPD

The Georgian Revival house has a finely detailed entrance with sidelights, topped by a semicircular opening. Tall first-story windows are divided by pilasters. It was originally the home of John C. Marsellus, chairman of the board of Marsellus Casket Company and former director of First Trust and Deposit Company, for which Melvin L. King designed several branch offices throughout the city.

43. 209 Sedgwick Drive, 1923
Architect: Paul Hueber, Syracuse

CSPD

The original owner of the Georgian Revival house was Robert Page, president of Merchants' Delivery Service, the first delivery service for parcels in Syracuse. A hipped roof of clay tiles covers a symmetrically articulated house that is square in plan and flanked by two lower wings.

44. 205 Sedgwick Drive, 1925
Architect: Gordon A. Wright, Syracuse

CSPD

An open-topped pediment of cast stone embellishes the entrance that also features a Doric frieze. The Georgian Revival house was designed for Albert F. Hills, who once was president of Crouse-Hinds Company.

45. 108 Sedgwick Drive, 1925

CSPD

The former Nelson Hyde residence with a stuccoed exterior, and its original red tile roof, grillwork above the entrance, and an arcaded gateway is an example of the Mission style.

James Street was once considered Syracuse's most exclusive residential area. During the second part of the nineteenth century, it became home to well-to-do Syracusans who seemed to vie with each other in the size and grandeur of their homes and gardens. As early as 1842, Moses DeWitt Burnet built his imposing Greek Revival house here when the street was known as Foot Street. At this time, John Wilkinson lived in a house that was surrounded by beautiful and extensive gardens, and was bounded by James Street and Hawley Avenue. One of the finest Greek Revival houses in the area, featuring a two-story Ionic portico and side wings, was the home of General Leavenworth and his family (1839–43; Elijah T. Hayden) at the corner of James and McBride streets. Architect and owner may have been inspired by designs published in Minard Lafever's *Modern Builders' Guide* (1833). The house was demolished in 1950, a time that marked the beginning of the destruction of James Street as a residential area. Measured drawings of the Leavenworth house were published in *Great Georgian Houses of America* (compiled by Architects' Emergency Committee, 1970). When in mid-nineteenth century the Romantic movement with its picturesque building styles captured people's imagination, Charles B. Sedgwick built a Gothic Revival cottage on James Street in 1845. It was designed by nationally known architect Alexander Jackson Davis. Before the Sedgwick house was destroyed in 1962, photographic records were made by the Historic American Building Survey for deposit in the Library of Congress. As houses on James Street became vacant in mid-twentieth century, city planners did not want to repeat the example of West Genesee Street. Once lined by handsome residences, surrounded by fine gardens, and shaded by trees, that street was taken over almost completely by car dealers by the 1960s. Residences were replaced by offices and apartment buildings in hopes of somehow preserving the genteel character of James Street. A few of the older homes (listed below) remain and allow a glimpse into the street's erstwhile elegance. Upper James Street to Teall Avenue (1100–1600 blocks), developed during the early decades of the twentieth century, is still relatively intact and predominantly residential.

Other notable houses and sites in the area but not on the tour follow.

W. E. Kane House, 1916
1208–1212 James Street
Design and construction: W. E. Kane, Syracuse

The imposing former residence is now used as an office building. The house is of poured concrete, and the exterior is stuccoed. A symmetrical main facade, exterior and interior details, and a grand entrance are classically inspired.

1111 James Street, 1925
Architect: Dwight James Baum, Syracuse
Renovation: 1981–85, Schopfer Architects, Syracuse

This elegant Spanish Colonial Revival house was designed for Mrs. Benjamin E. Chase. Later the home of prominent businessman Hurlburt W. Smith, the building is now adaptively reused and accommodates office space. It is one of the few remaining James Street mansions and is at present home to Schopfer Architects.

Corinthian Club, 1853
930 James Street
Additions and renovations: 1878, 1882, Joseph Lyman Silsbee, Syracuse; alteration and complete remodeling: 1893–94

Formerly known as the Barnes-Hiscock Residence, the house was originally built in 1853 as an Italian villa. In 1878, Silsbee made interior changes and added bays, dormers, porches, and a porte cochere. When Frank Hiscock became the new owner, Silsbee remodeled the dining room (1882). In the 1890s, a third story containing the ballroom was added, and the house received a Georgian Revival facade. Extensive gardens, including a water garden, required the care of three gardeners. The Corinthian Foundation, a not-for profit organization, purchased the house in 1947 and rented it to LeMoyne College one year later. Essentially unchanged, the house is at present used by the Corinthian Club, a private women's club that has occupied the building since its founding in 1949.

405 Oak Street, 1890
Architects: Kirby & Bates, Syracuse
Renovation: 1982, Zausmer-Frisch Associates Inc., Syracuse

This handsome Queen Anne house was once the residence of Justin Seubert and his family, and is now adaptively reused to accommodate office and residential space. Seubert had a wine cellar in his basement and a parlor big enough for chamber concerts. He had the parlor ceiling insulated with tanbark so that concerts would not disturb sleeping children upstairs (the parlor is now the reception area for one of the tenants).

213 Highland Avenue, ca. 1856
Architect: James Coburn, Syracuse
CSPD

James Coburn, listed in the *Syracuse City Directory* as "Master Builder," designed this handsome Italian villa for Lyman Stevens. The size of the house and the attention paid to details—ornamental brackets supporting overhanging eaves, the cornice line emphasized by a scalloped frieze, finely detailed Palladian windows—indicate that the owner was prosperous. Spacious rooms have high ceilings, ornate cornices, and ornamental fireplaces. Stevens was a salt merchant and was mayor of Syracuse in 1855. He built three houses for his three daughters next door at

209, 207, and 205 Highland Avenue, ca. 1874
CSPD

These are also good examples of the Italian Villa style. Rectangular in plan, these brick houses have overhanging eaves, tall, narrow first-floor windows—all windows have ornate surrounds—and low-pitched hipped roofs with towers. Only 209 Highland Avenue still has the original Italianate entrance porch. The porches of 207 and 205 Highland Avenue have been changed.

110 Highland Street, 1913
Architect: Ward Wellington Ward, Syracuse

The former Frank A. Garrett residence is stuccoed and has ornamental latticework on its main facade and a false thatched roof. This kind of roof was sometimes used on Tudor Revival houses to mimic the picturesque thatched roofs of rural England but with modern materials. Surrounding the fireplace in the inglenook is an original tile mosaic mural depicting St. George and the dragon. It was made by Henry Chapman Mercer and gives an English tapestry effect.

Rose Hill Cemetery

Bounded by Lodi, Willow, Highland, and Douglas streets is Rose Hill Cemetery, which was established during the early nineteenth century as a municipal burial place and closed in 1914. Although now used by some as a park, others choose to vandalize the remaining gravestones. It was once defined by a stone wall along Lodi Street; there was a small caretaker's house, and a handsome entrance designed by Horatio Nelson White. Near Highland Street is an imposing mausoleum that marks the graves of Harvey Baldwin (Syracuse's first mayor) and his family. The older, grander monuments have a view of the city from their hilltop location. Ethnic groups are segregated here. In the northwestern quarter of Rose Hill are the graves of "Africans," according to the map. Then there are sections for Irish, Germans, English, Americans, orphans, and members of the Society of Concord.

Baldwin mausoleum

Fireproof Houses in Eastwood, early 1920s

Architect: Paul Hueber, Syracuse

A group of concrete houses, poured in place, was constructed by Hueber Brothers in the Shotwell Park area. Exterior walls are of concrete, as are floors and interior partitions. Advertised as "fireproof homes," they were built for speculation. Designed in a variety of popular architectural styles of the time, the houses remain relatively unchanged for obvious reasons. Some examples are 236, 256, and 260 Shotwell Parkway.

It has been said that what Brooklyn is to New York, Eastwood is to Syracuse. At one time, it was good farmland and was given to an American Revolutionary soldier. By 1896, a thriving little community had developed with a stable population of Irish, Italians, and Poles. Eastwood was annexed by Syracuse in 1926.

Fireproof houses in Eastwood

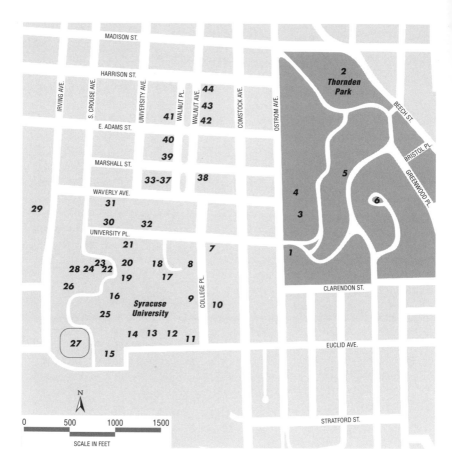

MADISON ST.

HARRISON ST.

IRVING AVE.

S. CROUSE AVE.

UNIVERSITY AVE.

WALNUT PL.

WALNUT AVE.

COMSTOCK AVE.

OSTROM AVE.

E. ADAMS ST.

MARSHALL ST.

WAVERLY AVE.

UNIVERSITY PL.

COLLEGE PL.

BEECH ST.

BRISTOL PL.

GREENWOOD PL.

CLARENDON ST.

EUCLID AVE.

STRATFORD ST.

**2
Thornden
Park**

5

4

3

6

1

44

43

42

41

40

39

38

33-37

31

32

30

29

21

7

23

28 24 22

20

18

8

19

17

26

16

9

10

25

*Syracuse
University*

14 13 12

11

27

15

N

0   500   1000   1500

SCALE IN FEET

EAST SIDE

Rose Garden and Thornden Park

Estimated walking time: 45 minutes (Nos. 1–6). To walk from **No. 6** *to* **No. 7** *requires about 20 minutes.*

1. Edmund Mills Rose Garden, 1924

At the southwest corner of Ostrom Avenue and University Place is a delightful rose garden with a pavilion, trellises, and approximately 10,000 roses that were developed from 300 to 400 varieties. Originally three times its present size, it began as the Syracuse University rose garden but fell victim to the expansion of the campus. The city included a rose garden in Thornden Park at the request of the Syracuse Rose Society, which has maintained it since 1923. During peak time, the garden is enjoyed by many, and has recently become a favorite spot for wedding parties.

1. Edmund Mills Rose Garden

2. Thornden Park

CSPS

Thornden Park evolved from farmland, to a private estate, and finally to a public park. In 1855, James Haskins, a wealthy salt manufacturer, bought the land from local farmers (the Ostroms), built his house there, and cultivated his garden. After Haskins' death in 1875, Alexander H. Davis purchased the estate, named it Thornden, and built a larger Tudor style house around the older core building. With the help of his chief gardener David Campbell, who later became superintendent of parks in Syracuse, Davis further improved the grounds. He became a collector of trees that would survive the harsh Syracuse climate. Sections of his estate were developed as hunting grounds for deer and pheasant; part of it was a small golf course. After an unsuccessful attempt at being elected to the United States Congress, Davis left the country to live in Europe.

During World War I, the land was used by an Italian truck farmer who raised vegetables and wheat. Later, a variety of functions were suggested for the park. At one time, it was considered as a site for the Everson Museum as well as for a junior high school and a housing tract. In 1921, the city bought the estate, which included the Davis house and various outbuildings on seventy-five acres of land. With a fine existing collection of ornamental plants, the park was "ready-made." During the 1920s and 1930s, part of the English garden landscape that once surrounded the house was converted into recreational areas. The Thornden swimming pool opened in 1927, and the amphitheater on the former site of Haskins' trout pond was dedicated in 1930. Plans were made to renovate the Davis mansion for use as a community house, but it burned in 1929. Many of the formal gardens were removed in the 1960s, and recreational facilities were emphasized instead. The Thornden Park Association was formed in 1983 to improve and restore the park.

3. Rock Grotto
Restoration: 1986–, City of Syracuse Department of Parks and Recreation, and Thornden Park Association

A stone stairway leads to the rock grotto, which is a survivor of an extensive formal perennial garden. The lily pond and rock garden have been restored. A few steps beyond, among the remains of the park's pinetum, is the

4. Herb Garden
The herb garden has been restored to its original 1939 design. Although it is colorful and aromatic, few visitors to the park notice it. Formally dedicated in 1941, it is maintained by the Home Garden Club.

5. Amphitheater, 1930
Restoration: 1989, City of Syracuse Department of Parks and Recreation

A WPA project, the amphitheater was built on the site of an old fish pond and included six rock-faced terraces, each supporting two rows of wooden benches. After years of neglect and nonuse, the amphitheater functions again as a place for concerts and special festivities.

5. Amphitheater

6. Elon P. Stewart Reservoir, 1925

The reservoir stands guard on top of Thornden Park Hill. Named after a former city water engineer, it was built to provide adequate service to the East Side. Steel tanks holding water are enclosed in limestone and brick. Appropriately, Neptune's head and tridents beckon from the Neoclassical portal.

Syracuse University

The information is based on the article "A Place to Learn", 1984. *Syracuse University Alumni News* , 64 (3) (Spring): 16–33.

*Estimated walking time: 1 hour (**Nos. 7–32**). To walk from **No. 32** to **No. 33** requires about 5 minutes.*

Were Andrew Dickson White, prominent Syracusan and first president of Cornell University, to have had his way, "the Hill" would be home to Cornell rather than to Syracuse University. A few years before the trustees of Syracuse University bought the site, White suggested it as a location to Ezra Cornell, founder of the university that is named after him. But Cornell had other plans—his own farm in Ithaca—and so the great view from the hill of the city and of Onondaga Lake would be enjoyed by all who attended and worked at Syracuse University; Cornellians were obliged to settle for Cayuga Lake and a picturesque landscape. The Hill, indeed, is a fine site, and on a clear day one has a splendid view of the city and the surrounding countryside. The architectural collage that came to be built on that hill was considered by some as "deplorable in the crudity of the parts and absence of anything that can decently be called whole" and by others as "a rich panorama." It might be best to keep an open mind and view it in the context of history.

In 1870, a committee appointed by the board of trustees of the recently chartered university bought a farmland tract of fifty acres, most of which belonged to George F. Comstock. Three years later, Syracuse University

Syracuse University campus, late 1880s, looking northwest, Crouse College, Administration Building, Hall of Languages (l–r). Courtesy Onondaga Historical Association, Syracuse

moved from its downtown location in the Myers Block (on the southeast corner of Montgomery and East Washington streets) to its new home on the Hill and into its first building, the Hall of Languages (**No. 20**). Because of the economic depression that followed the Panic of 1873, it remained the university's only building for fourteen years. The first chairman of the board of trustees, the Reverend Jesse Peck (Syracuse University was closely affiliated with the Methodist church), proposed a campus plan that would include seven buildings. Like so many subsequent plans, it was not realized. In the 1880s, three more buildings were constructed (**Nos. 22, 26,** and **28**), designed in accordance with the popular architectural styles of the time. In the early 1890s, the Women's Gym (demolished) was built, open space behind the buildings was graded, and a playing field known as the Old Oval was created.

The size of the campus doubled at the turn of the century. The university bought Yates Castle (now demolished) and its surrounding fourteen acres of grounds. Four new buildings were constructed (**Nos. 18, 25**), and Winchell (1900) and Haven Hall (1904),the first two dormitories (both demolished). Mount Olympus, later to become the site of another dormitory complex, was then used as a golf course. A contest to plan the campus was opened to twenty architects who had graduated from Syracuse University. The winning plan of 1906, by S.U. architecture professors Frederick W. Revels (1869–1937) and Earl Hallenbeck (1876–1934), attempted to order the hitherto anarchic building activities and shape the campus. The plan oriented the campus on a north-south axis. It changed the Old Oval to a central quadrangle that was to be bordered on all sides by new buildings. Many of the structures were designed by Revels and Hallenbeck between 1904 and 1921. In keeping with the popular Beaux-Arts trends, the architects chose a modified Renaissance mode as a unifying style. Frederick L. Olmsted, Jr., son of the famous landscape architect, was hired to develop a landscaping plan. He submitted a number of them, one of which was accepted but never implemented.

These were the days of Chancellor James Roscoe Day, who, according to writer Upton Sinclair, was obsessed with the growth of the university as well as with the "evils of socialism" throughout his term (1894–1922). During World War I, Dr. Day showed his patriotism by converting SU into an army center with a mess hall behind Sims dormitory. "Hell is too good for young men unwilling to serve," said he, and ROTC (Reserve Officers' Training Corps) came to SU in 1917 at Day's insistence. Alarmed, the university trustees lobbied for his resignation and, not being too successful with it, enlisted the help of the *Post-Standard*, according to Sinclair. The chancellor was presented with his forthcoming resignation on the front page and had to comply. Dean Henry A. Peck was appointed as acting chancellor but soon thereafter died of a heart attack. Day returned and did not formally retire until 1922.

Between the two world wars, the building activities of the university slowed down; but again there was to be a new order. In 1927, nationally known architects John Russell Pope (1874–1937) and Dwight James Baum (1886–1939) developed a new fifty-year master plan: the eclectic architecture was to be unified, and related academic disciplines were to be grouped together in a series of quadrangles. The plan also called for the Old Oval to be divided into two quads, with Hendricks Chapel (**No. 16**) as a focal point, and for the College of Forestry (now the State University of New York–College of Environmental Science and Forestry—SUNY-ESF) to occupy a third quadrangle. An enlarged medical center was to be located across Irving Avenue. To unify this new group of buildings stylistically, the then-popular Georgian Revival style was chosen. A few Georgian buildings were constructed before the Great Depression intervened. The Pope-Baum plan was implemented in part: their suggestion of a main quadrangle with Hendricks Chapel as its centerpiece was followed, and all subsequent plans included the design of a series of quadrangles as they had proposed.

There were feverish building activities between 1942 and 1969: of the sixty major buildings on the campus today, forty were built then. And in 1948 local landscape architect Noreda Rotunno unveiled yet another master plan: it called for the demolition of several older buildings, Yates Castle among them. The pace of construction to fit urgent building needs modified his plan.

To alleviate a housing crisis, 300 temporary structures had to be built for students entering the university after World War II, 200 of which were located south of the campus off East Colvin Street. That area, now known as Skytop, has evolved into South Campus, where student housing and administrative buildings are located. Permanent dormitory complexes were developed on Mount Olympus and north of the campus facing Thornden Park as well.

New York-based architect Lorimer Rich (1892–1978) and his local associates Harry A. and F. Curtis King attempted to make the new campus buildings—among them the Ernest I. White Law College (1954), the Women's Building (1953), and various dormitories—conform to the existing architecture. It was not an easy task. To be consistent with materials used for the older buildings, they employed brick facing with limestone trim, but the modern buildings added yet another layer to the architectural collage of the campus, as did the two most recent additions of Post-Modern persuasion, the Science and Technology Center and the Dorothea Ilgen Shaffer Art Building.

Because of space limitations, not all campus buildings are included in the walking tour, nor are the buildings of the SUNY-ESF campus directly south of the Syracuse University campus. The tour covers the Comstock Tract ("Old Row") buildings (National Register Historic District), as well as a few recent buildings. Sculptures by faculty and students are an integral and enhancing part of the campus, but because their placement is often changed, it is not possible to list them in this walking tour. A guide to the artwork may be obtained from the Joe and Emily Lowe Art Gallery at Syracuse University.

7. Psi Upsilon House, 1898
101 College Place
Architect: Wellington W. Taber, Syracuse
NRHP

The Neoclassical Revival building is one of two fraternity houses left on College Place. Located on a prominent site, the exterior of the building has two monumental porticoes (one on the west, the other on the north facade), an octagonal cupola, and classically inspired details.

Wellington W. Taber (1866–1943) graduated from the School of Architecture at Syracuse University and was a member of Psi Upsilon. He worked as superintendent of buildings in this city and as New York State supervisor of construction for several state buildings, Auburn and Attica penitentiaries among them.

8. Lyman Hall, 1907
Corner of College Place and University Place
Architects: Earl Hallenbeck and Frederick W. Revels, Syracuse
NRHD

This building of modified Beaux-Arts style anchors the west end of the campus It is said that the crown of its tower is a scaled-down version of the third century a.d. temple of Venus at Baalbek. Originally known as Lyman Hall of Natural History, it was funded with money given by trustee John Lyman as a memorial to his two deceased daughters. A Natural History Museum was once located on the top floor. Unfortunately, a fire in 1937 destroyed many of the artifacts. The large lobby lends itself well to sculpture exhibits. Oak woodwork, ornamental balustrades, and mosaic floors are among its interior features.

Said architectural critic Montgomery Schuyler, "the Hall of Languages and the College of Applied Sciences are the sincere efforts of an incompetent designer...and as such are almost immune from criticism. They have not the outrageous self-complacency and aggressiveness of such creations as the Natural History Building of which it is so clear that the author has never been forewarned with Emerson, that the vice of the times and the country is an excessive pretension." The only campus building Schuyler considered to of be "positive architectural interest" was Archbold Stadium, which has since been demolished to make way for the Carrier Dome (**No. 26**).

9. Slocum Hall, 1918
Architect: Earl Hallenbeck, Syracuse
NRHD

The building's exterior is of granite and limestone, and was to house the College of Agriculture. Its imposing main entrance, topped by a balcony and framed by monumental columns, faces College Place. The building originally had four entrances; three are left. Slocum Hall was given to the university by Margaret Olivia Slocum Sage in honor of her father, General Joseph H. Slocum, who was apparently one of the first in the country to be interested in the scientific development of agricultural education. Since the College of Agriculture was discontinued in 1933, the building has housed a number of schools and colleges. The School of Architecture, which formerly had occupied space in Crouse College and Bowne Hall, moved into the building in 1919 and remains there today.

10. Science and Technology Center, 1989
Architects: Kling Partnership, Philadelphia, and
Koetter, Kim and Associates, Boston

The Post-Modern structure covers a five-acre lot between University and College places and Euclid and Comstock avenues. It houses research and educational facilities in computer science, electrical and computer engineering, information studies, and chemistry, as well as the Center for Advanced Technology in Computer Applications and Software Engineering (Case Center). Said former Chancellor Melvin Eggers, "this is a state-of-the-art center, which will serve to strengthen the area and state economy. Through increased University-industry collaboration, it will quicken the rate at which basic research conducted at the center will be translated into commercial application."

12. Dorothea Ilgen Shaffer Art Building

11. Sims Hall, 1907

Architects: Frederick W. Revels and Earl Hallenbeck, Syracuse
Renovation: 1989–91, Design and Construction, Syracuse University
NRHD

The reinforced concrete structure, faced with marble, red brick, and terra cotta, was originally built as a dormitory for men, which explains the confusion one experienced in its interior until recently: the building had several entrances that were not connected by hallways and stairs. Since 1963, it has housed classrooms and offices. The building was named after Charles N. Sims, Syracuse University's third chancellor.

12. Dorothea Ilgen Shaffer Art Building, 1990

Architects: Koetter, Kim and Associates, Boston, and Fuligni-Fragola, Syracuse

Sculpture Court, 1991

Architects: Schleicher-Soper, Syracuse

Post-Modern in style, the building conforms stylistically to the Science and Technology Center. The enlarged Joe and Emily Lowe Gallery (1952; King & King, and Lorimer Rich) has become part of the new building, but most important, the Shaffer Building has consolidated previously dispersed sites of art education in one place. "It brings together numerous artistic disciplines from the earliest forms, painting and drawing, to the most modern computer generated design," says dean of the School of Art, Donald M. Lantzy. And to quote the former director of the School of Art and well-known sculptor Rodger Mack: "You can feel a sense of creative energy in the building. What we planned to happen, has happened." A commanding drum, which allows painters to get northern light exposure, anchors the building to the quad and firmly states its presence.

The sculpture court between the Shaffer Art Building and Bowne Hall accommodates three sculptures by Ivan Mestrovic, *Moses, Job,* and *Supplicant Persephone* (Mestrovic was a professor of sculpture at SU from 1947 to 1955), and Luise Kaish's *Saltine Warrior.* These are permanent installations. Two spaces are reserved for changing exhibitions of work by faculty and students.

13. Bowne Hall, 1907

Architects: Frederick W. Revels and Earl Hallenbeck, Syracuse
NRHD

Named after university trustee Samuel Bowne, the tile-roofed building with its Neoclassical exterior of brick and terra cotta was hailed as fireproof and was originally designed to house the chemistry department. Some of the chemistry labs are still used; otherwise the building serves as classroom, office, and administrative space.

14. Carnegie Library, 1907

Architects: Frederick W. Revels and Earl Hallenbeck, Syracuse

NRHD

In Beaux-Arts fashion a grand stairway leads to the columned portico that shelters the entrance (now closed) to the library. Carnegie Library and Bowne Hall face the main quadrangle and close off its southern border. Originally designed as Syracuse University's main library, it now houses the Science and Technology Library. The steel-frame building faced with gray brick and terra cotta was named after its donor, Andrew Carnegie.

15. Archbold Gymnasium, 1908

Architects: Frederick W. Revels and Earl Hallenbeck, Syracuse

Renovation and addition: 1952, Lorimer Rich, New York

NRHD

Flanagan Gymnasium, 1990

Architects: Bohlin, Powell, Larkin & Cywinski, Wilkes-Barre, Pa.

Flanking Carnegie Library to the west stands the building named after its donor, John D. Archbold, friend of Chancellor Day, chairman of the board of trustees of Syracuse University, and president of Standard Oil of New Jersey. He was an important benefactor during Chancellor Day's term. Archbold Gym was built in conjunction with Archbold Stadium (1907; demolished). In 1947, the building was nearly destroyed by fire, and consequently only the front outer walls are original to the structure. Lorimer Rich designed an addition with a swimming pool in 1952. Flanagan Gymnasium, connected to Archbold Gymnasium by a skybridge, was built for intramural athletics.

16. Hendricks Memorial Chapel

16. Hendricks Memorial Chapel, 1930

Architects: John Russell Pope and Dwight James Baum, New York
Restoration of interior: 1984, Design and Construction, Syracuse University
NRHD

Bequeathed by New York State Senator Francis Hendricks in memory of his wife Eliza Jane Hendricks, the chapel was designed by John Russell Pope and Syracuse alumnus Dwight James Baum. Modeled after Jeffersonian prototypes such as the Rotunda at the University of Virginia, the brick and limestone building is topped by a steel-framed, lead-covered dome. Its plan is based on the octagon, the circle, and the Greek cross. Monumental steps lead to a classically inspired portico with Ionic columns. The core of the building is a handsome auditorium. Here the geometry of the plan is repeated in its Neoclassical ornament, in the shape of the skylight, and in some of the window openings. A complex space, it is well worth a visit. According to Pope and Baum's master plan, the building was meant to be the focal point between two important quadrangles. The Women's Gym, which had been on this site, was removed. The location of interdenominational Hendricks Chapel reflects its architectural importance as well as its central role in the life of the university community.

16. Hendricks Memorial Chapel, interior

17. Machinery Hall, 1907

Architects: Gaggin & Gaggin, Syracuse
NRHD

The reinforced concrete and steel building, with rough-cut masonry block facing and covered with a tile roof, is straightforward and factorylike. It reflects its original purpose—to carry the load of heavy laboratory equipment. After various other uses, the building has functioned as a computer center since 1964.

18. Lyman Cornelius Smith Hall, 1902

Architect: Edwin H. Gaggin, Syracuse
NRHD

The building was given to Syracuse University to promote mechanical engineering. The donor, Lyman Cornelius Smith, originally a gunmaker, turned to the manufacture of the L. C. Smith typewriter, to later establish the Smith-Corona Company. (At one time, the manufacture of typewriters was an important local industry.) The exterior is of rough-cut masonry. Fronting University Place, the building's main facade is symmetrically articulated with classically inspired ornamentation and a porticoed entrance flanked by arcaded towers. The building was originally designed to have laboratories in the basement, machine shops on the first floor, and classroom and offices above.

19. Huntington Beard Crouse Hall, 1962
Architects: King & King Architects, Syracuse
The Passion of Sacco and Vanzetti, 1966–67
Artist: Ben Shahn

A mosaic and enamel mural triptych covers the east facade of the modern building known as HBC. It depicts the political activities, trial, and death of two Italian immigrants who were convicted of a 1920 robbery and murder, which they may not have committed and for which they were executed in 1927. The three-paneled mural was designed and executed in France and installed here in 1966–67.

The building was named after Huntington Beard Crouse, who founded the Crouse-Hinds Company with Jesse C. Hinds in 1897. It was the first completely air-conditioned building on campus. A welded-rod sculpture of bronze and steel, *The Syracuse Nova* (1961), by Harry Bertoia, hangs from the lobby ceiling. The landscaped area between HBC and the Hall of Languages was designed by landscape architect Noreda Rotunno of Syracuse.

20. Hall of Languages, 1871–73
Architect: Horatio Nelson White, Syracuse
Remodeling of interior: 1979, Sargent Webster Crenshaw & Folley, Syracuse; design consultants, Architectural Resources, Cambridge, Mass.
NRHP NRHD

On 8 May 1873, students and faculty assembled for the last time at the Myers Block downtown, from where they walked in formal procession to "Piety Hill" to dedicate their first campus building, the Hall of Languages, known as HL. According to Professor Harley J. McKee, plans for the building had been submitted by several architects, W. L. Woollett of Albany and Archimedes Russell of Syracuse among them. Although the trustees chose Horatio Nelson White's Second Empire style design, Woollett and Russell must have been retained in some capacity because Woollett was paid $300 and Russell $200 for architectural services, and they also received "thanks for donating the remainder of their bill." In 1873, HL was surrounded by a hayfield; a $200 profit from the sale of hay helped with mortgage payments but not with payments for the architects, or so it seems. The cost of the building was $136,000. Of Onondaga limestone and having an H-shaped plan, the building housed the whole university for sixteen years. A chapel occupied the entire central portion on the top floor, and the two towers held tanks of water in case of fire, a necessary precaution for a building

20. Hall of Languages

with a wooden floor system. A central cupola above the clock was added in 1887. The name "John Dustin Archbold College of Liberal Arts" was placed into the arch of the front entrance in 1914 to honor the Standard Oil executive who was a university trustee and benefactor. In 1979, the interior was gutted and completely remodeled.

21. Place of Remembrance Memorial, 1990
Architects: Schleicher-Soper, Syracuse

The entrance to the university from University Place is axially aligned with the entrance to the Hall of Languages. The esplanade contains a memorial dedicated to Syracuse University students who were killed in 1988 by a terrorist attack on Pan American Flight 103 over Lockerbie, Scotland.

22. William Pearson Tolley Administration Building, 1888–89 (former von Ranke Library)
Architect: Archimedes Russell, Syracuse
Addition of west wing: 1903, Frederick W. Revels, Syracuse
NRHD

The structure was built to house the famous book collection of German historian Leopold von Ranke that was donated to the university by the Reverend John M. Reid, one-time president of Genesee College at Lima, New York, where Syracuse University originated. The Romanesque Revival brick building with corner towers and turrets sits on a granite base and originally had an asymmetrical plan. The terra cotta flower detail in the pediment of the entrance bay is a Queen Anne element, and the large entrance arch is a Richardsonian Romanesque feature. The building's design is related to that of Crouse College, which was built at the same time. Because it was to function as a library, its interior was made as fireproof as was then possible. The Administration Building's form was changed and made symmetrical with the addition of the west wing. In 1907, the books were moved to the Carnegie Library, and the building was remodeled and renamed. The first cafeteria on campus was located in the building's basement.

23. Abraham Lincoln, 1930
Sculptor: James Earl Fraser

A bronze sculpture depicting the young Lincoln as the "strong woodsman, the man of poetic vision, and the philosopher" was placed on the east court between Maxwell and the Administration Building in 1968. This casting was made especially for Syracuse University. The sculptor James Earl Fraser was known as the designer of the buffalo nickel. He also designed *The End of the Trail*, another depiction of the young Lincoln, which may be found on the SUNY-ESF campus south of Archbold Gymnasium.

24. Maxwell School of Citizenship and Public Affairs, 1937
Architects: John Russell Pope and Dwight James Baum, New York
NRHD

The building did not appear on the original Pope-Baum plan of 1927. Money for its construction was donated two years later by the North American Holding Company, owned by George H. and Carrie A. Maxwell. The architects Pope and Baum suggested placing the Georgian Revival style structure on Irving Avenue, where they had also wanted the university's main entrance to be. Monumental steps and a colonnade were to lead to the campus, and Maxwell was to be placed on this axis of entry. In accordance with the chancellor's and the donors' wishes, however, the building stands between the Administration Building and Crouse College, thus destroying the architectural coherence between the two older buildings. An imposing portico with composite monumental columns supporting a pediment marks the entrance facing University Place. Its main entrance faces the Administration Building and leads into a lobby with marble floors, a copy of Jean-Antoine Houdon's statue of Washington, and a wall inscription of the Athenian oath of citizenship. Besides office and classroom space, there is an auditorium on the first level; offices and classrooms are upstairs.

25. Steele Hall, 1898
Architect: Edwin H. Gaggin, Syracuse
NRHD

The building is of rock-faced Onondaga limestone and was originally built for the Department of Physics. Dr. J. Dorman Steele, after whom the building is named, taught courses in what was then called "natural philosophy" (now physics). At present, it functions as an administrative building.

26. Holden Observatory, 1887

Architect: attributed to Archimedes Russell, Syracuse

NRHD

Constructed of rock-faced Onondaga limestone with walls two feet thick and a lead-covered dome, it was the second building erected on campus. The donor was Erastus F. Holden, a local coal dealer and vice-president of the board of trustees. It was named in honor of his son, Charles Demarest Holden. He equipped the observatory with an eight-inch Alvan Clark telescope with an electric clock drive, three-inch reversible transit, comet seeker, chronograph, and chronometer. To keep the dome viewing slot in line with the telescope, the dome, set on rollers, is rotated manually. "One of the observatory's brightest moments was in 1939, when Mars passed close to Earth and throngs of people often waited in line until 3 a.m. to catch a glimpse," noted the local paper. By the 1920s, the building was used not for research but for teaching. According-

ing to SU archivist Amy Doherty, "from 1947 to 1956 Holden housed radioactive isotopes used for atomic experiments throughout the university." Although the physics department still uses the telescope for instruction, the space is also used for other purposes. In 1991, the sturdy little structure was moved 200 feet from its location on "Science Hill" to make room for a planned second Maxwell building, Eggers Hall.

26. Holden Observatory (being resettled)

From here you can see the

27. Carrier Dome, 1980

Architects: Finch, Heery, Hueber, Atlanta and Syracuse

Syracuse University attracted architectural attention by the construction of a $27-million building, whose major private donor was the Carrier Corporation. It replaced Archbold Stadium, which when built in 1907 was the largest concrete stadium in the United States. "Notre Dome" has impressive credentials: the fifth largest of six air-supported stadia in the country, the Dome is the only enclosed football stadium on a university campus, and it seats 50,000 people. By creating a difference in air pressure between the exterior and the interior, sixteen fans hold up the building's roof of fiberglass panels that cover an area of six and one-half acres. The Dome also houses the Ernie Davis Room, a small museum that features sports-related exhibits.

28. Crouse College, 1887–89

Architect: Archimedes Russell, Syracuse
Partial restoration: 1974, Design and Construction, Syracuse University
NRHP NRHD

The building has an imposing location on top of the hill. With a commanding view of the city and the surrounding countryside, it originally overlooked Chestnut Street, soon to become Crouse Avenue. The Romanesque Revival structure, with its towers and turrets and a full complement of Queen Anne-inspired ornamentation, is of Longmeadow brownstone and has a granite foundation. From University Avenue, a long staircase leads to the main entrance, which, surrounded by elaborate stone and terra cotta ornamentation, is placed in the large bell tower that has become a symbol of Syracuse University. The building was given to the university by John R. Crouse, a well-to-do local merchant. He wanted the building to be "the best in the country" and asked that it be named Crouse Memorial College for Women. From its beginning, it housed the College of Fine Arts, now the College of Visual and Performing Arts. Crouse, greatly involved with the building, supervised much of the construction. He died before the building was finished, and his son, D. Edgar, continued his father's role as benefactor. The chimes, consisting of nine bells, as well as a Roosevelt organ were also gifts of John Crouse. A grand interior staircase is guarded by a copy of the *Winged Victory* of ca. 300 b.c. (restored in the late 1960s by Professor Rodger Mack and a group of graduate students) and leads to the Memorial Music Hall that occupies the second floor and seats 1,200 people. (The space was for chapel services before Hendricks Chapel was built.) With its

28. Crouse College (r) and Maxwell School of Citizenship and Public Affairs (l)

28. Crouse
College, detail

open-timber ceiling and stained-glass windows, it is one of the finest interior spaces at the university. You may want to sit here on an afternoon when the stained-glass windows color the rays of the sun that model the room's surfaces and highlight its tactile qualities. Imagine that you are sitting on molded wooden chairs (they were replaced by the present seating in the 1950s) and that you are looking at a colorful peacock design in the organ recess. It was covered over when the Roosevelt organ was replaced by a larger Holtcamp organ in the 1950s, and the stage was enlarged.

The College of Fine Arts at Syracuse University began offering a course in architecture in 1873 and was one of the few schools in the United States to do so at that time. Local architects such as Archimedes Russell and Joseph Lyman Silsbee were the first to teach courses in architecture there (without pay). The college even counted a woman among its early graduates in architecture. Early twentieth-century architectural critic Montgomery Schuyler did not like Crouse College either, with its "random aggregation of unstudied form and features." He warned that the "course of architecture at Syracuse will fail of its purpose unless it inculcates upon its students the pri-

Yates Castle, early 1900s, looking northwest from University Hill.
Courtesy Onondaga Historical Association, Syracuse

mary necessity of refraining from doing anything like the buildings of the campus."

Walk around Crouse College and enjoy the intricate detailing on the building's exterior as well as a fine view. Looking northwest toward Irving Avenue, you will see a low stone wall that remains of Yates Castle (1852–55; James Renwick) and its surrounding landscaped gardens, which once included a moat. The twenty-four-room castellated Gothic Revival mansion was variously referred to as Renwick Castle, Longstreet's Folly, and Yates Castle. During its construction, Renwick (1818–95) had also drawn plans for the Smithsonian Institution in Washington, D.C. and was to begin St. Patrick's Cathedral in New York. Built for clothing merchant Cornelius Tyler Longstreet, "the Castle" stood on sixteen acres of landscaped gardens and was sold to Longstreet's partner Alonzo Chester Yates in 1867 when the Longstreets moved to a house on James Street. In 1905, Syracuse University became the owner, and the Castle functioned successively as the home for Syracuse University Teachers' College and the School of Journalism. By the 1950s, it was wedged between four hospitals and the medical school built on or around grounds that had by then shrunk to less than two acres. In 1954, the Castle with its gardens, one of the grandest local expressions of the Romantic movement, was demolished to make way for the addition of a new wing to

29. College of Medicine, Weiskotten Hall, 1937
Architects: John Russell Pope and Dwight James Baum, New York
Addition: ca. 1954

This building was constructed as part of the university's fifty-year plan and designed in the Georgian Revival style. In 1950, Syracuse University sold the College of Medicine to the state of New York.

30. Newhouse I, 1964

Architect: I. M. Pei Associates, New York, and King & King Architects, Syracuse

The modern building occupies the site of Haven Hall, one of the first dormitories. The plan of the pre-stressed concrete structure is of a Greek cross with three stories underneath a flat roof. Combining architectural and sculptural forms and carefully considering the site, its well-known architect, I. M. Pei, saw it as "an iceberg," since most of its spaces are underground. It is named after its donor, Samuel I. Newhouse, university trustee and owner of a publishing empire. The building houses the Newhouse School of Public Communications and was the first of a planned three-building complex connected by a concrete terrace that would coordinate the structures into an architectural unit. Only two were built. At the dedication ceremony in August 1964, President Lyndon Johnson delivered the first part of his Gulf of Tonkin speech. I. M. Pei received the First Honor Award in 1965 from the American Institute of Architects for the design of the building.

30. Newhouse I

31. Newhouse II, 1974

Architects: Skidmore, Owings & Merrill, New York

It is the second of the planned three-building communications complex and houses classrooms and studios for broadcast and film, television and radio.

32. Schine Student Center, 1985

Architects: Edward Larrabee Barnes Associates, New York
Sculpture: Jon Isherwood

A student union building appeared as part of the 1927 Pope-Baum plan but was never built. Sixty years later, the construction of a student center was made possible by a gift from the Schine family. During the early part of the twentieth century, when tickets for the movies could be bought for a nickel, J. Myer Schine owned and operated three movie theaters in downtown Syracuse. The brick-covered modern structure faces inward. Four building blocks, each different in size and function, are connected by a closed court topped by a pyramid. This separation of functions into connected wings is characteristic of modern architecture. The blocks contain a cafeteria and lounge, a meeting hall and student services, a bookstore, and an auditorium. An existing bookstore was incorporated into the new structure. The building can be entered conveniently from four sides. Exterior architectural elements such as large round-arched openings visually refer to older campus buildings across the street. The abstract welded-steel sculpture in the center of the court was created in 1987. The building is not part of the Historic District.

Other Syracuse institutions of higher education but not on the walking tour are:

Onondaga Community College (OCC) on Onondaga Hill

(see South Side tour)

LeMoyne College, 1948

LeMoyne Heights
Architects: Eggers & Higgins, New York

The four-year, coeducational Jesuit college was established in Syracuse in 1946. Its beginnings were humble: classes were held in a building at 254 East Onondaga Street and, later and less humbly, in the former Hiscock Mansion at 930 James Street. In 1948, the college moved into its new home on the former Gifford farm. It was named after French Jesuit Simon LeMoyne, who did missionary work among the Iroquois Confederacy between 1654 and 1662. A notable recent addition to the campus is the LeMoyne College Library (1981; Quinlivan Pierik & Krause, Syracuse).

Walnut Park and Vicinity

NRHD

Because of space limitations, not all properties of the Walnut Park Historic District have been included.

Estimated walking time: 30 minutes (Nos. 33–44)

Reminiscent of a village green, the small park, originally the Stevens farm, was laid out in 1870. George F. Comstock, with a shrewd eye for real estate investment, bought 200 acres of the farm's land and established Walnut Park in 1872. Comstock was a prominent local banker who had also been influential in the metamorphosis of Genesee College (Lima, New York) into Syracuse University. He deeded Walnut Park to the city provided that it would be improved by plantings and landscaping and "would be maintained in suitable order as a public park." Accordingly, elm trees were planted. They died in the 1950s but were replaced twenty years later, because Syracuse University students had raised the money for replanting.

As Syracuse University expanded, properties surrounding Walnut Park owned by Comstock were sold as individual plots. He insisted that it be an enclave for the well-to-do. A local newspaper echoed Comstock's sentiments when it reported that "those that bought their lots of Judge Comstock very early know well that he would not allow a house built unless it reached certain proportions as to price." Built between 1897 and 1930, these houses have similar proportions, are set back at equal distance from the greensward, and with few exceptions are designed in the Neoclassical and Colonial Revival styles, popular at the time of their construction. After 1900, many of the houses were acquired by SU fraternities and sororities. "Fraternity Row," originally located on Irving Avenue, began to move to Walnut Park. Between 1920 and 1930, Greek societies were responsible for the architectural development around the park, and affluent national and alumnae/alumni organizations provided their chapters with new houses.

33. 310 Walnut Place, ca. 1925

NRHD

The large Neoclassical Revival house was originally built for the Sigma Phi Epsilon fraternity. Symmetry, a pedimented classical entrance porch extending the full height but less than the full width, as well as a centrally placed open-topped doorway are distinguishing features.

34. 308 Walnut Place, 1898

NRHD

Originally built as a private residence, it later became home to the Alpha Phi sorority. Its symmetrically articulated five-bay facade, stepped gables, and brick-faced end walls, together with prominent dormers and a Federal style door, make this building a good example of the Colonial Revival style. The fanlight of stained glass bears the sorority's emblem.

35. 306 Walnut Place, 1928
Architect: Marjorie Wright, Syracuse
NRHD

The Tudor Revival house exhibits characteristic features, such as an entrance surrounded by stone tabs, false half timbering, and steep gables. The house was built for Kappa Alpha Theta, of which Marjorie Wright was a member. She worked in the office of her father, the prominent local architect Gordon A. Wright.

36. 304 Walnut Place, 1899
Architect: Gordon A. Wright, Syracuse
NRHD

The Colonial Revival house was designed for George Larrabee, manager of the National Biscuit Company. Prominent dormers and chimneys, shell ornamentation above second-story windows, and a front porch with Ionic columns distinguish the exterior.

37. 300 Walnut Place, 1903
Addition: ca. 1923
NRHD

So popular was this area for the social elite of Syracuse that the Denison family built a large Georgian Revival style house here to be used only for entertainment purposes. The Tri-Delta sorority bought the house twenty years later. It was then that a Doric portico was added to reflect its Greekness.

38. 901 Walnut Avenue, 1907
Addition: 1940s
NRHD

The house is a good example of the Tudor Revival style. It was originally built as a private residence and now houses the Delta Gamma sorority. Only a few changes have been made to the house since it was built; in the 1940s, a side wing was added and a side porch enclosed.

39. 210 Walnut Place, 1897
Alterations: 1920s
NRHD

The Colonial Revival house was built as a residence for prominent local clergyman Bishop Huntington. The house later became a social club for men and subsequently the Phi Beta Phi sorority house. In the 1920s, the building was renovated and gained its present appearance.

40. 200 Walnut Place, ca. 1900

NRHD

Built originally as a residence for the Reverend E. McChesney, the house now is home to the Kappa Phi Delta fraternity. The frame house with its hipped roof and prominent dormers—the central dormer has a Palladian window—and its symmetrically articulated facade divided by Ionic pilasters is a fine example of the Colonial Revival style.

41. John G. Alibrandi, Jr. Catholic Center, ca. 1899

110–112 Walnut Place
NRHD (112 Walnut Place)
Addition: 1982, Hueber Hares Glavin, Syracuse

Much altered since it was built as a residence, the house became the St. Thomas More Chapel. With a modern addition, the complex is identified as the John G. Alibrandi, Jr. Catholic Center, memorializing John Jr. and recognizing the gift by the Alibrandi family that made the building possible. At the center of the new section is the Reservation Chapel, which can be entered from the narthex, or main entrance hall. A folding oak-paneled partition leads to the St. Thomas More Chapel. The addition also contains offices, a multipurpose room, and a kitchen. An open loggia identifies the main approach to the center, creating a small courtyard and bringing both new and old into a uniform scale.

41. John G. Alibrandi, Jr. Catholic Center

On the east side of the park behind a stone wall are three imposing residences that exhibit the wealth and prestige of their former owners.

42. 705 Walnut Avenue, 1905
Architect: William H. Miller, Ithaca, N.Y.

NRHD

William H. Miller designed the house for Albert E. Nettleton, founder of the A. E. Nettleton Company, Syracuse's well-known shoe manufacturing firm, and later president of the Paragon Plaster Company. Faced with Roman brick and covered with a tile roof, the building's main facade features a grand semicircular entrance porch flanked by two hexagonal towers and overlooks Walnut Park. Alpha Chi Omega sorority sisters live there now.

42. 705 Walnut Avenue

43. 703 Walnut Avenue, 1905 (former Horace Wilkinson House)
Architects: Gaggin & Gaggin, Syracuse
Renovation and partial restoration: 1988, Crawford & Stearns, Syracuse

NRHD CSPS

Former President Theodore Roosevelt slept here. That was in 1915, when he was a guest of the Wilkinsons during the Barnes-Roosevelt libel suit. The castlelike stone house was built for Horace S. Wilkinson, founder and chairman of the board of the Crucible Steel Company of America and associate of the typewriter magnate, Lyman C. Smith. Its steeply pitched tiled and gabled roof, its towers and turrets, its battlemented porches and porte cochere, an interior ornamented with fine woodwork, an elaborately carved walnut staircase, and a Moorish room all reflect the intention to impress.

Since mid-twentieth century, the house has been the home of Phi Delta Theta fraternity.

43. 703 Walnut Avenue

44. 701 Walnut Avenue, 1901
Architects: Benson & Brockway, Syracuse
NRHD

The house of Indiana limestone trimmed with red and black brick was built as a residence for William Nottingham, a distinguished local attorney and university trustee. The stately twenty-room house is located on two acres bounded by Comstock Avenue, Harrison Street, and Walnut Park. The structure features massive entrance arches, steep gables, and prominent dormers and chimneys. Woodwork and paneling of oak from England and Canada, ornate fireplaces, and leather-lined walls in the library create a rich interior. A carved central staircase leads to a third-floor grand ballroom, which is no longer used. At one time, there were stables and an ice house on the landscaped grounds. The house was purchased by Syracuse University and became the home of Chancellor James Roscoe Day in 1915. It has continued to be the home of Syracuse University chancellors.

Other buildings of interest in the area but not on the tour are:

Two houses designed by Ward Wellington Ward: **519 Walnut Avenue**, 1911, built as a residence for Herbert Walker, now used as an apartment house, and **604 Walnut Avenue**, 1910, built for Samuel Cook, at present also used as an apartment house, with another entrance at 920 Madison Street.

44. 701 Walnut Avenue

Madison Court Condominiums, 1917 (former Madison School)
Corner of Madison Street and Walnut Avenue
Architect: James A. Randall, Syracuse
Renovation: 1983–85, Stephen Whitney, Rochester

A former city school was recycled into condominiums. The original corridors were kept, and former schoolrooms were gutted and combined into apartments. The auditorium and its stage on the first level were also recycled and became part of the new condominium space.

The firm of Randall & Vedder was responsible for the design of many city schools in the 1920s; among them the Percy Hughes School (1929) at 345 Jamesville Avenue, the first school in the country that was designed for children with disabilities.

Grace Episcopal Church, 1876
819 Madison Street
Architect: Horatio Nelson White, Syracuse
NRHP

A Gothic Revival structure of rock-faced limestone, this church was designed to resemble English village churches. Once, its tall tower could be seen from afar. For safety reasons the upper part of the tower was removed, but otherwise few changes have been made.

Temple Society of Concord, 1910
910 Madison Street
Architect: Alfred C. Taylor, Syracuse, and Arnold W. Brunner, New York
Addition: Mabel Weisberg Religious School, 1960

The imposing Neoclassical Revival temple sits on a commanding site. The first Jewish congregation was formed in the city when twelve Jewish immigrants came to Syracuse from New York. Within three years, the congregation had a synagogue and a cemetery. Their first building was erected in 1851 at Harrison and State streets (Elijah T. Hayden; demolished). The implementation of reformist ideas caused a group of dissenters to leave and form the congregation Adath Yeshurun. The Temple Society of Concord continued to thrive. The congregation still occupies the temple on the hill site. *The Tree of Life*, a stained-glass window designed by Stanley Worden of Henry Keck Stained Glass Studio, was installed there in 1965.

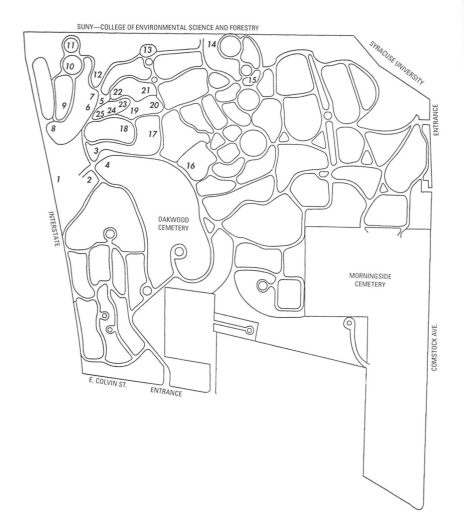

SUNY—COLLEGE OF ENVIRONMENTAL SCIENCE AND FORESTRY

SYRACUSE UNIVERSITY

ENTRANCE

INTERSTATE

OAKWOOD
CEMETERY

MORNINGSIDE
CEMETERY

COMSTOCK AVE.

E. COLVIN ST.

ENTRANCE

Oakwood Cemetery

Prepared by Christine B. Lozner

NRHD CSPS
*Estimated walking time: 1 hour, 30 minutes (**Nos. 1–25**)*

Since its founding in 1859, Oakwood Cemetery has played a dual role in the life of the Salt City. A tranquil and beautiful resting place for the deceased, it is also a historic picturesque landscape filled with art and architecture, and carefully planned for the enjoyment and enrichment of the living. The original sections, located on the west side of today's 160-acre cemetery, are most important historically as a nineteenth-century American landscape type called the rural cemetery. Of considerable interest as well is the grand array of monuments and mausolea that form a virtual outdoor museum of funerary sculpture and architecture, while mirroring the lives of Syracuse's Victorian families.

The 1850s was a period of dynamic growth for Syracuse, and efforts to build a rural cemetery began as early as 1852 with a search for an appropriate site. By this time, the rural cemetery was considered a necessary institution for a truly civilized, successful city. Civic leaders in Syracuse shared the period's moral uneasiness over the seeming chaos and confusion that accompanied growing urbanization. The word cemetery, used for the new burial grounds nationwide, was a good indicator of their founders' intent; derived from the Greek word for sleeping chamber, a rural cemetery was considered a next home, of a sort, where relatives and friends could sleep in peace. The city center, with problems of vandalism and of expansion into older burial grounds, could not provide the sense of sanctity desired for a final resting place. In addition, Syracuse's older cemeteries, like those in other cities, were crowded and, with their noxious fumes, were considered a health hazard. At work too was a growing nostalgia for the vanishing rural landscape. The response to these issues was the establishment of a new burial ground outside the city limits.

The first rural cemetery in the United States was Mount Auburn, established in Cambridge, Massachusetts in 1831. From there the idea spread to become, as a period source said, "all the rage" nationwide by the 1860s. Though established later than the first great rural cemeteries, Oakwood remains a particularly fine example of the form. With its many natural advantages, the current site was the unanimous choice of the 1852 search committee. In 1859, after several delays, Elias Leavenworth and Hamilton White led the final push resulting in the formation of Oakwood. Its importance today derives from its largely intact plan, created by New York City landscape gardener Howard Daniels (1815–63), to conform to the then-popular picturesque ideal in landscape design. Though less widely known than his contemporary Frederick Law Olmsted, Daniels was one of the country's early and important landscape gardeners, the predecessors of today's landscape architects. During the 1850s, he studied in Europe, published his theories in widely read horticultural journals, and designed at least fifteen rural cemeteries; Oakwood is his last known and arguably his finest.

However large or small, all rural cemeteries shared certain design principles reflecting a Romantic outlook on nature. City founders in Syracuse and elsewhere were often avid amateur horticulturalists familiar with the work of Andrew Jackson Downing, the father of American landscape architecture. They, along with the landscape gardeners they hired, were guided by the Romanticism of the time with its principal tenet that natural scenery had a salubrious impact on the mind. The rural cemetery, designed as a series of landscape pictures, could become a place of spiritual fulfillment for the living as well as a resting place for the dead. What could not be avoided could at least be made beautiful. Important design features included a location outside the urban center—not so far as to be inaccessible but sufficiently distant to present a rural prospect and relief from the crowded city. Ideally the location allowed a view to the distant city. An overall picturesque effect was achieved through varied topography, irregular land divisions, serpentine roads and paths, and controlled internal views. The curvilinear layout of a rural cemetery contrasted with the crowded gridiron plan of most cities and underscored the intended difference between the two spaces. Daniels's circulation system at Oakwood was particularly successful. The land was contoured where necessary, and formal circular paths were placed at the top of hills with long, winding paths following the natural drainage swales down the slopes. To increase the cemetery's sylvan appeal, roads and paths were given such evocative names as Lake View, Sun Set, and Pine Ridge. The broken remains of iron street signs still stand here and there.

Vegetation in a rural cemetery was always naturalistic in form and type. Oakwood's extensively varied terrain and venerable old trees provided Howard Daniels the opportunity to use all the design principles previously described. The original ninety-two acres included about sixty acres of dense oak forest interspersed with pine, ash, hickory, and maple. With a crew of sixty laborers, Daniels "thinned and grouped" the trees, accentuating distinctive groves and stately specimens. The presence today of many 150-year-old trees attests to his careful selection. A final universal ingredient for a rural cemetery was a formal entry with a gate and a grouping of necessary buildings.

Oakwood was an immediate success following its dedication in November 1859. Visitors numbering in the thousands led to the establishment of omnibus service to the cemetery gates. Additions to the original acreage were laid out in a manner sympathetic to the original design. The broad use of cemeteries like Oakwood as "pleasure grounds" directly generated the call for public parks nationwide. New York's Central Park was established in 1858. Syracuse followed the national trend with the creation of Burnet Park in 1886.

While the cemetery tour includes individual buildings and monuments, it is important to remember that overall design is Oakwood's most significant asset. As an 1871 guidebook stated, "there is presented to the eye at every turn and from every point a feast of panoramic splendor which cannot fail to charm the beholder." The cemetery's charm remains intact, and the visitor should be constantly on the lookout for internal and external viewpoints, for the old main roads and traces of the original path system, for ancient native trees along with picturesque groupings of introduced trees and shrubs. Monuments and mausolea on the tour are located in the oldest sections of the cemetery. The visitor is encouraged, however, to venture into the newer sections, which also contain interesting and significant sites. Of particular note is the L. C. Smith Mausoleum near the Comstock Avenue entrance. Built in 1910, its stained-glass window by the Tiffany Studios is one of Oakwood's artistic masterpieces.

The tour begins on the west side of the cemetery near the entrance arch. Enter from East Colvin Street, proceed to the top of the hill, turn left at the circle containing the Hundred Year Monument, and follow the road to the bottom of the hill. The entrance arch stands at the west edge of the property; the old office is immediately to the west; and the mortuary chapel stands across the road to the east. Although the text indicates cemetery section numbers for most sites, often those numbers are missing from the section itself. Persistence and sharp eyes may be necessary to locate some tour stops.

1. Entrance Arch/D.L. & W. Railroad Bridge, 1902
Architect: H. Q. French & Co., New York

This Romanesque style granite entrance replaced an earlier Egyptian Revival style gate. The new arch was donated to the cemetery by James J. Belden and was planned to conceal as fully as possible the "unsightly railroad bed and rails." The entrance area is the portion of the cemetery most significantly altered over time. With the construction of Interstate 81 in the 1960s, the entrance arch and roads along the west edge of the cemetery were filled, and the main entrance was moved to Comstock Avenue on the east side of the property. These changes to the circulation system severely compromised the integrity of Daniels' 1859 design for the cemetery entrance.

1. Top of entrance arch

2. Old Office, 1902
Architect: H. Q. French & Co., New York

Like the entrance arch, the old office was donated by James Belden and designed by H. Q. French & Co. in the Romanesque style. It replaced the original Gothic Revival gatekeeper's cottage built in 1862 just inside the entrance gate. Nineteenth-century visitors stopped at the gatekeeper's cottage for a visitor's pass and a copy of the cemetery's "Rules and Regulations" before going on to enjoy an afternoon in the cemetery. To house the cemetery's collection of tropical plants, greenhouses were constructed in 1902 directly across the road from the Old Office.

3. Mortuary Chapel and Receiving Vault, 1879
Architect: Joseph Lyman Silsbee, Syracuse

The mortuary chapel is an example of a then-new architectural form necessitated by the removal of cemeteries from their traditional location next to churches. A protected space for services was needed within the new rural cemetery. Built of Onondaga limestone, the chapel is detailed with Gothic and Romanesque elements. Terra cotta cresting tops the steeply pitched slate roof while a Greek cross completes the central tower. Note the playful use of carved spiderwebs to detail the rear chimneys.

3. Mortuary chapel and receiving vault

4. Lion, 1982
Sculptor: Thomas A. Haggerty

The bronze lion memorializes the sculptor's brother, Michael, who died in his teens. This site is not part of the National Register Historic District.

Walk along the road west of the chapel to:

5. Dedication Valley, 1859

Originally accessible from the west gate, Dedication Valley is the heart of the oldest part of the cemetery. Here the cemetery's unique terrain is apparent with a sharp rise to the west and more gradual slopes to the east and northeast. The regularity of the hillocks to the east reflects the contouring done by Daniels. With great fanfare, parades, and speeches, Oakwood was dedicated on 3 November 1859. A grouping of introduced plants—bald cypress, yellowwood, and bottlebrush buckeye—at the east end of the valley typifies the period's picturesque approach to landscape design.

View looking west

6. Lewis H. Redfield Monument, ca. 1866, Sect. 3
Sculptor: John C. Esser, Syracuse

A respected newspaper publisher and printer, Redfield erected this monument during his lifetime. The Gothic style Onondaga limestone marker features a medallion portrait of Redfield carved by local sculptor John C. Esser (1839–1905), who carved other monuments at Oakwood as well as elsewhere and who is credited with having been the first artist to sculpt in local limestone. In addition to his monument work, Esser carved the letters on the former Syracuse Public Library building and produced ornamental carving for the state capitol in Albany.

7. Cornelius Tyler Longstreet Mausoleum, ca. 1875, Sect. 3

As the grandson of early Onondaga Valley settler and salt producer Comfort Tyler, Longstreet may well have chosen this site for its prominent vantage point. The massive stone pyramid surmounted by a cross stands on a hill whose natural form was improved in the cemetery's early days. The hillsides were evenly sloped and the top leveled to become an earthen base for the monument. Tablets west of the pyramid commemorate Comfort Tyler and his wives, Deborah and Elizabeth.

Walk southwest along the hilltop and note the views west to Onondaga Valley.

8. General Amos P. Granger Mausoleum, 1870, Sect. 3
Architect: Archimedes Russell, Syracuse

Designed in the High Victorian Gothic style, this tomb is noteworthy for the variety of materials used to create a polychrome effect. The base is of Onondaga gray limestone. Nearly square, the monument consists of paired pointed arches that spring from marble capitals that, in turn, top Scotch granite columns. A stone cross once stood at the peak of the rusticated stone pediment now topping the structure. Granger became a general following service in the War of 1812 and, as an active politician, played an important role in the city's growth and prosperity.

9. J. R. Whitlock Monument, ca. 1878, Sect. 4
Sculptor: John C. Esser, Syracuse

Erected by city Alderman J. R. Whitlock, the monument was touted for its "originality, beauty of design and delicacy of finish." Esser is said to have used his daughter as the model for the marble statue of the Angel of Peace that originally faced east under the limestone arch. A draped urn considered to have been the "finest piece of sculpture ever attempted from Onondaga limestone" remains in place atop the arch.

10. General Edwin Vose Sumner Mausoleum, ca. 1865, Sect. 8

Among the Sioux, whom he fought as a cavalry colonel, Sumner was known as "the Chief who slept with one eye open." During the Civil War, he served under General McClellan as commander of the Second Corps of the Army of the Potomac. In 1863, en route to a new command in Missouri, Sumner died while visiting his daughter, Mrs. William W. Teall, at her home on Fayette Park. Though Sumner was a Massachusetts native, he was buried in Syracuse. His Gothic Revival style tomb, covered in the nineteenth century with luxuriant woodbine, stands at the top of a hill in an area laid out with circular plots. With reference to the inspiring view to the west, the path surrounding the plot was called Sun Set. The foliage on the copper beech and the weeping beech to the east of the monument is spectacular in the spring.

11. James R. Lawrence Monument, 1866, Sect. 7
Sculptor: John C. Esser, Syracuse
Grove Lawrence Monument, 1862, Sect. 7
Designer: Linihan & Hinsdale Monument Co., Syracuse

Like the adjacent Sumner plot, the Lawrence family property is circular and afforded visitors a view of the city and Onondaga Lake from its surrounding path, Fair View. Underbrush and new construction obstruct the view today, but sections of the low stone wall outlining the property remain in place. A prominent attorney and judge, James Lawrence served as US district attorney under Millard Fillmore in the 1850s. Lawrence's portrait on the north face of the monument was carved by John C. Esser. An 1866 newspaper commentary encouraged the use of carved medallions by "all lot owners in Oakwood," but only the Lawrence and Redfield busts are known to have been executed. The nearby Grove Lawrence Monument is smaller in scale and represents an earlier style of design. Made of marble, its ornamentation is naturalistic with the family name carved in rustic letters with an intertwined vine.

12. Captain Austin Myers Mausoleum, 1862, Sect. 9A

Austin Myers was a successful businessman with a line of canal packet boats and real estate investments in Syracuse. The mausoleum, built like a miniature Gothic cathedral, with once-towering pinnacles atop the buttressed corners, looks down to exotic bald cypress trees and bottlebrush buckeye shrubs in the valley to the northeast.

Walk down the slope south of the mausoleum, turn left, and walk northeast, noting traces of the original cobblestone gutters lining the road along the way.

13. Benjamin F. Colvin Plot, ca. 1870, Sect. 20
Sculpture: Wm. S. See & Co., New York

An 1871 Oakwood guidebook stated that "this lot and its attractions receive perhaps more attention from visitors than any other in the cemetery." The Victorian reverence for nature, inherent in the rural cemetery, is present in the marble tree stump with clinging ivy symbolizing strength and devotion. Colvin family history is recorded on the tree stump, while the stone dog conveys faithfulness. A spectacular copper beech shades the east side of the plot.

An uphill walk to the east leads to:

14. Onondaga County Orphan Asylum Monument, 1894, Sect. 44
Sculptor: Ralph Cook of Francis & Co. Monuments, Syracuse

This monument, given by Christina Colvin, commemorates the Orphan Asylum dead with a statuary group representing Charity. The statues were carved by Ralph Cook, a sculptor for one of the local monument companies that prospered following Oakwood's opening. The monument stands part way up a compound hill that terminates to the east with a series of concentric circular plots along the highest ridge. In 1859, the view to the northwest was not obstructed by the State University of New York College of Environmental Science and Forestry (SUNY-ESF), now a very near neighbor along the north edge of the cemetery. At the west edge of Section 44, alternating yellowwood and Japanese katsura trees outline the base of the hill.

15. Frederick Wolf Mausoleum, 1910, Sect. 42

This mausoleum is the only fully articulated Egyptian Revival structure at Oakwood. Though built in the early twentieth century, it stands at the eastern edge of the acreage laid out in the mid-nineteenth century. From the vulture-and-sun-disk symbol on the cornice to the palm leaf capitals and stylized foliate gates, the monument is complete in its detailing and is typical of classical revival styles popular at the turn of the century.

The walk southwest to the next site is longer than other intervals on the tour. Along the way are many internal viewpoints to the west where the sense of an enveloping, picturesque landscape is apparent. The copper roof of **No. 16** can be seen from a distance and is the best available guide to the site.

16. General John A. Green Mausoleum, 1866, Sect. 25
Architect: Horatio Nelson White, Syracuse
Sculptor: John C. Esser, Syracuse

A Utica native, Green made his riches in the wholesale grocery business in Syracuse and served as a brigadier general in the Civil War. Local architect Horatio Nelson White designed the mausoleum, which cost over $25,000 in

1866. With elaborate stonework by John C. Esser, it features boldly scrolled, Flemish stepped gables and is the cemetery's most flamboyant structure. White experimented with the use of tapering pilasters at the entrance and corners and later used them to detail his S. A. & K. (1869) and Gridley (1867) buildings in downtown Syracuse. From the Green plot, there is a good view south down the slope to Oakwood's Midland Avenue, one of the principle routes through the cemetery.

16. General John H. Green Mausoleum

17. John M. Wieting Mausoleum, 1880, Sect. 15

Dr. John Wieting, donor of the historic Wieting Opera House that once stood on Clinton Square, earned his fortune as a lecturer on physiology and other topics. Avid, observant travelers, he and his wife, Mary, went

around the world in 1875. It is specu-
lated that his curious mausoleum,
built during his lifetime, may take
the shape of a stupa, a Buddhist
architectural form used to mark a
sacred spot. Wieting had visited
India and may well have decided to
use this form for his own monument. Built of rough-cut granite, it
was originally christianized with a
cross at its peak.

17. John M. Wieting Mausoleum

18. Lester Tucker Monument, 1869, Sect. 14

Filled with sentimentality, little Lester Tucker's chair, cape, and baby shoes
are symbolic of Victorian family life. Rendered permanently in stone, they
were intended to comfort the bereaved relatives with the suggestion that
treasured earthly traits could not be entirely extinguished by death.

19. John Crouse Mausoleum, 1884, Sect. 16
Architect: H. Q. French & Co., New York

With his brother James, John Crouse made a fortune in the wholesale grocery business, J. & J. Crouse. When he died in 1891, Crouse was thought to
be Syracuse's wealthiest man. The donor of Richardsonian Romanesque
style Crouse College (1887–89), he had a mausoleum built that befitted his
position in the community. The English Gothic style structure was
designed by the New York firm of H. Q. French, who would later design the
cemetery's gate and office. Noteworthy features include the near absence of
vertical joints, the magnificent bronze doors with lion's head motifs, and the
massive slab of granite forming the walk.

20. Robert Gere Monument, 1866, Sect. 17

A tall simple obelisk marks the grave of Robert Gere, a contractor for the
original Erie Canal and for the first railroads in Syracuse. Gere was a
founder of the Geddes Coarse Salt Company and had an interest in lumber
and iron businesses as well. The Gere Building on Hanover Square was
built in his honor by his son-in-law, James J. Belden, who is also buried in
this plot.

21. Burr Burton Mausoleum, 1866, Sect. 12

Architect: Horatio Nelson White, Syracuse

Burr Burton was one of the city's leading salt manufacturers during the industry's height in the 1850s. He was shot and killed at his home by a prowler in 1865. His Gothic-inspired, Onondaga limestone monument was designed by Horatio Nelson White, who was particularly fanciful in his use of ornamental detail. Flowerlike finials top the buttressed corners and forty-foot pinnacle. In the nineteenth century, the area to the east of the Burton plot was considered the finest vantage point for an internal view of the cemetery. Still today the winding paths and gracefully rounded hillocks form a delightful scene.

22. Horace and Hamilton White Monument, 1868, Sect. 12

Hamilton White made his fortune in banking and railroads before Syracuse was incorporated as a city in 1848. One of Oakwood's founders, he is best known today for the magnificent Greek Revival mansion he built in 1842. It is the only survivor of the many elaborate houses that once lined Fayette Park. Massive but unostentatious, the White tomb is surrounded by family graves marked with Celtic crosses. A hitching post at the base of the steps is a reminder of the cemetery's horse-and-carriage days.

23. Elias W. Leavenworth Mausoleum, ca. 1885, Sect. 13

A Yale-educated New Englander who studied law with William Cullen Bryant, Leavenworth was one of Syracuse's most prominent citizens. His offices included mayor and congressman, and, as an avid horticulturalist, he supervised the laying out of the city's earliest parks. He was the guiding spirit in the founding of Oakwood and served as president of its board of trustees from 1859 until his death in 1887. As an 1894 history stated, he "loved every pathway, knoll and spreading tree." His massive Gothic mausoleum also honors Judge Joshua Forman, founder of Syracuse and Leavenworth's father-in-law. The massive white oak to the east of the tomb appears as a sapling in an 1871 illustration of the site. Just to the west stand small markers detailed with carved flowers.

24. James Crouse Monument, 1860, Sect. 13

Designer: Sidney Stanton, Syracuse

James Crouse and his brother John were in the grocery business. James' elegant white marble monument was the first to be erected in Oakwood. The Crouse family, having been among the first to choose a lot, selected a prominent knoll in the heart of the original cemetery. On the north face of the monument, a carved angel surrounded by an ivy wreath commemorates an infant child.

25. Orrin Welch Monument, 1879, Sect. 13

Architect: Archimedes Russell, Syracuse

This unusual monument, in the form of a sarcophagus with a canopied spire, was erected in memory of Welch by his Masonic brothers, and its installation featured a parade with full Masonic regalia, speeches, and hymns. Built of Quincy granite, the monument is noteworthy for its architectural detail, particularly the ornate moldings and the carved Masonic symbols tracing Welch's rise through the order.

Of note but not on the walking tour is the dwelling at:

953 Comstock Avenue, 1960

Architect: Louis Skoler, Syracuse
Landscape design: Reimann Buechner Partnership, Syracuse

The design of this fine modern house takes full advantage of its site. Closed off toward the street and cemetery beyond, the house opens up to a patio and a landscaped garden in back. A large window faces south, but the view toward the crematorium is blocked off by a large brick chimney. The original owners, Dr. and Mrs. Dakota Greenwald, spent time in Finland and were impressed with Finnish houses, especially Alvar Aalto's architecture. A sauna has access to a small entry court that is protected by moveable wooden slats. The entry court serves as a focal point for the first-floor apartment and the living and dining areas above. Skoler's designs were influenced by those of Frank Lloyd Wright and Richard Neutra, as well as by the traditional Japanese house.

953 Comstock Avenue

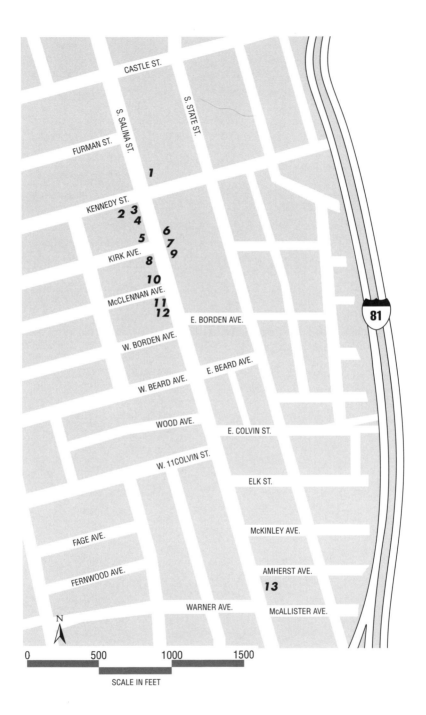

CASTLE ST.

S. SALINA ST.

S. STATE ST.

FURMAN ST.

1

KENNEDY ST.

2 *3*
4

5   *6*
7
9

KIRK AVE.   *8*

10

McCLENNAN AVE.

11
12

E. BORDEN AVE.

W. BORDEN AVE.

E. BEARD AVE.

W. BEARD AVE.

WOOD AVE.

E. COLVIN ST.

W. 11COLVIN ST.

ELK ST.

McKINLEY AVE.

FAGE AVE.

AMHERST AVE.

FERNWOOD AVE.

13

WARNER AVE.   McALLISTER AVE.

81

N

| 0 | 500 | 1000 | 1500 |

SCALE IN FEET

SOUTH SIDE

South Salina Street National Register Historic District

The South Salina Street National Register Historic District (NRHD) *consists of twenty-nine properties, of which only twelve are included in the tour.*

Estimated driving time: 20 minutes (Nos. 1–13)

In 1824, General Thaddeus M. Wood, a veteran of the War of 1812, bought large land holdings here and named the settlement Danforth after his father-in-law General Asa Danforth, an American Revolutionary soldier who had come to this area in 1788 at the invitation of Ephraim Webster. Because Wood was not able to pay for his land, ownership reverted to the state of New York. In 1843, William B. Kirk purchased the unsettled land from the state and developed what became known as the Kirk Tract. He gradually subdivided his land, and by the time of his death in 1886, most of the Kirk Tract had been sold. Kirk Avenue and Kirk Park bear his name.

Surrounded by good land, Syracuse was considered a center of farming activities. By 1825, New York had become a dairy state. Agricultural societies and journals as well as county and state fairs became important tools in educating farmers in agricultural principles and improved farming methods. Fairs were also a place for fun and entertainment. An important annual event in New York, the state fair was held on the South Side, west of Onondaga Creek, on and around Academy Green, in 1858. The attraction of that fair was an exhibition of live rattlesnakes, one of which, it is said, bit the exhibitor, who luckily survived. Before Syracuse became permanent host to the New York State Fair in 1890, it hosted the event at various times and locations: between Syracuse and Salina on the grounds that surrounded the second Onondaga County Courthouse in 1841, and on James Street Hill eight years later.

In 1874, Danforth was incorporated as a village. The horse-drawn Syracuse and Onondaga Railroad ran along South Salina Street and connected Danforth with Syracuse to the north and with Onondaga Hollow to the south. Danforth became part of Syracuse in 1887. People were attracted by the bucolic surroundings and built their suburban houses there. Amidst landscaped lots, set back from the street and sheltered by trees, house designs exhibit architectural fashions of the day; some may have come from catalogues.

In mid-twentieth century, demographic changes altered the neighborhood. The construction of Interstate 81 resulted in the loss of housing stock belonging to Pioneer Homes, and many of the residents settled on the South Side. During the 1950s, the city's African-American population grew by 144 percent. Many of the newcomers had migrated from the South. It was reported that of all cities with a similar number of blacks the proportion of Southern blacks in Syracuse was the largest. As many new residents settled in the older "streetcar suburbs," the South Side being one of them, urbanites moved to middle-class enclaves. Since then, one-family homes have been divided into multifamily units or are adaptively reused; some buildings are vacant, while others have been replaced by parking lots.

Start your driving tour at South Salina and Kennedy streets. The northeast corner is occupied by the

1. Sumner Hunt Building, 1878
1555 South Salina Street
Renovation: 1991–, Crawford & Stearns, Syracuse
NRHD

The Second Empire style brick building is the only commercial building in the historic district and visually dominates it. It served the community as a general store for many years. A newspaper clipping at the Onondaga Historical Association quotes the original owner Sumner Hunt as saying, "all this property around here was a big woods in which girls and boys used to hunt sassafras roots." General Thaddeus M. Wood purchased the land from New York State, which referred to it as "Indian Reservation." The slate patterns in the polychrome mansard roof spell the date of construction and the letter H, the original owner's initial. The interior was altered in the 1950s, and it is now being converted into an apartment building; the exterior will be restored.

2. Renetta C. Palmer House, 1868
111 West Kennedy Street
NRHD

This Italian villa constructed of brick is one the best of its kind in the city. Tastemaker and writer Andrew Jackson Downing recommended the Italian Villa style house as the "perfect residence for the captain of industry ... in a leafy suburb away from the place of work." The house is distinguished by a prominent tower, broadly projecting bracketed eaves, ornamental lintels, bay windows, and an ornate veranda. The Italian villa differs from the Italianate house in that it has a tower, usually placed off-center and sometimes at the corner of the house. The original owners were Renetta C. and Anson N. Palmer. Renetta was the daughter of Charles Tallman, settler of the Tallman Tract (north of the Kirk Tract). Tallman and his son-in-law Anson Palmer contributed to the development of south and southwest Syracuse.

2. Renetta C. Palmer House

3. Anson Palmer House, 1890
1606 South Salina Street
NRHD

The house embodies the picturesque, eclectic stylistic features of the late Victorian era. It is constructed of brick and has a variegated roofline, large plate-glass windows, and an abundance of ornament.

4. Justus Newell House, 1872
1622 South Salina Street
Renovation and partial restoration: 1985–86, Mary Ann Smith, Syracuse
NRHD

Handsomely restored, this fine Italianate house reflects a once prosperous neighborhood. Cubic massing, a low-pitched roof with projecting eaves supported by ornate brackets, a cupola, as well as ornamental hood molds are characteristic of the Italianate style. An arched cornice gives the house special distinction, as do quoins that articulate the corners of the facades. Elaborate porches shelter front and side entrances. The structure was built of concrete blocks and represents a very early example of this type of construction, which was to become a common building technique by the beginning of the twentieth century. Newell, owner of the Syracuse and

Onondaga Railroad, also owned a sand and gravel company. His earlier experiments with concrete construction had failed, but his own house was a success. Grained painted woodwork and all existing original light fixtures in the interior were restored. At present, the house accommodates apartments.

4. Justus Newell House

5. Erastus B. Phillips House, 1869
1632 South Salina Street
NRHD

A more common interpretation of the Italianate house with hipped roof and paired brackets is represented here. Plain stone lintels and a deeply recessed doorway with rectangular transom and sidelights are part of the Greek Revival vocabulary of an earlier time.

6. 1631 South Salina Street, 1850–55
NRHD CSPS

The earliest construction in the community occurred between Kennedy Street and Kirk Avenue. A survivor of these early buildings is this Gothic Revival cottage. It has distinctive characteristics, such as a steeply pitched, cross-gabled roof with pinnacles and pendants, and pointed-arch windows with label molds. The door with rectangular sidelights and transom are

Greek Revival style elements and show the persistence of an earlier building tradition.

7. New Jerusalem Church of God in Christ, 1884–85 (former Danforth Congregational Church)
1641 South Salina Street
Architect: Asa L. Merrick, Syracuse
Addition of rear wing: 1899, Wellington W. Taber, Syracuse
NRHD CSPS

The Romanesque Revival church with decorative brick detailing and round-arched openings is given ready visibility by a prominent bell tower and steeple. Sheltering the entrance is a porch complete with buttresses and Gothic pointed-arch openings, representing yet another example of the eclectic mix of stylistic elements seen in **Nos. 5** and **6**. The building's scale and picturesque massing harmonize with the residential character of the street. A modern brick addition at the front of the tower is stylistically inappropriate.

8. 1704 South Salina Street, 1907
Renovation: 1991–, Wolff J. Garritano, Fayetteville, N.Y.
NRHD

The house, symmetrically arranged and exhibiting Neoclassical Revival details, was originally a one-family house, later a funeral home, and then a rooming house. At present, it is being recycled for the Salvation Army, which will use it as a refuge for homeless women.

9. Dunfee-Kelly House, 1908
1709 South Salina Street
NRHD

With its stuccoed and false half-timbered exterior, it stands out as the only Tudor Revival house in this area. The original owners of the house were Joseph Dunfee, a prizefighter turned contractor, and his wife, an opera singer.

10. 1730 South Salina Street, ca. 1890
NRHD

Intricate woodwork and cutout ornamentation distinguish the exterior of this picturesque frame dwelling. Such Eastlake ornamentation of pierced vergeboards in panels with cutout ornamentation above windows, and entrance porches with spindle friezes, turned posts, and balustrades reached the height of their popularity during the 1870s and 1880s, celebrating ornamentation made possible and affordable by the machine. A large carriage barn behind the main house on McLennan Avenue is a good example of the attention given to support structures during the Victorian era.

11. All Saints Episcopal Church, 1923
1804 South Salina Street
Architects: Taylor & Bonta, Syracuse
NRHD

The Onondaga limestone structure is designed in the Late Gothic Revival style and harmonizes with its neighboring residential buildings in size and massing. Good craftsmanship and detailing such as buttressing, pointed-arch openings, clerestory windows with quatrefoil ornamentation, and a fine rose window are notable features. Several windows were designed and installed by the Henry Keck Stained Glass Studio in the 1920s and 1930s.

12. Alvord House, 1890
1818 South Salina Street
Architect: Archimedes Russell, Syracuse
NRHD

A broad veranda and porte cochere emphasize the horizontal massing of this imposing Queen Anne house. Classically inspired ornamentation and a variety of textures enliven the facades. An elegant Colonial Revival style carriage is part of the property, which was originally owned by local physician Dr. George E. Gridley. The house functioned as office and residence. Much of the interior woodwork is of cherry, and the living room has a frescoed ceiling as well as an elaborate mantelpiece. Dr. Gridley sold the house to Anson Alvord, descendent of salt manufacturer Alisha Alvord. A barn on the property once housed Anson Alvord's racehorses.

13. Reformed Presbyterian Church, 1861
2517 South Salina Street

The small Romanesque Revival building with bell tower was also known as the Church of the Covenanters, a Scottish sect. Organized in 1849, the congregation counted among its members pioneer settlers who owned land in the area.

13. Reformed Presbyterian Church

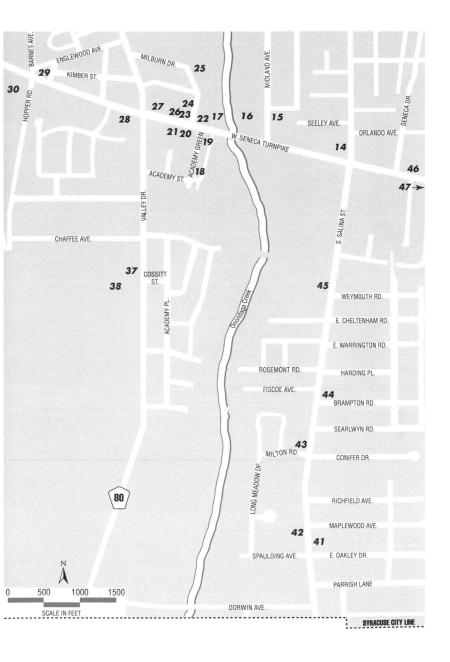

BARNES AVE.

ENGLEWOOD AVE.

MILBURN DR.

29 KIMBER ST.

30

HOPPER RD.

28

27 26 23 24

21 20 19

ACADEMY ST.

ACADEMY GREEN

18

22 17

25

16 15

MIDLAND AVE.

SEELEY AVE.

W. SENECA TURNPIKE

ORLANDO AVE.

SENECA DR.

14

46

47 →

VALLEY DR.

CHAFFEE AVE.

37 COSSITT ST.

38

ACADEMY PL.

45

S. SALINA ST.

WEYMOUTH RD.

E. CHELTENHAM RD.

E. WARRINGTON RD.

ROSEMONT RD.

FISCOE AVE.

HARDING PL.

44

BRAMPTON RD.

SEARLWYN RD.

43

MILTON RD.

CONIFER DR.

Onondaga Creek

80

LONG MEADOW DR.

RICHFIELD AVE.

MAPLEWOOD AVE.

42

41

SPAULDING AVE.

E. OAKLEY DR.

N

PARRISH LANE

0 500 1000 1500

SCALE IN FEET

DORWIN AVE.

SYRACUSE CITY LINE

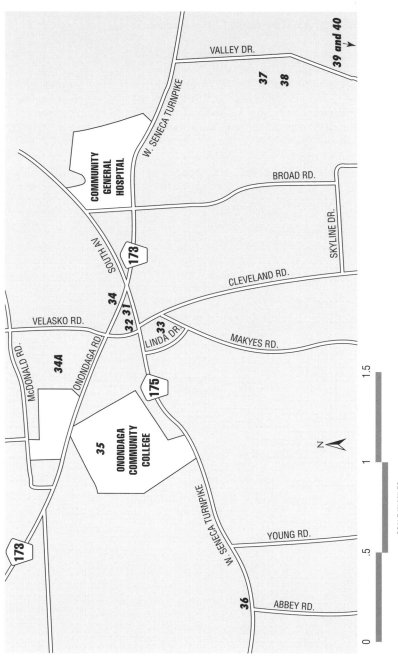

VALLEY DR.

39 and 40

37

38

W. SENECA TURNPIKE

COMMUNITY
GENERAL
HOSPITAL

BROAD RD.

SKYLINE DR.

SOUTH AV

173

CLEVELAND RD.

34

VELASKO RD.

32 *31*

33

LINDA DR.

MAKYES RD.

McDONALD RD.

ONONDAGA RD.

34A

175

35

ONONDAGA
COMMUNITY
COLLEGE

W. SENECA TURNPIKE

N

173

YOUNG RD.

36

ABBEY RD.

SCALE IN MILES

0   .5   1   1.5

Onondaga Valley and Onondaga Hill

Estimated driving time: 1 hour, 15 minutes (Nos. 14–47)

Turn right on West Seneca Turnpike and go west. Although it is not a historic district, you will be driving through an area that was settled earlier than Salina or Syracuse. After the Onondaga land went to the state, the first European settlers arrived to settle in Onondaga Hollow. Ephraim Webster came to live in the Hollow, as did Asa Danforth and Comfort Tyler. From here Danforth and Tyler walked six miles to the north to gain salt from the salt spring at Onondaga Lake. Tyler, intrigued by grander schemes, became involved with Aaron Burr's plans to set up his own country in the southwest. Arrested for treason, he was acquitted and later settled in Montezuma, where he became an ardent supporter of the canal ticket.

While Tyler still lived in the Hollow, he saw the need for a good east-west road and helped bring it into existence. Before Onondaga County was established in 1794, all pioneers traveled along Indian trails through the wilderness. In the early 1790s, a first road was cut through the region from Whitestown to Canandaigua. Enlarged and improved by the state government, the "State Road" was the only thoroughfare until 1800, at which time the Seneca Turnpike was built. It closely followed the original road and passed through all the important settlements that had sprung up along it, stretching from Utica in the east to Canandaigua in the west. Over this road, New Englanders pushed their way westward. Many of them settled along the route, enticed by productive but cheap farmland, plenty of timber, and water. They formed the nucleus of the county's population, and several of them became important figures in the history of Syracuse. As new arteries of commerce were established to the north, the old "pike" lost its erstwhile importance.

Since transportation was difficult, building materials came from the immediate area. Wood was plentiful and by tradition New Englanders built timber-frame houses. In many instances, a hand-hewn frame dwelling or a log cabin was constructed when the land was cleared. Barns and other farm buildings consisted of a skeleton of squared beams pegged together and covered with a skin of horizontal or vertical barn boards. Roofs were covered with hand-split wooden shingles. As the farmer prospered and the family grew, the earlier dwelling would be enlarged by additions covered with a "saltbox" roof or replaced by a more substantial frame house, in this area often added to the front of the earlier smaller structure. The latter was usually a two-story house covered with clapboards, if of frame or plank construction. With a central hall flanked by two rooms and a centrally located fireplace, it was a substantial and comfortable house for its time and place. None of the late eighteenth-century dwellings have survived, but a number of wood, brick, and limestone houses built during the first half of the nineteenth century still stand. Another building material, unique to this area, especially between Rochester and Syracuse and along the shoreline of Lake

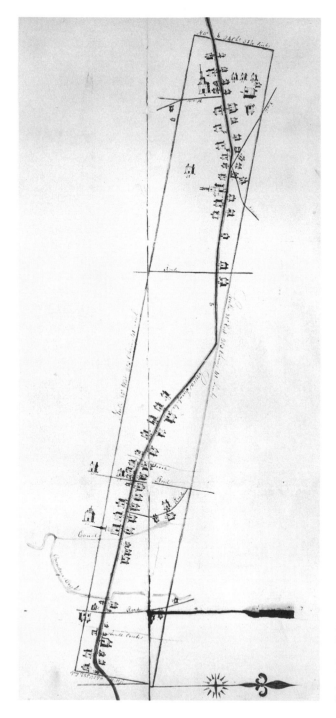

Settlement along
Seneca Turnpike,
Brewster map, 1823.
Courtesy Onondaga
Historical
Association,
Syracuse

Ontario, was cobblestones. Ice Age glaciers left cobbles in the field, and when these were used up by the settlers, water-rounded cobbles from Lake Ontario replaced them as building material. An example in Onondaga Valley is the Oliver Bostwick House (**No. 37**). Established in 1798, the Town of Onondaga has changed considerably in size. It is not part of Syracuse and contains Nedrow, South Onondaga, Onondaga Hill, Cedarvale, Split Rock, Howlett Hill, and Taunton. Danforth, once belonging to the town of Onondaga, became part of the city of Syracuse in 1887. The Elmwood area was incorporated into the city in 1899, and the valley section (the Hollow) in 1927. Farmland and open country have been converted into building lots. It continues to be a desirable residential area.

14. Valley Vista Apartments, 1974
122 West Seneca Turnpike
Architects: Hueber Hares Glavin, Syracuse

An Urban Development Corporation-sponsored project, the prefabricated apartment units of reinforced poured concrete are occupied by tenants with low and moderate income. The architects received an Award of Merit from the American Concrete Institute.

15. Fire Station No. 18, 1990
3801 Midland Avenue
Architects: Hueber Hares Glavin, Syracuse

The use of cube, cylinder, and circle create an attractive design for this modern brick-faced firehouse that is placed behind an earlier, now-defunct firehouse (1927, Randall & Vedder). Semicylindrical glass-block towers recall the firehose drying towers that were discontinued in the 1970s. Here the towers contain desks and workstations on the first level, which is also occupied by space for the trucks, a common room for the firefighters, and a kitchen. Upstairs are dormitories, the officers' quarters, and bathrooms. Large circular windows and the glass-block towers create a very light interior. The architectural firm built the structure as a model for other firehouses.

16. Gordon Needham House
222 West Seneca Turnpike

This was one of the earliest houses on Webster's Mile Square, land granted to Webster by the state of New York with the approval of the Onondaga. The house was destroyed by fire in 1829. Walls surrounding the living room, the fireplace, and the rooms behind it were saved, but there are no records to indicate when the rest of the house was rebuilt. It received additions and a veranda, as well as Gothic Revival ornamentations such as trefoils and gingerbread details (probably in the 1850s). These ornamental details became fashionable in mid-nineteenth century and were made possible by the invention of the jigsaw. Related to Joshua Forman by marriage, the original owner of the house, Dr. Gordon Needham was, according to Marian K. Schmitz (1983), "Onondaga county's first physician."

17. Joshua Forman House, ca. 1810
266 West Seneca Turnpike

Joshua Forman came to Onondaga Hollow in 1800 and practiced law. A promoter of the Erie Canal, he moved to the village of Syracuse and functioned as its president at the time the canal opened in 1825. Forman, who is sometimes referred to as the father of Syracuse, lost his house, which was surrounded by one of the finest gardens in the valley, at a sheriff's sale. After the Kellogg-Sabine family had occupied it, the house was sold in 1845 to the Onondaga Valley Academy (formed primarily because of Forman's interest in education) for use as a seminary. Since the 1850s, the house functioned as a residence and had many owners, who made considerable changes over the years. Walls, hand-hewn timbers, and a cooking fireplace in the basement kitchen are all that is left of the original house. George Palmer, who bought the house in 1901, raised the roof three feet, replaced fireplaces with bays, and probably added the porch. He also built the carriage house in back and the house next door.

18. William Sabine House, ca. 1816
9 Academy Green
Renovation and restoration: 1974–, Gillis and Laetitia Murray, Syracuse

The house was located in the center of Onondaga Hollow and is a fine example of the Federal style as built in this area. The brick house, which may have been built earlier than 1816, features stepped gables with an elliptical fanlight and recessed arches and pilasters that articulate the window bays. William Sabin (the e was added later) came to the Hollow from Connecticut in 1800, practiced law with Joshua Forman, and became his brother-in-law.

18. William
Sabine House

As the Sabine family was growing, a bedroom wing was added to the east side of the house. It remained in the family until 1944 and had several owners and functions until 1973, when the present owners, Gillis and Laetitia Murray, the latter a descendant of William and Sallie Sabine, bought the house and renovated it. The outbuildings, including Sabine's slave house, have not survived. Around the turn of the century, the house was surrounded by fine gardens and chestnut trees. At one time, rows of locust and chestnut trees led to the house, which was then called Locust Lawn.

Academy Green, once the property of William Sabine and now a public park, was also the location of the first log-cabin schoolhouse at the rear of the Onondaga Valley Presbyterian Church. It was used until 1813 when the first building that housed the Onondaga Valley Academy was built. It was the first and, for many years, the only high school in Onondaga County; the building was destroyed by fire in 1919.

19. Onondaga Valley Presbyterian Church, 1924
275 West Seneca Turnpike
Architect: Earl Hallenbeck, Syracuse

The brick structure replaced the earlier church building (1810) that burned in 1922. The site was donated by William Sabine, and the original church, one of the finest Federal style churches in this area, served the oldest religious congregation in the Hollow. Local architect Edward A. Howard had drawn up plans to build a replica of the earlier building, but they burned in the Bastable Block fire of 1923. It was decided that to copy the old church would have been too expensive.

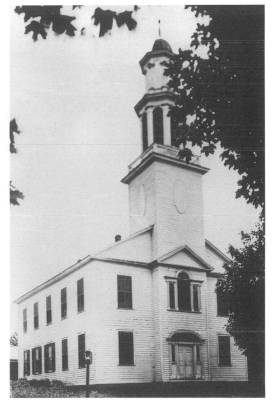

Onondaga Valley Presbyterian Church, before 1923. Courtesy Onondaga Historical Association, Syracuse

20. Wood Store, ca. 1815

305 West Seneca Turnpike

The wood-frame house is now a private residence but was originally used as a general store. This well-maintained house with side door and gable end facing the street features a small round window in the gable and block designs along the cornice line—design elements borrowed from Georgian architecture.

21. Brick Store, ca. 1815

313 West Seneca Turnpike

Pilasters divide the gabled main facade of the brick house into three bays. The first-story window and door openings are set into recessed elliptical arches, which is a Federal style feature. The Brick Store and the Wood Store were built for William Sabine, who intended to rent or sell them as general stores, and both are located on land that was part of Webster's Mile Square. At one time, Gordon Needham, who came to Onondaga Hollow in 1795, ran the store, then referred to as Needham's Store. He also practiced medicine and opened the first school in 1796. The house is now privately owned and occupied.

22. Ashbel Searle House, ca. 1812 (former Gidding's Tavern)

290 West Seneca Turnpike

The two-story, central-hall frame house with flanking chimneys was originally built as a tavern on land belonging to Joshua Forman. It was later remodeled as a residence, was purchased by physician Dr. Ashbel Searle in 1854, and remained in the family for seven generations. The porch and Acorn brackets supporting the cornice were later additions. Survivors of the early interior are wide floorboards and two open fireplaces on the main floor.

23. Unity Church of Truth, 1884
(former St. Paul's Methodist Church)

300 West Seneca Turnpike

St. Paul's, the oldest Methodist society in Syracuse, was organized in 1816. This frame building was the congregation's second building. It was designed in the form of a meetinghouse with a tower at its southeast corner. The structure was enlarged and renovated in 1915 and was sold to the Unity Church of Truth in 1958. Unity grew out of the New Thought Awakening that had started as a healing movement and swept the country in the 1880s. It had a profound influence on Norman Vincent Peale. The frame building features Stick style elements in the tower as well as Eastlake ornamentation in the gables and between windows. Large volutes support gables above the front and side entrances. One of the stained-glass windows is dedicated to Edwin Sumner Chatman, an African-American who lived in Onondaga Valley. Julius Chatman, a servant of General Edwin

Sumner, once visited Syracuse with Sumner. After the general's unexpected death, Chatman decided to stay. Son Edwin served as town clerk and, with the help of his sister Frances May, ran a general store in the valley.

24. Lewis Hamilton Redfield House, ca. 1812
314 Milburn Drive

Lewis H. Redfield built this modest one and one-half-story frame cottage. Fronting the street (Mill Street until named Milburn Drive, a more dignified appellation some thought) is a facade covered with flush boarding to imitate masonry construction, while the rest of the exterior is clapboard covered. A front porch was removed, and the house was renovated by a recent owner. Here Redfield, who liked to dabble in politics and who described journalism "as the power behind the throne," printed the weekly *Onondaga Register* in 1814. If you had no money, you could trade food for a copy. It has been said that the zealous publisher of the area's first newspaper had to print a lot of retractions because he was in the habit of writing obituaries of people who were still alive. Thurlow Weed, who eventually became a newspaper editor, briefly worked for Redfield as an apprentice. Weed, together with Horace Greeley and William H. Seward, later controlled New York State politics. When Greeley applied for a job with Redfield, the latter refused to hire him because he thought the young man was lazy and loutish. This did not discourage Greeley from becoming the founder of the *New York Tribune* and from running for president. In 1820, Redfield was postmaster, and the house served as post office. Ann Maria Redfield wrote books on natural science, some of which were used as textbooks. Her collection of books and objects became the nucleus of Syracuse's first library. Lewis Redfield moved the *Register* to the growing village of Syracuse in 1829. He proudly pointed out that his printing office was located in a new brick building opposite the Syracuse House (at the present site of the Gridley Building). After having merged with the *Syracuse Gazette*, the paper was sold in 1832. Renamed the *Syracuse Argus*, it went bankrupt two years later.

Before the house was moved to the present location from its original site on West Seneca Turnpike (now the site of Unity Church), it functioned as the parsonage of the Methodist church between 1884 and 1900.

25. Lee's Feed Store, 1846 (former Mercer's Mill)
207 Milburn Drive

The often-maligned Onondaga Creek was an important source of waterpower for the early settlement. On this site in 1813, Joshua Forman built a gristmill, which burned in 1845. A new four-story mill with a deep basement was constructed on the remains of the old structure. In 1858, it was outfitted for grist and was called the Onondaga Valley Mill; but it was commonly referred to as Mercer's Mill, after the owner's name. In 1949, the creek was straightened, and the mill has since been operated by electricity. It is now used mainly to grind cattle feed. According to Sue Campbell (1986), the structure "is so solidly built with its main floor supports, 14" x 18" beams, and floor joists that are 4" x 14", that Lee is still able to store 100 tons of feed on the second floor of the mill."

25. Lee's Feed Store

26. 310–312 West Seneca Turnpike, ca. 1807
(former Masonic Temple School)

Much changed now, the two-story New England farmhouse is said to be the oldest house still standing in Syracuse. From its location next to the creek, it was moved to its present site in 1813. It is said that Dr. Needham erected it as a schoolhouse; the structure was built jointly by the residents of Onondaga Hollow and the Freemasons. Schoolrooms were downstairs, while the Masons occupied the second floor. At one time, the Odd Fellows took over the building, and later Onondaga Hollow held town meetings on the first floor. Before it being recycled as a two-family home, it was used as a roller rink. When in the 1980s wooden clapboards were replaced by vinyl siding, a brick wall underneath the siding was found to extend to the second story. The green space in front is public land, where at one time during the early nineteenth century the militia drilled.

27. 328 West Seneca Turnpike, 1830

The frame structure is ornamented with classical details, such as a fanlight in the gable, block ornamentation along the cornice line, and pilasters framing the entrance.

28. Samuel S. Forman House, 1812

417 West Seneca Turnpike

HABS

Samuel Forman, brother of Joshua Forman, practiced as a lawyer. The house he built exhibits Federal style elements such as stepped gables with elliptical fanlight and a main facade with pilasters forming elliptical arches that frame window bays. Especially noteworthy is the deep-set entrance with semielliptical leaded glass transom and sidelights. At one time, the property was also known for the beauty of its gardens. Unfortunately, the house has been changed in the twentieth century by commercial additions. "Nowhere in this country has there been a more complete revolution in point of general improvement and comfort of living," wrote an early nineteenth-century English traveler; and "nowhere in this country have early post-colonial buildings suffered more at the hands of progress," said a contemporary local architect. This building is an example.

28. Samuel S. Forman House, 1915. Courtesy Onondaga Historical Association, Syracuse

29. Harrison House, ca. 1830

612–614 West Seneca Turnpike

The seventeen-room farmhouse has a twelve-foot-high cellar, and the twelve-by-twelve-inch boards used for the foundation are tongue and groove fitted without nails. The house and its surrounding land was purchased in the late 1880s by William Henry and Clarice Harrison, who farmed the land. Their descendents lived there until the beginning of the twentieth century. It may have been in mid-nineteenth century that the exterior was "gothicized" with board and batten, a pointed-arch window in the gable, and brackets along the cornice.

30. Jasper Hopper Homestead, 1814
711 West Seneca Turnpike

Originally a brick structure, it was probably built in two parts. Construction consists of brick nogging (brick infill) between twelve-foot square posts with clay being used instead of mortar. The exterior is now covered with clapboards, and the house has undergone considerable alteration. At present, it is a two-family dwelling. The Jasper Hopper family were among the earliest European settlers in the Hollow. Politically active, Hopper was postmaster of Onondaga Hollow and a storekeeper who kept troops supplied during the War of 1812. Hopper's Glen, a popular place for picnics in the late 1800s, was named after him.

On this tour, only those buildings visible from the road are marked. For more information on the town of Onondaga, see *Onondaga Landmarks* (Cultural Resources Council of Syracuse and Onondaga County, Inc. 1975).

County government existed in the English colonies and was used after the American Revolution to organize and administer newly settled lands. After Onondaga County had been established in 1794, county court was held first in the corn house of Asa Danforth and later in various other locations until the first Onondaga County Courthouse was erected on Onondaga Hill. The site of the courthouse was the subject of heated debate between Onondaga Hill and Onondaga Hollow. The designation as county seat meant prestige and, usually, an influx of new settlers and commercial growth. Residents of the Hill maintained that their location was superior to that of the Hollow because it was less marshy and malaria-ridden. Their argument seemed sufficiently persuasive to secure the courthouse site near the center of the village. It has been reported that the popular General Lafayette, when visiting the area on his way from Washington to Boston, was impressed with the great improvements that had been made here since he had been in command of the northern frontier during the Revolution.

31. Easton Store House, 1823
4863 West Seneca Turnpike
HABS

This was used as a blacksmith shop, a general store, a wagon shop, and a stagecoach stop between Buffalo and Albany. The vernacular Greek Revival building with low-pitched gable and gable-end returns (gable with a gap in the base molding) is constructed of Onondaga limestone. Notice the 15/15 double-hung windows and centrally placed doorways at three levels. The porch above the second-level doorway was added when the house was renovated in 1939. For the construction of this building, twenty-eight-inch stones were cut in the quarries near South Avenue with the help of the Onondaga. Water was poured into natural or artificial cracks in the stone. When the water froze, the stones broke into the desired sizes.

31. Easton Store House

32. First United Methodist Church of Onondaga Hill, 1874
4845 West Seneca Turnpike

Originally built as the First Methodist Episcopal Church, it served the congregation that had formed two years earlier. The frame building with its steeply pitched roof and small belfry, pointed-arch openings, and ornamental buttressing is a good example of a Gothic Revival village church.

33. Josiah Bronson House, 1814
4811 Makyes Road
Renovation: late 1980s, Richard and Elaine Wisowaty; Preservation Consultant: Randall T.Crawford, Syracuse

Stepped gables and an elliptical attic light distinguish this vernacular Federal style house, which also has a handsome door featuring semielliptical transom and sidelights. An entrance porch was added later, as were the bay window and brackets along the cornice. Josiah Bronson, an early settler and innkeeper, built this fine brick house to be used as a residence. It is still a one-family house.

34. Plaque in Front of 4801 West Seneca Turnpike (Town Hall)
The plaque marks the site of the timber-frame building that functioned as the first Onondaga County Courthouse and jail from 1807 to 1830. Despite much opposition, the county seat was moved to Syracuse, and Onondaga County's second courthouse was erected at a location between

34 A. Van Dyn Home and Hospital, 1827–1953
Route 173

The original two-story section of Onondaga limestone was built as the Onondaga Poor House. A third story and wing were added in 1868. Other additions were made between 1854 and 1953. This is the oldest extant institutional building in Onondaga County, and deserves listing in the National Register of Historic Places.

35. Onondaga Community College (OCC), 1968–73

Route 173
Architects: Clark Clark Millis & Gilson, Syracuse
Landscape architects: Duryea and Wilhelmi, Syracuse

OCC, a two-year college, started in 1962 in what was then called Midtown Plaza. Soon more space was needed, and in 1968 a master plan was approved by the Onondaga County legislature. The move to the new campus on Onondaga Hill was completed in 1973.

36. General Orrin Hutchinson House, ca. 1825
(now Inn of the Seasons)

4311 West Seneca Turnpike
HABS

The house was built by James Hutchinson, who came here from Connecticut in 1802. It was later owned by his son Orrin, who became brigadier general in the militia and supervisor of the town of Onondaga. Located west of Onondaga Hill, the design of this Onondaga limestone building incorporates elements characteristic of the vernacular Federal style house, such as stepped gables with elliptical fanlight. Unusual is the second-story porch on the east facade. At that time, porches were frequently used on taverns but rarely on residences. Additions have been made to the rear of the house, and the entrance has been changed.

36. General Orrin Hutchinson House

37. Oliver Bostwick House, 1830
1942 Valley Drive

Oliver Bostwick, a prosperous dairy farmer, bought about a hundred acres of farmland that were part of Webster's square mile. He built a stone house and then added to the front the cobblestone house with walls two feet thick. A side wing was added in 1840. The cobbles came from the land, as did the stone used for the foundation, quoins, sills, and lintels. The exterior of the house is embellished with Greek Revival elements, such as an entrance with block designs on the transom and sidelights framed by pilasters, and a triangular attic light in the low-pitched gable. Changes have been made to the side wing. All of the outbuildings of this one-time working farm are gone except a large barn that is at present used by the Anglers' Club. It has been said that Joseph Forman (father of Joshua) housed his slaves on the property behind the Bostwick House.

37. Oliver Bostwick House

House built by Joseph Forman allegedly for his slaves, 1923. Courtesy Onondaga Historical Association, Syracuse

38. Webster's Pond

The artificial pond, named after Ephraim Webster, is fed by Kimber Brook and maintained by the Anglers' Club. According to some sources at the Onondaga Historical Association, Webster built his house in back of 1942 Valley Drive after he had abandoned his earlier dwelling near the cemetery close to the hills. Others maintain that the frame house that once stood behind the Bostwick House was a slave house owned by Joseph Forman. The pond is located on the ninety-three-acre Rand Tract and was deeded to the city by Herbert and Alma Rand in 1944 with the exception of their house (**No. 37**). When the Anglers' Club leased the wetlands in the 1960s, it was little more than a marshy dump. In 1966, they received a conservation award for the improved three-acre pond, which harbors mallards and is a stopover for ducks and Canadian geese. Designated as a conservation-education area, the pond has been under the supervision of the City of Syracuse Department Parks and Recreation since 1971.

39. Caleb Alexander House, ca. 1820
2321 Valley Drive

The two-story New England farmhouse with semicircular fanlights in gables was changed considerably over the years. It was built by Caleb Alexander, who served as pastor of the Presbyterian churches of Onondaga Valley and Salina, was principal of the Onondaga Valley Academy, and helped with the founding of Hamilton College. The house originally faced an Indian trail to the north.

40. WSYR Transmitter Building, ca. 1936
Valley Drive

The streamlined look is characteristic of the Modernistic style represented in this small structure built for WSYR. In 1922, WSYR was started as WMAC in the home of its founder, Clive Meredith, in Cazenovia.

41–42. 5721 and 5700 South Salina Street

Both houses exhibit exterior features characteristic of the Gothic Revival style, such as pointed-arch windows with label stop molding (**41**) and lacy gingerbread ornamentation in a steeply pitched gable (**42**). The entrance porch on **No. 41** is a later addition.

43. Harvey Tolman House, ca. 1850
5516 South Salina Street

The house was built as a farmhouse. The main house and wing are constructed of brick with stone lintels and sills, employing modified Greek Revival details.

41. 5721 South Salina Street

44. Nathaniel Searle House

44. Nathaniel Searle House, 1849

5323 South Salina Street
Restoration: 1965–80, Carl Steere Myrus, Syracuse
NRHP

Andrew Jackson Downing's dictum that the Gothic cottage should be the heart of the picturesque landscape has been realized here: the house is set back from the street and is surrounded by trees and landscaped gardens. Its name, Acorn Cottage, comes from the finial in the gable that ends in the shape an acorn, a symbol of hospitality. The authentically restored frame structure is a fine example of a Gothic cottage. It features board-and-batten siding, a steep gable with vergeboards and a finial, a red cedar shingle roof, brick chimneys, and a front porch framed by Tudor arches. The interior has the original floors and woodwork of yellow pine, a hard pine no longer to be found in the northeast, as well as two fireplaces and a cherry balustrade.

45. John F. Clark House, ca. 1851

4954 South Salina Street

John F. Clark, active in local and state politics, bought ninety-seven acres of land in 1846 and a few years later planted trees along the street, now South Salina Street. The house he built was occupied by his family for over ninety years. The hipped-roofed house has a one-story rear wing. Since its construction, many changes have been made to the brick building, including the addition of a Neoclassical Revival front porch.

46. John Gridley House, 1812

205 East Seneca Turnpike
HABS NRHP

This is one of the oldest homes in Syracuse still used as a residence. Sturdy and almost fortresslike, the house is constructed of Onondaga limestone with walls three feet thick. It has stepped gables with elliptical fanlights and a fine Federal style entrance. John Gridley built the house during the War of 1812. A Masonic emblem is carved into the stone lintel above the front door. Legend has it that the emblem was to ward off victorious English soldiers believed to be members of the Masonic Lodge. The only English soldiers who came by, however, were those who were taken prisoner. The interior has its original flooring and woodwork, and seven working fireplaces, of which six have mantels supported by fluted columns faced with carved sunbursts. The seventh, in the old kitchen in the basement, has its original crane and oven. The interior is unusual in that the entrance opens into a reception room rather than into a hall. An enclosed stairway is centrally placed in the hallway.

46. John Gridley House

47. Bronze Tablet in front of 302 East Seneca Turnpike

To commemorate the site of the Onondaga Arsenal, the tablet was given by the Onondaga County Chapter of the Daughters of 1812. The arsenal was located one and one-half miles east of Onondaga Valley. Onondaga County was considered to be of military importance in the state. Wary of a possible invasion, the state legislature passed an act in 1808 to deposit arms and ammunition and to build a place for their storage. In 1809, Cornelius Longstreet, son-in-law of Comfort Tyler, deeded land to the state to erect an arsenal. It was built in 1811 of native limestone and was ready in time for supplies to be sent from here to Canandaigua during the War of 1812. Soldiers on their way to the Niagara frontier used it, as did captured English soldiers on their way to prison camps.

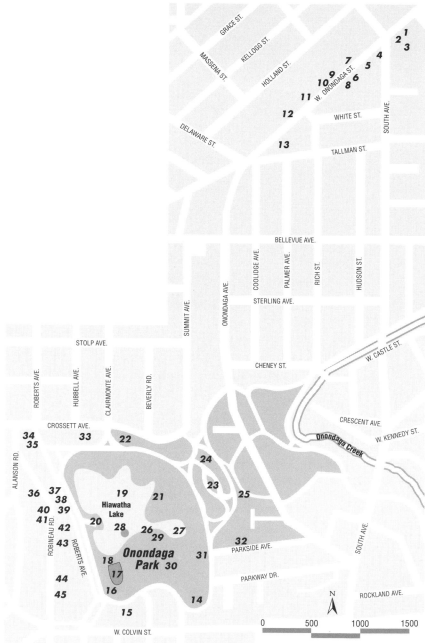

WEST SIDE

West Onondaga Street

*Estimated walking time: 30 minutes (**Nos. 1–13**); driving time: 15 minutes.*
*To drive from **No. 13** to **No. 14** will take 5 minutes.*

Today it is simple enough to get from South Clinton Street to South Avenue. But before 1830, travelers trying to traverse the area would have found themselves in the midst of a large swamp. It is said that West Onondaga Street started out as Cinder Road, so called because a man with a horse cart put down cinders all the way to the edge of Elmwood Park to create an access road to Mickle's Foundry, a producer of arms for the War of 1812. When the swamp was drained in the 1830s, the area was opened for residential development. Before long, a number of Greek Revival mansions shaded by elm trees lined the street. Henry W. Slocum, a local attorney, lived on the northwest corner of West Onondaga Street and Slocum Avenue, then called Russell Avenue. He entered the service as an artillery captain during the Civil War. By 1864, Slocum was promoted to major general and participated in Sherman's famous march from Atlanta to the sea. The Greek Revival home of Syracuse's first mayor, Harvey Baldwin, stood on the northwest corner of West Onondaga and South West streets. During the later part of the nine-

West Onondaga Street, early 1900s. Courtesy Onondaga Historical Association, Syracuse

teenth century, the area was favored by well-to-do Syracusans who liked to live in Queen Anne homes and occasionally made do with a Second Empire or a Richardsonian Romanesque-inspired residence.

West Onondaga Street experienced its Queen Anne heyday during the latter part of the nineteenth century, and in 1879 the street was advertised as "second to none." But architects and plan book designers who did their clients' bidding and lined suburban streets with Queen Anne houses and their variations were not necessarily liked by everyone. Architectural critic Montgomery Schuyler called architects who build in the Queen Anne style "a frantic and vociferous mob, who welcome the new departure as the disestablishment of all standards, whether of authority or of reason, and as an emancipation from all restraints, even those of public decency." It is obvious that Schuyler preferred the more restrained Greek Revival and Italianate elegance of Fayette Park. The decline of West Onondaga Street came when residents moved away into suburbs and exurbs. Their homes were replaced by parking lots or modern apartment houses during the mid-twentieth century. Few of the remaining houses now serve as residences for their owners.

1. 515 West Onondaga Street, 1877
NRHP

Syracuse lumberman William J. Gillette built this Second Empire style house for his family. Elaborate detailing around windows and doors and a mansard roof covered with multicolored tiles, topped by iron cresting, are hallmarks of the style. All of the wooden elements on the exterior and interior were fashioned in Gillette's own molding mill. The house was purchased by Trinity Episcopal Church in 1957 to be used as an exchange shop. Since 1989, the Alternative Efforts Center of Central New York has used the house as an AIDS Hospitality Center, the first in Central New York.

1. 515 West Onondaga Street

2. Trinity Episcopal Church of Syracuse, 1914–15

523 West Onondaga Street

Architects: Brazer & Robb, New York

The building is faced with stone and was designed in the Late Gothic Revival style. Especially noteworthy are the stained-glass windows, some of which were designed and installed by the Henry Keck Stained Glass Studio between 1948 and 1965. The tower had to be taken down for structural reasons in 1992. Directly behind the church stands the

3. Trinity Parish House, 1871

523 West Onondaga Street

The structure was moved to this site to make room for the church building. The picturesquely massed frame house was built by Reuben Porter for local newspaperman Carroll Earll Smith, son of Vivus. A multicolored tile roof with an elaborate cornice, pointed-arch openings, and Eastlake detailing distinguish the building. When the church was built, Trinity Episcopal Church bought the building for use as a parish house.

4. Marker on the Southwest Corner of West Onondaga Street and South Avenue

The inscription on the marker indicates that it was on this site on 17 June 1856 that the New York State Republican party was organized under an elm tree on the property of local newspaperman Vivus W. Smith. The founding of a new "northern party" seemed necessary to many because the probable passage of the Kansas-Nebraska Act threatened to open new territory to slavery. Horace Greeley, editor of the *New York Tribune,* came to Syracuse to discuss the issue with Smith, then publisher of the *Western State Journal,* and Thurlow Weed of the *Albany Argus.* They met at Smith's home on West Onondaga Street, and since it was a hot June day, they came out on the lawn and stood in the shade of an elm tree. The elm, which no longer stands, became Syracuse's most famous tree and was listed in *Who's Who in Outstanding Trees* (published by the U.S. Forest Service).

Vivus W. Smith came to Onondaga Hill in 1824 and three years later edited the *Onondaga Journal.* When Smith moved to neighboring Syracuse, which promised to become the leading community of the county, he was a co-founder of the *Onondaga Standard.* In its early years, the paper loudly denounced the practice of allowing pigs, cows, and geese to scavenge in the streets, by many considered a useful practice before the advent of municipal garbage collection. In jest, Smith was appointed "hog reeve" for the village of Syracuse, an appointment he accepted with enthusiasm, and he soon filled the village pound with straying barnyard animals.

5–7. 627, 636, and 637 West Onondaga Street

With a few exceptions, in the 600 block Queen Anne reigns supreme. Houses are of irregular massing and feature towers, turrets, textures, tall chimneys, bays, porches, and ornamentation. A stylized sunflower and a spiral pie motif were much liked. 627 West Onondaga Street (**No. 5**) is an example. Here a stylized sunflower fills the gable. The house was originally the home of Monroe Smith, brother of L. C. Smith and an executive for L. C. Smith Company. At one time, all three Smith brothers lived on West Onondaga Street. The exterior of 637 West Onondaga (**No. 6**) is textured and embellished with sunflower and pie motifs. Ornate hood molds, often used in Second Empire style houses, and a detailed cornice distinguish 636 West Onondaga (**No. 7**).

8. 643 West Onondaga Street, 1903
Architects: Benson & Brockway, Syracuse

Different from the surrounding Queen Anne houses, this is a large brick house of two gables; one is stepped, as might be found on seventeenth-century Dutch houses, the other curved and of Flemish inspiration. Built for Willis A. Holden, it was used as a residence until 1925, at which time it became an American Legion post, then a lodge for the Loyal Order of Moose, and finally the Church of Grace Tabernacle.

9. 652 West Onondaga Street, 1893
Architect: Charles E. Colton, Syracuse
Restoration: 1989, Hueber Hares Glavin, Syracuse

The form, the use of materials that create textural richness, and the eclectic exterior ornament indicate that the house was designed for a well-to-do entrepreneur. The original owner was W. L. Smith, an executive in the typewriter manufacturing firm of his brother L. C. Smith. Notice the Palladian windows in the gables and the stylized flower motifs, swags, and garlands in the porch frieze. The house was restored and functions again as a one-family house. Originally two separate houses, 652 and 658 West Onondaga were connected in 1971 to accommodate medical offices as well as a psychiatric clinic, Twin Elms, the precursor to the Benjamin Rush Center.

10. 658 West Onondaga Street, ca. 1890
Renovation and partial restoration: 1991–, Hueber Hares Glavin, Syracuse

This is a fine Queen Anne house with an octagonal corner tower, small panes in the upper sashes of windows, a large chimney, an exterior of brick and wood shingling, and Stick style elements in the main gable. The spacious interior with high-ceilinged rooms, outstanding woodwork, and stained-glass windows is now occupied by the Simon J. Volpert Environmental Center, a group of nonprofit organizations concerned with the environment and world peace.

9. 652 West Onondaga Street

10. 658 West Onondaga Street

11. 672 West Onondaga Street, 1890

Architect: Archimedes Russell, Syracuse
Renovation of interior: 1900, Gordon A. Wright
Renovation and partial restoration: 1987, Dr. H. Y. Jung

When built, this brick house with stone trim, prominent chimneys, and sunflower ornamentation above windows was considered to be one of the largest and most valuable houses in this section. It was designed for Dr. George D. Whedon. The interior is resplendent with fine woodwork of mahogany and oak, stained and beveled glass, fireplaces with ornate mantels, and parquet floors and canvas ceilings decorated with paintings or plasterwork. From 1904 to the mid-1980s, the house was used as a Catholic rectory. It was then that dropped ceilings were installed; they have since been removed by the present owner. He also converted part of the house into a museum for his collection of bronze sculptures, which he makes available to the public by appointment.

11. 672 West Onondaga Street

12. Alexander T. Brown House, 1895
726 West Onondaga Street
Architect: Gordon A. Wright, Syracuse
Renovation and partial restoration: 1969, Hueber Hares Glavin, Syracuse
NRHP CSPS

Displaying irregular massing, the use of masonry, and good craftsmanship, the house was designed in a style made popular by well-known
American architect Henry Hobson Richardson. It was a style soon to be
eclipsed, for suburban houses, by the Colonial Revival. Its design may
have been directly inspired by the Wickwire mansion in Cortland, with
which the original owner, Alexander T. Brown, was familiar. Large
Richardsonian arches and red Potsdam sandstone with carved details
distinguish the exterior. The roof is covered with red clay tiles. Leaded
glass and woodwork of mahogany, cherry, and oak embellish the interior.
An unusual feature was a hydraulic-powered elevator that ran from basement to attic. A combination of gas and electric lighting fixtures indicates
that electricity was not completely trusted in these early years. The third
floor is illuminated by a skylight of glass tile of the same configuration as
the clay roofing tiles. Brown, a prominent industrialist and inventor,
was one of the founders of the Brown-Lipe-Chapin Company, later to
become a part of General Motors. Among his many inventions were the
Smith Premier typewriter, the L. C. Smith breech-loading shotgun, and
numerous automotive gear assemblies and other devices. After the death
of Mary Seaman Brown (Alexander's wife) in 1932, the house had several

12. Alexander T. Brown House

owners, and the interior was extensively altered in 1947 when a group of physicians occupied it. Fortunately, much of the "debris" left from that remodeling job consisted of the original hardwood trim, mantelpieces, paneling, and sliding doors, enough to restore most of the interior to its original elegance.

The large carriage house on the property contained space for up to ten automobiles, with a turntable in front of the door. The second floor had rooms for the chauffeur and a private workshop for Brown. A hand-powered elevator with a counterbalanced pulley system could lift vehicles to the shop area for inventive tinkering. The building has been adapted for drafting room facilities. The local architectural firm Hueber Hares Glavin owns the Brown house and the former carriage shop.

13. 749 West Onondaga Street, 1894
Architect: Archimedes Russell, Syracuse

Textural variety and ornamentation as well as a corner tower and prominent chimneys distinguish this house as a good example of the Queen Anne style. It was designed for Francis Gridley, president of Salt Springs National Bank and one-time owner of the Gridley Building on Clinton Square.

Continue on West Onondaga Street, turn left on Onondaga Avenue, right on Bellevue Avenue, and left on Summit Avenue. Continue south on Summit Avenue to begin the Onondaga Park tour.

Onondaga Park
(Main Park Tour and Park Tour West)

Some of the information here is taken from "The Onondaga Park Neighborhood: A Walking Tour," prepared by the historical committee of the Onondaga Park Association (OPA).

Because of space constraints, only the park itself and part of Park Tour West are discussed here. For the complete tour, as well as for areas to the north, south, and east of the park, see the OPA's pamphlet. See also the brochure "Historic Landscapes of Syracuse" (City of Syracuse, Department of Community Development, Syracuse Landmark Preservation Board 1991).

A Brief Review of Syracuse's Park Development

In announcing the opening of the new Onondaga Park, the local paper reported in July 1898: "The city's new park...is now open to the public. Alderman Sager of the 13th ward, who succeeded in having 71 acres of the city's land dedicated by the common council as a park, has ordered all trespass signs removed, and the men, women and children of this city, who enjoy the pure fresh air and the pleasures to be found in a picturesque spot in a beautiful and healthful stretch of land may now visit the new park at any hour of the day or evening and call it their own."

Words such as "healthful" and "pure fresh air" echo the concerns of the public health movement of the 1890s. In architecture, general acceptance of the germ theory of disease provided the momentum for the "sanitary house." Interiors were to be free of features that collected dust; sleeping porches and screened-in sun parlors that could be glazed in the wintertime provided fresh air and sunshine, as did rooftop kindergartens in the larger cities. In his book *How the Other Half Lives* (1901), Jacob Riis called attention to the plight of tenement dwellers, with the result of some reforms and improved tenement designs.

Another expression of this trend was the development of landscape parks, sometimes referred to as "lungs for the poor." These urban green spaces were considered to be a panacea against the evils of urbanization brought about by the Industrial Revolution. Here the city dweller could walk and contemplate, inhale fresh air, and uplift the spirit. Frederick Law Olmsted (1822–1903), known as the father of landscape architecture in the United States and designer of Central Park in New York among many other parks, strongly felt that refinement and happiness would come to all who experienced the pastoral beauty of the park.

Syracuse's parks grew with the increase of population, and in 1917 the City of Syracuse Department of Parks and Recreation was organized. The city's park system, covering about a thousand acres of land, was created from public squares and from some early cemeteries. When in 1886 John B. Burnet gave his property to the city to be used as a public park, city officials hesitated to accept the gift because the owner stipulated that a certain amount of money be spent annually for improvements. Now the county's

Burnet Park Zoo is part of Burnet Park, as is a municipal golf course, said to be one of the first in the country. When Mayor McGuire decreed the golf course he was ridiculed, but he insisted that it was the "coming thing." The zoo, covering four acres, was established during the first decade of the twentieth century and was owned and administered by the city. Onondaga County acquired and expanded the zoo area in 1979. Three years later, major renovations began with local architects Hueber Hares Glavin in charge of major site planning. The Onondaga County Parks and Recreation staff, working with outside consultants, designed the exhibits. The architects for the new main building, which incorporates an earlier one, were Sargent Webster Crenshaw & Folley of Syracuse. The new Burnet Park Zoo, officially reopened in 1986 and well worth a visit, now covers sixty acres.

Onondaga Park is second in area to Burnet Park. With the seventeen-acre Hiawatha Lake within its boundaries, it was destined to become a place for recreational activities. The lake was the site of the Wilkinson Reservoir, constructed in the 1870s to supply water to the city. Woodland Reservoir, three blocks to the west, replaced it in 1895, and Wilkinson Reservoir was recontoured in 1911 to become Hiawatha Lake. The city had bought the reservoir and the land in 1892 and six years later opened the area as a public park. It had to compete for department funds: $1,500 remained in the park budget in 1898, and Alderman Sager suggested that these funds be used to "keep the grass cut and clear out the creek for bathing"; he added, "it is the intention to improve and beautify Onondaga Park from year to year and make it a delightful place for people to go." Those who visited the park on any Sunday—and there were many—must have thought so too.

In 1903, thirteen acres of woodland at the southeastern edge of the park, known as Bissell Woods, or Olmstead Grove, had been added to the park. Roads were improved and trolley car tracks extended to transport anticipated crowds. Under the guidance of a parks commission established by the mayor, the park was further landscaped and developed.

In the 1920s, Onondaga Park was at its most beautiful. The attraction of

19. View of Hiawatha Lake and bathhouse

the lower park was Star Lake, complete with jets of water. A covered garden walk of Japanese design was a popular spot for wedding pictures. The wintry park, too, had its attractions. Thousand of visitors came during the annual Ice Carnival to watch skaters on frozen Hiawatha Lake, enjoy dogsled exhibitions, and admire ice sculptures. In the late 1950s, maintenance problems threatened the park and its structures. Ten years later, several neighborhood groups saved the park's green space from becoming a public school campus. There have been other changes since: shrubbery was removed to reduce maintenance costs, and the swimming pool was installed. The bathhouse was renovated, retaining some of its architectural integrity, and the deteriorating picnic pavilion was rebuilt according to original plans. A children's sprinkler has been installed and a grass beach created to the south of the new pool. In 1980, the Onondaga Park Association was founded. Its members' efforts have made significant progress toward historic restoration and increased usage of the park.

Main Park Tour
CSPS
(Upper Onondaga Park Landscape Preservation District)

Estimated walking time: 45 minutes (Nos. 14–31)

14. The Elmwood Engine House is located east of Roberts Avenue at the highest point of the park. The small structure was designed by Thurber J. Gillette around 1913. It is covered with a hipped roof and dormer and has projecting rafters. Leaded-glass windows have been removed to be restored in the future. No longer an active fire station, the building is used as a city of Syracuse safety training site, an election day polling place, and a place for occasional comunity activities.

The **tennis courts (15)** were constructed in the early 1940s on the corner of West Colvin Street. Slightly to the north is the **stone grotto (16)**, which is near the site of the former reservoir inlet pipe that brought in water from Raynor and Wardsworth springs. Today's Olympic-sized **swimming pool (17)**, built around 1974, has replaced the lake for swimming, and Victorian bathing restrictions are no longer adhered to. The pool is located in the former women's bathing area, which was connected to the lake by an opening through the bathhouse. Although these modern facilities are safer for swimming, the geometric shape of the pool seems at odds with the picturesque landscape of the park. The concrete pier and the **bathhouse (18)**, featuring Colonial Revival style elements, were constructed about 1914 to divide the lake into two swimming areas, one for each sex. Besides dressing rooms, the bathhouse had an opening for the passage of swans and canoes from one swimming area to another (regardless of sex). The original balconies (now replaced) had slides from which swimmers could dive or slide into the lake.

In 1911, Wilkinson Reservoir metamorphosed into picturesque **Hiawatha Lake (19)**, a focal point of the park and once a lovely spot for

Sunday afternoon boating. During the formation of the lake, the **peninsula and west path (20)** leading to it were created. Catalpa trees, with their large heart-shaped leaves and foot-long seed pods, line the path. The small piece of land jutting into the lake is a favorite spot for anglers. It once featured two umbrella-like shelters, now removed because of maintenance problems. On the east side of the lake is a **slate floor (21)** marking the location of the original gatehouse (ca. 1870) that served the Wilkinson Reservoir. In 1930, the gatehouse was replaced by a gazebo and only the floor remains.

In the **Northside field area (22)**, a double row of trees was planted to form a natural extension from Beverly Avenue into the park, and a circular drive on top of the knoll, called **Round Top (23)**, provides a scenic view of the city, the park, and the lake. Plans to build a pavilion there were never realized. To the east, the **basketball courts (24)** are located on the original site of the park's tennis courts, and the eastern slope of the upper park is planted with lilacs, a delight in the spring. Lilacs also border the path, **Lilac Walk (25)**, that parallels the park road. **A footbridge (26)** crossing a lagoon surrounded by lush plantings was built around 1913. The arched masonry and stone bridge is a favorite background for photographing local wedding parties. It once connected the lake with the **eastern lagoon (27)**. The area was filled in and allowed to develop naturally. Large willows add to the picturesqueness and form a perfect backdrop to the lagoon. A small island to carry a **bandstand (28)** was created near the shore. People would line the western lawn to enjoy summertime band concerts. Musicians were transported from the shore to the bandstand by a train that ran on tracks just below the water level. Park engineer George Helmstetter designed the structure around 1913. It has a concrete foundation and a stone balustrade that supports six wooden columns. The roofline echoes the curves of the bathhouse roof. It fell into disrepair in the late 1950s but was saved from demolition in 1967 by the construction firm of a park neighbor, Ted Spodatto. In 1990, the structure was restored by the local architectural firm of Quinlivan Pierik & Krause. Concerts again delight summer listeners. To the southeast, a replica of the original **pavilion (29)** was built around 1978. The earlier structure had been demolished.

Named after its original owner, Louis Olmstead, the **Olmstead Grove (30)** is now a popular picnic area. This patch of wooded land was given to the city by his daughter Evella Grassley, while the rest of Olmstead's property was traded for other city property. Large oak trees developed as secondary growth under the original maple and beech stands. A small stone building held maintenance equipment. The curved stone bench is the perfect place from which to contemplate the water flowing from a waterfall, built in a tree-covered knoll, into the lovely **lily pond with rustic fountain (31)**.

Park Tour West (in part)

Estimated walking time: 45 minutes (Nos. 32–45)

32. 192 Parkside Avenue, 1915
33. Ames Residence, 1918
317 Crossett Avenue
Architect: Merton E. Granger, Syracuse

Both Tudor Revival houses were designed by Merton E. Granger and show Ward Wellington Ward's influence. Early in his career, Granger had worked in Ward's office. The Crossett Avenue house features several pieces of stained glass by Henry Keck as well as by Stanley Worden, Keck's long-time associate. The house on Parkside Avenue also has Keck windows and Mercer tiles, and was designed for Adon Hoffman, inventor of the steam press dry-cleaning machine.

Roberts Avenue is lined with detached one-family houses that one might have found in the pages of a catalogue from Sears, Roebuck or some other mail order company or in a monthly publication of the Architects' Small House Service Bureau, Inc. The latter was founded in 1921 with the intention of controlling part of the suburban market and was officially sponsored by the American Institute of Architects. Offering conservative designs and emphasizing modern appliances and economy in construction, the office produced stock plans for three- to six-room houses, charging $6 per room. For larger houses, the services of an architect were recommended. Although they are given various classifications such as "Dutch Colonial," "Colonial Revival," "Spanish Colonial," and "Tudor Revival" (depending on particular ornamental detail and massing), they were nevertheless modern American houses with maximum equipment within a minimum of space.

32. 192 Parkside Avenue

34–35. 500 and 508 Roberts Avenue ca. 1912

These houses are examples of the American Foursquare, a popular house that appeared in the suburbs in great numbers during the first decades of the twentieth century. This classic two-story box was comfortable and inexpensive, and was sold through many mail-order catalogues. It seemed to symbolize solidity. Both houses have a simple square plan and a low-pitched hipped roof with gables, and both feature bays and wide front porches. 500 Roberts Avenue (**34**) is embellished with modest classical features, while 508 (**35**) is stuccoed and shingled, with wrought-iron light fixtures on the porch that are Craftsman hallmarks.

Go north on Roberts Avenue, turn left on Crossett Avenue, and go south on Alanson then Robineau Road, a picturesque area with houses that have a harmonious relationship to their immediate landscape and a splendid view.

36. 176 Robineau Road, ca. 1919
Architect: Ward Wellington Ward, Syracuse

Ward designed this Mission style house for Arthur White. A flat or low-pitched tile roof, arched entryways, and smooth plastered or stuccoed walls are common features of Mission style houses, as is the floor plan that pays attention to "convenience," which was of concern in the early decades of the twentieth century. The clean design of many of these houses anticipates the modern house.

37. 185 Robineau Road, ca. 1920
Stuccoed surfaces and exposed roof rafters give this bungalow the Craftsman look. Gustav Stickley, who liked to feature bungalows in his Craftsman magazine, saw the relationship between the house and its setting as important as a harmonious interior: open, flowing spaces that lent the house a sense of spaciousness, a fireplace with an inglenook as a central core, built-in

37. 185 Robineau Road

furniture, and the use of natural materials. Exposed ceiling beams and roof rafters, rough brick or stone chimneys, and fireplaces would add to the allure of the Craftsman house.

38. 193 Robineau Road, ca. 1981

Architect: Arthur McDonald & Associates, Syracuse

The modern house, designed by architect/owner Arthur McDonald, uses the site on a steep slope to its best advantage. An energy-conscious design provides for private spaces to be protected by being built into the hill while the public areas on the upper levels have full benefit of a panoramic view.

38. 193 Robineau Road

39. 205 Robineau Road

The stuccoed villa has the roofline of a (modest) medieval castle, is built into the hill, and overlooks the lake and park below.

40. 206 Robineau Road, 1904

Architect: Catherine Budd, New York
CSPS

"Four Winds" was originally the home of Adelaide Alsop Robineau, renowned ceramic artist, Samuel Robineau, who published *Keramic Studio,* and their children. Robineau wrote to Fernando Carter, then director of the Syracuse Museum of Fine Arts: "Syracuse has at least two unique boasts to make: There is the salt which gives it savor, and there are the Robineau Porcelains! And when the Syracuse Art Museum is quoted in future articles as having a fine example of the work of this or that artist, it will be added that Syracuse's unique glory is its collection of the porcelains of its

40. 206 Robineau Road

townswoman, the only individual maker of art porcelain in this country one of the few—the very few—in the world and the only woman to attain such prominence in ceramics. All of which sounds very conceited of me but which is true nevertheless."

The Everson Museum has a fine collection of Adelaide Robineau's work, and the National Ceramic Exhibition was organized in her honor in 1932, three years after her death. The house was designed by a friend, architect Catherine Budd. The form of the house and its steeply gabled roof that shelters a porch are features borrowed from earlier Shingle style houses as well as from English cottages. The Craftsman style interior of the house displays oak paneling, geometric architectural details, ceramic fireplace tiles designed by Robineau, and an inglenook.

41. 208–210 Robineau Road, 1903
CSPS

Adelaide Robineau's former three-story studio, now used as a residence, housed her kiln on the first floor while the pottery was on the second level. The third floor was used as a playroom for the children. In its review of the Robineau homestead, American Homes and Gardens in 1910 considered this a "drastically modern" innovation. The house opens to a finely landscaped garden uniting the studio and the house.

42. 225 Robineau Road, 1919
Architect: Ward Wellington Ward, Syracuse

Fortresslike, embellished only with Neoclassical detailing on door and windows, the house is unusual in several ways. It is constructed of Onondaga limestone, a material not often used for residential architecture. Stone masons were brought from Italy to complete the work, which is said to have cost over $100,000. The design itself was not customary for Ward Wellington Ward, because he generally favored bungalows or the Tudor Revival and English cottage styles developed by English Arts and Crafts architects.

43. 229 Robineau Road, ca. 1907
Designer: William Henry Peters, Syracuse

The design of the house, with its sheltering slate roof, dormers, wide overhang, casement windows, and a prominent chimney, may have been inspired by Shingle style cottages. It is a house that is part of its landscape. The original owner was William Henry Peters, who owned orchards, vineyards, and rose gardens on either side of the road, sites now occupied by houses. He is also responsible for the design of the house. It is reputed to have had the first attached garage in central New York and was featured in *House and Garden* of 1911.

43. 229 Robineau Road

44. 255 Robineau Road, 1919
Architect: Ward Wellington Ward, Syracuse

The house was built for Dr. Harry Webb. Stained-glass panels in the front door, designed by Henry Keck, read "East, West, Home is Best." There are canvas ceilings in the interior, as well as eighteen Keck-designed stained-glass windows. The roof is covered with slate shingles; its arches form inverted Ws, which are said to have been a symbol for Ward's signature.

45. 257 Robineau Road, ca. 1928
Architect: John C. Seamans, Syracuse

This is a good example of the Tudor Revival style. Note the carved coats of arms, the slate roof, the herringbone brickwork, and the styled downspouts. The designer, John C. Seamans, is listed in the Syracuse City Directory as "Draftsman," and the house was built for Mr. Bourke of the Salt Springs National Bank, which fell victim to the Depression. Between 1930 and 1979, it was the home of Roland B. Marvin, mayor of Syracuse for four terms, and his family.

Other houses in this area designed by Ward Wellington Ward
but not on the tour are:

265 Robineau Road, 1926
The house was built for Julius Hunziker.

206 Summit Avenue, 1914
CSPS

Built for Annie Dunfee, the house features Henry Keck glass as well as ceramic tiles by Henry Chapman Mercer.

111 Clairmonte Avenue, 1914
Ward designed this house for the Fairchild family. Note the F above the front door and the Mercer tiles around the door frame.

1917 West Colvin Street, 1920
The house was built for Harold H. Clark.

Glossary of Architectural Terms

American Foursquare (popular ca. 1900–1940): Boxlike with rooms of nearly equal size and with side stairway, the two-story house has a pyramidal roof with dormers and sits on a high basement with steps leading to the front door. A veranda runs the full width of the first story. Conveying a sense of massiveness and stability, the Foursquare was popular among suburbanites.

Art Deco or Modernistic style (ca. 1905–1930): The Exposition des Arts Décoratifs, held in Paris in 1925, provided the impetus for Modernistic architecture and designs, which looked toward the future rather than toward the past. Mainly a style of ornament, it employs chevrons and zigzags in low relief and smooth shiny materials; it expresses modernity, the machine age, and the jazz age. Art Deco ornamentation was often used on early skyscrapers, designed in setback form.

Art Nouveau (ca. 1890–1915): Architectural and decorative style based on a sinuous, interlacing line derived from natural forms.

Arts and Crafts movement: A movement starting in England during the second half of the nineteenth century, it was a revolt against mass-produced objects. Craftsmanship was to be revived and pride and satisfaction brought back into work.

balustrade: A series of upright supports (balusters) for a rail.

Beaux-Arts style (ca. 1890–1915): Named after the École des Beaux–Arts, the leading school for art and architecture in Paris, the style stood for grand compositions. Its architects looked to Rome and the Renaissance for inspiration but employed modern structural methods. Coupled columns, monumental flights of steps, arched and rectangular openings, often between columns or pilasters, and a symmetrical plan are common features.The tone for public buildings in the United States was set when architects and planners of the White City at the World's Columbian Exposition in Chicago in 1893 employed the style extensively as a unifying element.

belt course: Also called stringcourse, it is a narrow horizontal band that projects from the exterior wall of the building, often defining floor levels.

board and batten: A method of siding a structure with vertical boards whose seams are weatherproofed with a thin vertical strip of wood (batten).

bracket: A small support element under eaves, shelves, or other overhangs: usually decorative rather than structural and often used in Italianate buildings.

bungalow (ca. 1900–1920): The bungalow comes in many styles, but they are secondary to planning considerations. In general an unpretentious small house of one-and one-half stories and about 800 square feet, it often has an open plan; it popularized the living room and the outdoor-indoor living space, and stressed harmony with the landscape. The bungalow provided suburbanites with an inexpensive and informal way of life. Mail-order houses offered do-it-yourselfers everything they needed. Bungalow magazines and specialized pattern books gave builders specifications for cobblestone chimneys and wooden roof brackets. The word bungalow comes from the Hindustani *bangla* which means belonging to Bengal and denotes a temporary dwelling.

buttress: A short section of wall built at right angles to the outer wall of the building, giving it support.

cantilever: A projecting beam or part of a structure stabilized by weight on its inner end.

capital: The head of a column or pilaster in classical architecture.

cartouche: An ornamental panel in the shape of a scroll, circle, or oval.

clapboards: A weathertight outer wall surface consisting of thin horizontal, overlapping boards.

classical architecture: The architecture of ancient Greece and Rome.

Colonial: Refers here to house forms derived from New England and the Hudson Valley, such as the salt box (one or one-and-one-half story cottage with extended sloping roof to cover an addition), the Cape Cod cottage (one or one-and-one-half stories), and the four-over four or two-pile house (four rooms on the first and four rooms on the second floor, divided by a central hallway). Large chimneys, central, or at each end of the house, and windows with small lights are typical features.

Colonial Revival style (ca. 1880–1920): A combination of various Colonial house forms and styles with contemporary elements, the Revival house is generally larger than its Colonial counterpart.

column: A vertical support, circular in plan, consisting of base, shaft, and capital. An exception is the Greek Doric column, which has no base.

composite order: A classical order with capitals ornamented with a combination of Corinthian and Ionic capitals.

corbel: A projecting block, usually of masonry, supporting a horizontal member. A range of corbels running below the eaves forms a corbel table.

Corinthian order: A classical order distinguished by capitals that are ornamented with leaf forms. It is the most ornate of the classical Greek orders of architecture.

cornice: A molding projecting along the top of a wall, pillar, or side of a building.

cupola: A small structure on top of the roof of a building.

curtain wall: An external wall that does not support any weight.

dentils: Small projecting blocks or teeth used in rows in classical cornices, an arrangement called denticulation.

Doric order: The oldest and simplest of the Greek orders, it is distinguished by fluted columns without a base, plain capitals, and a simple cornice.

dormer: An upright window projecting from a sloping roof.

Eastlake (ca. 1870–1890): It is a mode of ornamentation rather than a style and is usually applied to Stick style and Queen Anne houses. Decorative motifs borrowed from furniture are often employed, as are curved brackets and spindles (a small turned wooden element). The English architect Charles Locke Eastlake (1836–1906), after whom this ornamentation was named, was a precursor of the Arts and Crafts movement. He reacted against the Industrial Revolution and its ornamental excesses by promoting simplicity and good craftsmanship, and felt that he was thoroughly misunderstood in the United States.

Egyptian Revival style (ca. 1830–1850): Napoleon's Egyptian campaign during the beginning of the nineteenth century sparked an interest in Egyptian art and architecture. Columns with a bulge or resembling bundles of stalks, battered walls, smooth exterior finish, deep rounded cornices and the vulture- and-sun-disk symbol are distinguishing features for the first as well as the second Egyptian Revival style (ca. 1920–1930).

entablature: The horizontal part of the classical order above the columns or pilasters, consisting of architrave (the beam that spans a pair of columns as the lowest part of an entablature), frieze, and cornice.

facade (or elevation): The face of the building.

fanlight: A semicircular or semielliptical window above a door or window.

Federal style (ca. 1780–1820): The Federal style was also called the Adam style after the Scottish-born Adam brothers, architects in England between 1760 and 1780. Their design ideas were based on Hellenistic forms and ornament, and are characterized by lightness and airiness. Elliptical, semielliptical and circular forms are used, as are swags and garlands. Often a semicircular entrance porch contrasts with the rectilinear house form that usually faces the street with its broad side. Typical is the doorway with a semielliptical fanlight and with flanking sidelights, as are low roofs often hidden behind a balustrade. Federal houses in this area frequently have stepped gables.

fenestration: The arrangement of windows in a wall.

Flemish gable: A gable with stepped and sometimes multicurved sides derived from sixteenth-century Flemish architecture.

finial: an ornament at the top of a spire or gable.

flush boarding: Siding of horizontal boards that do not overlap.

fluted: having regularly spaced vertical parallel grooves or flutes on the shaft of a column or pilaster.

frieze: The middle part of an entablature; also a horizontal decorative band on a wall.

gable: The triangular upper part of the wall under the end of a pitched roof. A stepped gable is constructed with a series of steps along the roofline but is independent of it.

gambrel roof: A roof with two slopes of different pitch on either side of the ridge.

Georgian Revival style (ca. 1890–1915): It is based on the Georgian style (1780–1820), the first high style to be imported to the American colonies from England. The Georgian Revival house is rectangular in form with emphasis on symmetry and classical ornament. A central hallway, Palladian windows, and open-topped or broken swan's neck pediments above doorways are often used, giving the entrance prominence and relieving the severity of the rectilinear house form. Roofs usually have prominent dormers. Sometimes Federal style features are used as well.

Gothic Revival style (ca. 1840–1860): The style, associated with a Christian era, was favored for churches but also for residential architecture, reflecting changing attitudes toward nature. Rather than dominating over nature which is implied by classically inspired architecture, the Gothic building was meant to be part of the picturesque landscape, expressed in an informal, asymmetrical plan. Distinguishing features are pointed arches, towers, battlements, tracery, and leaded stained glass. Verticality is stressed, board and batten siding is often used. Gothic Revival houses usually have oriel and bay windows, porches, and ornamented verge- or bargeboards on steeply pitched gables. The jigsaw tracery used on vergeboards gave rise to the term Carpenter Gothic.

Greek Revival style (ca. 1830–1860): The new symbolic architecture was to express the nation's political ideals of freedom and democracy. There were strong associations with the oldest democracy in the Western world, and with the modern Greeks who fought for independence from the Turks in the 1820s. The Greek Revival building typically consists of a rectangular block with the gable end facing the street. Often the temple form is used and some adaptation of the classical orders; roofs are low pitched, frieze windows, columns, pillars or pilasters are often employed. Exterior facades are smooth and painted white to imitate marble. Symmetry is stressed.

Entrances are recessed and have sidelights and transom: arches are not used. Folk adaptations are the upright-and-wing (main house and side wing with porch), the upright and two lower wings, and the folk house with gable roof and returns.

half timbering: A type of construction in which spaces between the timber frame are filled with stones or bricks and the frame is left exposed.

High Victorian Gothic (ca. 1865–1890): Along with Gothic features, such as steep, gabled roofs and pointed-arch openings, a High Victorian Gothic building is often top heavy with complex rooflines and features contrasts in scale. External woodwork is solid, unlike the lacy gingerbread ornament of the Gothic Revival. Polychromy is the style's distinctive characteristic, but the color has to be inherent in the materials rather than applied.

High Victorian Italianate (ca. 1860–1890): That a building have character was as important to the designers of this style as it was for those of the High Victorian Gothic. Besides sharing forms and features with Italianate buildings, the High Victorian Italianate employs a variety of arch forms (except the pointed arch) for openings in the same elevation, shadow-forming moldings, and small-scale ornament, often of cast iron. In residential architecture, two two-story window bays on the front elevation are commonly used.

hipped roof: A roof with four uniformly pitched sides.

hood molding: Also called drip molding, it is a large molding over a window designed to direct water away from the wall.

Ionic order: An order of classical Greek architecture in which the capital is ornamented with two opposed scrolls or volutes.

Italianate style (ca. 1840–1880): It rivaled the Greek Revival style and was so popular that it was sometimes referred to as the "American style." Inspired by northern Italian farmhouses, the Italianate house is rectangular in plan, sometimes with side or front bay, with an almost-flat roof (sometimes crowned with a cupola), projecting eaves, and brackets, and with ornate entrance porches and window surrounds. Often quoins are used. The picturesque quality of the Italianate house had great appeal and allowed freedom in planning.

Italian Villa style (ca. 1840–1880): It shares its derivation, as well as features such as projecting eaves, brackets and ornate window surrounds, with the Italianate house, but it differs in form; it consists of asymmetrically grouped rectilinear blocks whose elevations as a rule are symmetrical. A tower is usually placed off-center, often at a corner, and rooflines have different forms. Houses most always have a veranda, classical ornament and quoins are often used, and there was freedom in planning.

keystone: A wedge-shaped piece at the highest point of an arch.

label stop molding: A molding above a door or window that extends horizontally across the top of the opening and vertically downward for a certain distance at the side.

lancet window: A narrow window with a pointed arch.

Late Gothic Revival (ca. 1890–1915): It is an architecture of masonry with pointed-arch openings featuring stone tracery. Frequently facing and details are of terra cotta. Verticality is stressed. The style was employed for churches as well as for educational (Collegiate Gothic) and commercial buildings. Early skyscrapers were often Gothicized in form and ornament.

lintel: A horizontal beam of stone or wood above a window or door to support the structure above it.

mansard roof: named after the seventeenth century French architect François Mansart, this roof covers the top story of a building, and has either concave, convex, or straight slopes to all four sides, as well as dormers to allow light into the attic story. The mansard roof is always used on Second Empire style buildings.

Mission style (ca. 1890–1915): The Mission style is California's answer to the East Coast's Georgian Revival. Arches and tiled, low-pitched roofs are general features. Curvilinear gables are often used, as are balconies. Towers or turrets often have pyramidal roofs. Walls are usually smooth and stuccoed. Sometimes the house is planned around an open courtyard and has second-story balconies.

Neoclassical Revival style (ca. 1890–1915): Like the Beaux–Arts style, the simpler Neoclassical Revival was popularized by the White City of the World's Columbian Exposition in 1893 and was often employed for public buildings. Flat roofs and broad expanses of plain wall surfaces are common. Usually the Greek orders are employed rather than the Roman.

ogee arch: An arch in the form of an S-shaped double curve, consisting of a convex and a concave part.

order: The basic structural system of the Greek temple, consisting of columns supporting an entablature. The Greeks had the Doric, the Ionic, and the Corinthian orders. The Romans adopted the Greek orders, adding them to their own Tuscan. The Renaissance adopted the Roman orders and added the composite. Each order had its own proportions and set of ornamental features.

Palladian window: A window with an arched central section flanked by lower side windows with entablatures above.

pediment: The gable end of a roof in Greek or Roman temples or a feature resembling it in classical architecture. A broken swan's neck pediment is one with a gap at its top or its base.

(the) picturesque: An aesthetic quality characterized by irregularity, asymmetry, and a variety of textures and forms.

pier: A masonry support, often rectangular or square in plan.

pilaster: A shallow column or pier attached to a wall and often modelled on an order.

porte cochere: A covered entrance attached to the building through which vehicles can drive.

portico:A covered entranceway or porch, usually with a pedimented roof supported by columns.

Post-Modern: Refers to the use of traditional architectural elements added as decoration to modern buildings.

Prairie style (1890–1915): Most houses designed in this style have two stories and one-story wings with low roofs. Wings sometimes shelter porches or carports. The house has an open plan, and horizontality is stressed. Sheltering overhangs protect terraces and gardens. Frank Lloyd Wright was known as the master of the Prairie House.

quatrefoil: An ornament composed of four lobes arranged around a common center.

Queen Anne style (ca. 1870–1890): The style was created by English architect Richard Norman Shaw, who combined late medieval domestic forms (including a large central hall) with semiclassical motifs. A sunflower motif is also much employed. The Queen Anne house has an irregular plan and massing, a great variety of textural wall surfaces, prominent chimneys, a variegated roofline, windows of many shapes (but never pointed-arched). Bay windows are often used, as are porches (sometimes with gazebos) and balconies. The corner tower or turret is a development of the later phase of the style.

quoins: Units of stone or brick used to accentuate the corners of a building.

Renaissance Revival style (ca. 1840–1860): In general, Renaissance Revival buildings are cubic blocks that fit into the urban grid system. Low roofs with massive cornices are the rule. Elevations are symmetrical and rectangular windows are often framed in architraves or have a complete entablature. They may vary in height in different stories and are sometimes linked by a beltcourse. Quoins are often employed. The style is a revival of High Renaissance palaces of Rome and Florence and was much liked for commercial buildings and clubhouses.

Richardsonian Romanesque (ca. 1870–1890): Richardsonian Romanesque, named after well- known architect Henry Hobson Richardson (1838–1886), was often employed for city halls, and commercial and residential structures. The buildings are of masonry construction and distinguished by a general massiveness and simplicity of form. Arched openings, lintels and other structural elements are often emphasized by being of different stone than that used for the superstructure. Round-arched and rectangular windows are divided by vertical stone dividers and transoms appear in the same elevation. The large Syrian arch is often employed, as are towers, turrets, and eyelid dormers.

Romanesque Revival (ca. 1840–1860): The style was mainly used for churches and public buildings and seldom for houses. A revival of the round-arched medieval style, semicircular arches are used for all openings. The form is repeated in arcaded corbel tables under eaves or belt courses. Towers frequently have a pyramidal roof.

sash window: A window of two or more sliding glazed frames running in vertical grooves.

Second Empire style (ca. 1860–1880): Architects of the style looked for sources to contemporary France, particularly Paris, where during the Second Empire of Napoleon III (1852–1870) ornate and monumental civic buildings with mansard roofs were being constructed. The mansard roof is the hallmark of the style. Dormer windows of many shapes are used. Classically detailed chimneys are important elements. Elevations, often embellished with classical ornament, have projecting and receding planes.

Second Renaissance Revival style (ca. 1890–1915): Buildings of this style share characteristics with the earlier Renaissance Revival but are usually larger. They are always faced with stone and sometimes with marble.

setback: An architectural design in which the upper stories of a building are set back from the lower stories in order to allow more light to reach street level.

shaft: The main part of the column between base and capital.

Shingle style (ca. 1880–1890): The Shingle style succeeded the Queen Anne in the 1880s and was considered to be the "Americanization of Queen Anne." Like its predecessor, it was a picturesquely massed house with porches and verandas (or with a gabled sheltering roof) and an open interior plan. But in contrast, its exterior was unadorned and faced with a skin of shingles. Most popular along the eastern seashore as vacation homes, Shingle style houses were often built near a body of water.

spandrel: The surface between two arches in an arcade.

Spanish Revival style (ca. 1910–1930): Like the Mission style, it originated in California reviving Spanish Colonial architecture. Usually smooth or textured stuccoed walls, tile roofs and masonry courses, wrought-iron grills and balconies, along with brick, tile, or stone floors and steps, are used.

Stick style (ca. 1870–1880): Inspired by wooden European houses and sharing characteristics with the Gothic Revival, the Stick style house is always of wood, and covered with board and batten or clapboards featuring an overlay of stickwork. Diagonal sticks are typical. Roof gables are steeply pitched; porches and balconies are common.

Sullivanesque style (ca. 1890–1915): Buildings in the style named after well-known architect Louis Henry Sullivan, are of straightforward skeletal form. They have flat roofs, usually large round-arched entrances and windows arranged in vertical bands. They are often faced with terra cotta and embellished with ornament (exterior and interior), which was Sullivan's answer to the European Art Nouveau. His designs consist of geometrical forms, natural as well as abstract.

temple front: The building facade of porch with columns and a pediment that resembles the end of a classical temple.

terra cotta: A fine-grained, fired clay used for tiles.

tracery: Ornamental work of stone, wood, or iron in the upper parts of Gothic or Gothic Revival windows.

transom: A horizontal, rectangular panel, usually glazed, above a door or window.

trefoil: An ornament featuring three lobes, similar to a clover leaf.

Tudor Revival (ca. 1910–1930): Loosely based on a variety of early English building traditions, the Tudor Revival house as it was built in U.S. suburbs, was decidedly American and rivaled the Colonial Revival in popularity. Identifying features are a steeply pitched roof, and one or more steep cross gables. Houses often have false half timbering, massive chimneys, and casement windows, sometimes with diamond-shaped small panes. Small stone tabs are at times used around doors. The Tudor (a flattened pointed) arch is also employed.

turret: A small tower, usually at the corner of a building.

tympanum: The space enclosed by the *lintel* or beam and the arch above it.

vergeboard: Also called bargeboard; a decorative board in the gable of Gothic Revival houses.

vernacular architecture: An architecture not designed by architects.

veranda: A space alongside a house sheltered by a roof supported by posts, pillars, columns, or arches. First used by the British in India, the word comes from the Portuguese *varanda*.

volute: A spiral or scroll.

wainscot, wainscoting: Paneling of wood or marble covering the lower portion of an interior wall.

Selected Bibliography

The American Renaissance: 1876–1917. Brooklyn, N.Y.: Brooklyn Museum, 1979.

Benjamin, Asher. *The American Builder's Companion.* 1827. Reprint. New York: Dover Publications, 1969.

_____. *The Architect, Or Practical House Carpenter.* 1830. Reprint. New York: Dover Publications, 1988

Blockson, Charles L. "Escape from Slavery: The Underground Railroad." *National Geographic* (July): 3–39, 1984.

Blumenson, John J. G. *Identifying American Architecture.* Nashville: American Association for State and Local History, 1983.

Bonta, Edwin. "Along the Seneca Turnpike." *Architectural Record* 40 (December): 505–15, 1916.

Bradley, James W. *Evolution of the Onondaga Iroquois: Accommodating Change.* Syracuse: Syracuse University Press, 1987.

Campbell, Sue. *Remember When ... The Valley Revisited.* Syracuse: Scotsman Press, 1986.

"Cathedral of the Immaculate Conception 1847–1959," n.d. Pamphlet at church archives, Syracuse.

Chase, Franklin Henry. *Syracuse and Its Environs.* 3 vols. New York and Chicago: Lewis, 1924.

Cheney, Timothy C. *Reminiscences of Syracuse.* Syracuse: Summers and Brothers, 1854.

City of Syracuse, Department of Community Development, Syracuse Landmark Preservation Board. "Historic Landscapes of Syracuse," 1991. Pamphlets at Onondaga Historical Association, Syracuse.

Condit, Carl W. *American Building.* Chicago: The University of Chicago Press, 1968.

Connors, Dennis J. "Boilers, Barons & Bureaucrats: A Tour of an Historic Syracuse Neighborhood." Syracuse: Salt Museum, Onondaga County Parks, 1986.

Davis, Barbara Sheklin. *A History of the Black Community of Syracuse.* Syracuse: Onondaga Community College, 1980.

———. *A History of the Jewish Community of Syracuse.* Sponsored by the National Foundation for Jewish Culture, the Syracuse Jewish Federation, and Onondaga County Community College, n.d.

Downing, A. J. *The Architecture of Country Houses.* 1850. Reprint. New York: Dover Publications,1969.

Eastlake, Charles E. *Hints on Household Taste in Furniture, Upholstery and Other Details.* 1878. Reprint. New York: Dover Publications, 1969.

Fowler, Orson S. *The Octagon House.* 1853. Reprint. New York: Dover Publications, 1973.

Gabriel, Cleota Reed. *The Arts and Crafts Ideal: The Ward House.* Syracuse: Institute for the Development of Evolutive Architecture, 1978.

Galpin, William Freeman. *Syracuse University: The Pioneer Days.* Vol.1. Syracuse: Syracuse University Press, 1952.

Gilder, Cornelia Brooke."Robert W. Gibson: Master of Many Styles." *Preservation League of New York State Newsletter* 10 (3) (May–June), 1984.

Gowans, Alan. *The Comfortable House.* Cambridge, Mass.: MIT Press, 1986.

Grow, Lawrence, ed. *Old House Plans.* New York: Universe Books, 1978.

Hamlin, Talbot. *Greek Revival Architecture in America.* 1944. Reprint. New York: Dover Publications, 1964.

Hand, M. C. *From a Forest to a City.* Syracuse: Masters & Stone, 1889.

Hardin, Evamaria. *Archimedes Russell.* Syracuse: Syracuse University Press, 1980.

———. "Courthouse." *Syracuse Scholar* (Fall): 35–48, 1988.

——— *Syracuse and the Underground Railroad.* Syracuse: Erie Canal Museum, 1989.

———. "The Niagara Mohawk Building: A Not-So-Tall Building Artistically and Historically Considered."*Central New York Architecture, 1989. A Desk Reference.* Syracuse: Publications Services.

Hennig, Calvin M. "The Outdoor Public Commemorative Monuments of Syracuse, N.Y., 1855–1950." Ph.D. dissertation, Syracuse University, 1983.

Heppel, Shirley G. "Carl W. Clark, Dean of Central New York Architects." *Preservation League of New York State Newsletter* 13 (4) (Fall), 1987.

Homefront: The Erie Canal in the Civil War. Syracuse: Erie Canal Museum, 1987

Horning, Elinore T. *Horatio Nelson White: The Man Who Changed the Face of Syracuse.* Mexico, N.Y.: Elinore T. Horning, 1988.

Jones, John Philip. *The Great Grey Spire.* Syracuse: Quartier Printing, 1985.

Jones, Robert., ed. *Authentic Small Houses of the Twenties.* 1929. Reprint. New York: Dover Publications, 1987.

Koolakian, Robert G. "The Erie—From Canal to Modern Thoroughfare." *The Canal Packet, Newsletter of the Canal Museum Associates* 2 (1) (February), 1978.

Landy, Jacob. *The Architecture of Minard Lafever.* New York: Columbia University Press, 1970.

Langdon, John W. "Against The Sky: 40 Years of LeMoyne College," 1986. Pamphlet at LeMoyne College archives.

Luke, Marion. "Historython: A Walk through Historic Syracuse." A Bicentennial Project of the Consortium for Children's Services, Syracuse, 1976.

McKee, Harley J., with Patricia Day Earle, Paul Malo, and Peter Andrews. *Architecture Worth Saving in Onondaga County.* Syracuse: Syracuse University School of Architecture, 1964.

"Mainly Spanish." *HHG Overview* 4 (2), n.d. Pamphlet in architects' office.

Maltbie, Annie C. *Picturesque Oakwood: Its Past and Present Associations.* Syracuse: Fred S. Hills, 1894.

Mansfield, Howard. "Was Yates Castle a Stop on the Underground Railroad?" *Syracuse University Alumni News* (Spring): 16–20, 1981.

Mitchell, Preston S. and Smith, Margaret."The Years of Plymouth," n.d. Pamphlet at church archives.

Monses, Anita. "Salt of the Earth." *Syracuse Alive* January–February): 30–35, 1985.

"Niagara Mohawk's Art Deco Building." Pamphlet from Public Relations Department, Niagara Mohawk Power Corporation, Syracuse, n.d.

O'Neill, Alexis. *Syracuse: The Heart of New York..* Northbridge, Calif.: Windsor Publications, 1988.

Onondaga County Public Library. "The Grand Opening of the Carnegie Public Library, March 23, 1905." Commemorative pamphlet, 1985.

Onondaga Park Association. "The Onondaga Park Neighborhood: A Walking Tour," n.d.

"A Place To Learn." *Syracuse University Alumni News* 64 (3) (Spring): 16–33, 1984.

Poppeliers, John, et al. *What Style is It? : A Guide to American Architecture*. Washington, D.C.: Preservation Press, 1983.

Public Art in Syracuse and Onondaga County. Syracuse: Onondaga Public Library and Cultural Resources Council of Syracuse and Onondaga County, Inc.,1985.

Pulfer, Donald Robert. "The early Work of Joseph Lyman Silsbee." M.A. thesis, Syracuse University, 1981.

Railroads in the Streets of Syracuse.. Marcellus, N.Y.: Central New York Chapter, National Railway Historical Society, Inc., 1979.

Reed, Cleota, ed. *Henry Keck Stained Glass Studio, 1913–1974* . Syracuse: Syracuse University Press, 1985.

Rifkind, Carole. *A Field Guide to American Architecture*. New York: New American Library, 1980.

Riis, Jacob A. *How the Other Half Lives: Studies Among the Tenements of New York*. 1901. Reprint. New York: Dover Publications, 1971.

Roseboom, William F. and Schramm, Henry W. *They Built a City: Stories and Legends of Syracuse and Onondaga County*. Fayetteville, N.Y.: Manlius Publishing Company, 1976.

Salt: A History of Salt Manufacturing in Onondaga County 1654–1926. Syracuse: Onondaga County Public Library in cooperation with the Salt Museum, n.d.

Schmitz, Marian K. *The Hollow and the Hill*. Parsons, W.Va.: McClain Printing Company, 1983.

Schramm, Henry W. *Empire Showcase: A History of the New York State Fair*. Utica, N.Y.: North Country Books, 1985.

Schramm, Henry W. and Roseboom, William F. *Syracuse from Salt to Satellite*. Woodland Hills, Calif.: Windsor Publications, 1975.

Schuyler, Montgomery. "Architecture of American Colleges." *Architectural Record* 30 (July–December): 565–73, 1911.

Scully, Vincent J., Jr. *The Shingle Style and the Stick Style*. New Haven and London: Yale University Press, 1971.

Shelgren, Olaf William, Jr. et.al. *Cobblestone Landmarks of New York State.* Syracuse: Syracuse University Press, 1978.

"Sixty Years 1915–1975; Hueber Hares Glavin; Architects, Landscape Architects, Engineers." n.d. Pamphlet in architects' office.

Sloan, David C. "The Living Among the Dead: New York State Cemetery Landscapes as Reflections of a Changing American Culture to 1949." Ph.D. dissertation, Syracuse University, 1984 .

_____. *The Last Great Necessity.* Baltimore: The Johns Hopkins University Press,1991.

Smith, H. P. *History of Oakwood Cemetery.* Syracuse: H. P. Smith & Co., 1871.

Smith, Mary Ann. *Gustav Stickley, the Craftsman.* 1983. Reprint. New York: Dover Publications, Inc., 1993.

Stepanek, Catherine Covert. "Founding of Park Central Church and Society," 1972. Pamphlet in church archives.

Stevenson, Catherine Cole and Jandl, H. Ward. *Houses by Mail.* Washington, D.C: Preservation Press, 1986.

Stickley, Gustav. *Craftsman Homes.: Architecture and Furnishings of the American Arts and Crafts Movement.* 1909. Reprint. New York: Dover Publications, 1979.

Syracuse-Onondaga County Planning Agency. *Onondaga Landmarks.* Syracuse: Cultural Resources Council of Syracuse and Onondaga County, Inc., 1975.

Tomlan, Mary Raddant. "The Work of William H. Miller: Far Beyond Cayuga's Waters." *Preservation League of New York State Newsletter* 1 (3) (May–June), 1985.

Tuck, James A. *Onondaga Iroquois Prehistory: A Study in Settlement Archaeology.* Syracuse: Syracuse University Press, 1971.

Weisman, Winston. "A New View of Skyscraper History." In Edgar Kaufmann, Jr., *The Rise of an American Architecture.* New York: Praeger, 1970.

Weiss, Peg. *Everson Museum of Art: Introduction to the Collection.* Syracuse: Everson Museum of Art, 1978.

_____., ed.*Adelaide Alsop Robineau: Glory in Porcelain.* Syracuse: Syracuse University Press in association with Everson Museum of Art, 1981.

Whitten, Marcus. *American Architecture since 1780: A Guide to the Styles.* Cambridge, Mass.: MIT Press, 1969.

Williams, Harrison E. "Golden Decades, 1914–1965. First Baptist Church, Syracuse, New York," n.d. Pamphlet in church archives.

Williams, John A. "Syracuse: A City in Transition," n.d. Unpublished article in John A. Williams Collection, George Arents Research Library, Syracuse University.

Wolcott, Fred Ryther. Onondaga: Portrait of a Native People. Syracuse: Syracuse University Press in association with Everson Museum of Art, 1986.

Wright, Gwendolyn. Building the Dream. New York: Pantheon Books, 1981.

INDEX